# B-29 Superfortress at War

Fighter at seven o'clock... he's comin' in!... watch him, I think he's gonna make another pass... And the turrets swing to cover this 500th BG Superfortress over a Japanese target area.
/ *Elmer Huhta Collection*

# B-29
# Superfortress
# at War

## David A. Anderton

Charles Scribner's Sons
NEW YORK

Bomb bay doors open, a Renton-built Boeing B-29A-5-BN (serial 42-93844) poses over Washington. / *Boeing*

Design by Anthony Wirkus LSIAD

1 3 5 7 9 11 13 15 17 19  I/C  20 18 16 14 12 10 8 6 4 2

Printed in Great Britain
Library of Congress Catalog Card Number 78-54608
ISBN 0-684-15884-1

This book is dedicated to the kids who were
there, and to the grown-ups who remember

9-26-79

The bombs are 500lb incendiary
clusters; the bombers are the
B-29s of the 98th Bomb Wing,
over the target in North Korea.
/ USAF 78774 A.C.

# Contents

# Acknowledgements

A-44 from the 871st Bomb Squadron, 497th Bomb Group is parked in the early afternoon sun and is the centre of some attention from the men around her. A thermos jug, canteen, and probably some food stand in the sun near the left nose wheel. Nonchalant pilot and aircraft commander, hands on hips, socks rolled down and shorts rolled up, stand and wait at the nose of the aircraft.
/ *Dr Lyman C. Perkins*

The response to my original request for assistance in telling the story of the Superfortress at war was overwhelming. Some of those who answered told their experiences by letter, by telephone, on tape, or — later — in interviews. Others loaned reference material: books, unit histories, clippings, copies of *Brief* magazine. Still others loaned their priceless collections of photographs, original negatives taken during the wars, collections of colour slides. A few did all of these.

Those who helped with this work, who made it possible, then and now, are listed below:

T. H. Brewer; Jack J. Catton; James B. Cliver; Gerald Coke; Ferd J. Curtis; Eugene L. Davis; William F. Dawson; H. W. Douglas; R. A. Ebert; Fleming Fraker, Jr; Paul Friend; James J. Garrity; Robert F. Goldsworthy; George S. Gray; Haywood S. Hansell, Jr; Charles B. Hawks; Ingram T. Hermanson; Don C. Hetrick; Robert B. Hill; H. D. Hallinger; Elmer Hahta; Mrs Thomas Isley; Mike Janosko; Richard M. Keenan; Philip J. Klass; W. B. Leake; Olinto F. Lodovici; John F. Loosbrock; Prescott Martin; David W. Menard; A. F. Migliaccio; Donald L. Miller; Francis B. Morgan; Charles R. McClintick; Glenn E. McClure; Bernard J. Mulloy; Kenneth E. Neff; W. A. Pearce; Alberto R. Pearson; Dr Lyman C. Perkins; Denny D. Pidhayny; Vern Piotter; J. R. Pritchard, Jr; Del Shafter; Murray Singer; Frederick M. Smith; Ben H. Tucker; E. L. Tyler; Roger Warren; Eric Weber; Gordon S. Williams; Fred Wolfe; Ron E. Witt; John Zimmerman.

Those who were there are further identified in the text. For their enthusiastic cooperation, I am deeply grateful.

The experiences related here, the quotations, the loaned materials are theirs; but the context, views and opinions are mine, and I'm responsible for them.

David A. Anderton

Ridgewood, NJ, USA
September 1977

# Notes on the photographs

Good photographic coverage of the B-29 in action was limited by a number of factors. The island bases were really isolated; everything had to be brought in from distant supply bases, and such luxuries as camera film were rare. Fine coral dust, sand and fungus attacked cameras and film. High temperatures plagued processing. Photo labs, like all other supporting units, had heavy work loads as routine, with little time available for private and unofficial work.

The bright sunlight overpowered many of the cameras and films of the day. It produced very high contrast between the highlights on a B-29 fuselage and the shadow under the aircraft. In the amateur films, paper and processing of the day, this resulted often in chalky white highlights and black blobs of shadows, devoid of any detail.

Photography in the air was another difficult matter. The pressurised B-29 had no open hatch or window for photography. All air-to-air pictures had to be taken through a layer of glass or plastic, with their inherent distortion, internal reflections, and other deterrents to good, clear pictures.

In spite of all that, the photographs in this book require no apologies, just explanations.

During the preparation of this work, at least 500 photographs were either printed from original negatives, or copied from loaned prints, then processed and printed. Several collections of negatives were loaned by their owners, and one of them demonstrated clearly the hazards of wartime photography on the islands. Several negatives had tiny grains of coral or fine sand embedded in the emulsion.

Copies of black-and-white photos were made with a Hasselblad 500C using the normal 80mm Zeiss lens and an extension ring, or a +1 diopter close-up lens, or both. Kodak Plus-X Pan Professional film was used, processed in Kodak Microdol-X in a 1:3 dilution.

All black-and-white photos, whether copied or printed from original negatives, were printed using a Beseler 23C enlarger on Ilfospeed paper of proper contrast grade, and processed in Ilfospeed chemicals.

Several collections of colour transparencies were loaned for this book. They were copied with a Canon F-1 and Canon FL bellows on Kodachrome II Professional (KPA135) film, using an Aimes-Hershey light box. Colour processing was done by Kodak.

Special thanks are due to Dr Lyman C. Perkins, who loaned his entire collection of hundreds of documentary negatives taken on Saipan during World War 2; to then Sgt William A. Dawson, B-29 gunner in the Korean war, for the loan of his negative collection; to Vern Piotter, a navigator in both wars, for loaning his colour transparencies; to Ingram T. Hermanson, for loaning a set of colour transparencies taken on Saipan by himself and Kenneth E. Neff; and to Eric Weber, then an engineering maintenance officer in the Second Air Force, for sending his collection of outstanding, professional-quality colour slides of the B-29s and their elegant noses.

There's always something to do on the damned engines; they're older now, and they've got a lot of time on them. So two of the 343rd Bomb Squadron's mechanics scramble over the cowling, wrenches in hand, and work on the engine in the Yokota winter sunlight.

# Introduction

The people who finally put the Boeing B-29 Superfortresses over targets in the Japanese home islands were pilots and file clerks, bombardiers and engineers, Rosie the Riveter and Rosey O'Donnell, and hundreds of thousands of Chinese farmers and Mao Tse-Tung.

The Chinese built the airfields in their country, the Indians in theirs. The US Naval Construction Brigades (Seabees) levelled and surfaced the Marianas runways.

The Army and the Marine Corps took the Mariana islands — Guam, Saipan and Tinian — where the B-29s were to be based. The Navy got them there, and softened the Japanese defences with shelling by warships and strikes by carrier-based aircraft.

And when the B-29 operations started, a closer liaison between the Army Air Forces and the Navy also began. The B-29s reported shipping locations and other maritime observations directly to the Navy on a secure communications channel. They flew reconnaissance missions from Guam with naval observers on board.

When the B-29 force shifted a portion of its effort to mine-laying in Japanese waters, naval mine fuse specialists assigned to B-29 units worked side-by-side with the air and ground crews.

Air-sea rescue was a joint operation that used both Army Air Forces and Navy aircraft for search and location, and Navy submarines and surface ships for pickup of crews from life rafts or sinking aircraft.

When the *Enola Gay* made her historic flight to Hiroshima, a naval officer was the first nuclear weapons specialist who went along to assemble and arm 'Little Boy', the first atomic bomb.

It was, in every sense, a joint operation all the way. True, there were high-level political moves to attempt to seize control of the B-29s, or their missions, or both. There were inter- and intra-service squabbles, jealousies, rivalries, and enmities that had to be factored in.

But at the working — and dying — level, the B-29 airmen understood that they were no more responsible for winning the war than soldiers or sailors or marines or even civilian production-line workers.

This is, properly, a book about the Boeing B-29 Superfortress in combat. For that reason, it must exclude with regret the story of the B-29 in many of its non-combat roles. There are no pictures of the B-29s that carried research aircraft aloft to their drop altitudes, no stories of weather reconnaissance flights out of northern bases during the Cold War, and nothing about the existing B-29s in museums or on flight status.

Further, this book is of finite size, and there is no way in the world that it could be, or pretend to be, the definitive history of the B-29 in combat. It took almost 400 pages in the official history of the United States Army Air Forces in World War 2 just to summarise the B-29 story in that war. This book had to be selective; the selection was the author's.

The Boeing B-29 saw combat during the closing days of World War 2, first from India and China, and later from the islands of the Mariana group. It had a brief rebaptism of fire during the Korean conflict, when Strategic Air Command and Far East Air Forces B-29s were assigned to bombing missions.

Its combat life was short, but its accomplishments were many and great. This book attempts to create the mood of those days, and to tell the story of the men and machines in the words of those who were there.

# Superfortress

She was born in Seattle, grew up in Wichita, and died in the skies over Japan. She was the Boeing B-29 Superfortress, loved and hated, Queen of the Skies and an aborting bitch.

She was graceful, with a long, sleek body that caught the sun in dazzling highlights. Her wings were wide, with a gentle taper and a slimness that hinted at effortless flight. Her power lay inside four huge engine nacelles, crowding forward from the uncluttered wing, bulging with steel and aluminium and magnesium that had been alloyed and shaped into cylinders, gears, rods, cases, and twin superchargers.

She was clean, aerodynamically smooth, with countersunk rivet heads lying flush with the aluminium alloy skin surfaces. Drop the landing gear, and her drag doubled.

She spawned superlatives: highest, fastest, biggest bomb load. Slowest-turning, biggest metal propellers. Largest cowl flaps. Heaviest and longest aluminium extrusion.

And the ultimate superlative: She dropped the first — and then the second — atomic bomb.

She was the pivotal airplane in the long and difficult transition from a subservient strategic air force to an independent United States Air Force.

Let's look at her from the start.

## The Beginnings
The United States Army Air Corps, as it was then, often organised boards of officers to study the needs of the growing air arm. Early

in June 1939, one such board began its deliberations with the goal of guiding future development of aircraft for the Air Corps. The board's report, issued at the end of the month, recommended among other things that several long-range medium and heavy bombers be developed during the next five years.

Late in 1939, Maj Gen H. H. Arnold sought and received the authority to let some study contracts for a very long range heavy bomber, and he gave instruction to Capt Donald L. Putt, then working in the Materiel Division at Wright Field, Ohio, to write the statement of military characteristics for the airplane.

On 29 January 1940, the Air Corps mailed its Request for Data R-40B to a number of aircraft companies. Four were to respond: Boeing, Consolidated, Douglas and Lockheed.

It took a while for the mail to get to Seattle, Washington, and the desk of Philip G. Johnson, then the president of the Boeing Aircraft Company. On 5 February Johnson read the letter and its enclosures: R-40B and Spec XC-218. They called for a proposal for the design of a bomber with a range of 5,333 miles, with more speed and bomb load than the Boeing B-17, then just entering service. And the letter asked for the designs to be submitted within 30 days.

Boeing beat the deadline with a week to spare and sent details of its proposed Model 341, a bomber that could carry 2,000lb of bombs and could fly faster than 400mph.

The exercise was not a completely new one for the company. They had been asked in March 1938 to submit ideas for pressurising the cabin of the B-17, and had begun work on two parallel studies. Design teams worked the Boeing XB-15 design into the Model 316 and altered the B-17 into the Model 322. The Boeing teams drew on that experience and forged ahead with their concepts of a heavy bomber. In January 1939, before the Air Corps had produced its own requirements,

Progenitor of the long line, the first experimental Superfortress stands in the September haze at Boeing's Seattle plant. She is officially XB-29-BO, serial number 41-002, and her lovely lines are swathed in olive drab and dark grey camouflage paint. She had three-bladed propellers, streamlined gunners' sighting blisters, and a fixed tail bumper. Her Sperry gun turrets were retractable. / Gordon S. Williams

Boeing had designed Model 333. It had tandem engines, tandem bomb bays, two pressurised crew compartments connected by a tunnel, and tail guns.

The design was refined further into Model 334-A, with a higher wing loading and other features that qualify that design, seen with the benefit of hindsight, as the first real ancestor of the B-29. By August, Boeing had the Model 341, with wing loadings as high as 64lb per sq ft, a 12-man crew, and the calculated ability to carry 2,000lb of bombs for 5,333 miles. Boeing was serious enough about the design to begin work on a full-sized mockup at company expense in December 1939.

By April 1940 the realities of modern war were sinking in. Early air combat in Europe at the beginning of World War 2 showed the many weaknesses of contemporary aircraft, with their conventional fuel tanks, little or no armour, small calibre machine guns. The Air Corps re-thought its needs and updated its request for proposals in a letter to the bidders: Include leakproof tanks, armour, heavier-calibre machine guns and cannon, and multiple gun turrets.

Out of this came the Boeing Model 345, powered by the new Wright R-3350 twin-row radial engines, and defended by four retractable turrets mounting twin machine guns and a tail turret with twin machine guns and a cannon. It was a pressurised airplane, capable of hauling one ton of bombs over 5,333 miles. Its maximum bomb load was to be 16,000lb. It had a 12-man crew. Its landing gear was tricycle, with double wheels all around. The wingspan was 141 feet 2 inches; length, 93 feet; design gross weight, 97,700lb. The formula was fixed, and on 11 May 1940, Boeing submitted the design for Model 345 to the Air Corps.

Later that month, Boeing and Lockheed were selected as winners of the competition, with the Model 345 considered to have the edge. The Air Corps gave it the XB-29 designation, and named Capt Putt as project officer. Lockheed's entry became the XB-30. In June, both companies received contract awards for mockups and wind-tunnel tests, and the Air Materiel Command was directed to begin negotiations for price and delivery dates of a pair of prototype aircraft, with an option to buy 200 production bombers.

On 24 August, the Air Corps decided on Boeing and signed a contract with the firm for the development and construction of two prototypes and a mockup at a cost of $3,615,095. By the time the contract had its official approvals on 6 September, Lockheed had made a policy decision to get out of bomber design, and Consolidated had been selected to develop the XB-32 as a parallel project. The remaining member of the original four bidders, Douglas, had been working its basic DC-4 transport configuration through a series of designs that might have become an XB-31, but the project never got beyond paper studies.

Late in the year, the Boeing mockup was inspected, and in November the company got an order for a third prototype and a fourth

airframe for static tests. The B-29 was on its way. Less than four years later — a remarkably short time for the design, development and deployment of a new weapon and its crews — the first B-29 mission was flown against the enemy.

## Building and Flying

All the times seem short, anyway. True, aircraft design was simpler in the 1940s. But the Boeing B-29 was as much of an advance over its contemporaries as a Mach 3 fighter is today. The first engineering drawings were sent down to the shop floor on 4 May 1941. The work statement called for the first airplane to be completed in August 1942: 15 months to go.

Then began the almost endless number of small and large changes, policy decisions, Air Corps — and after 20 June 1941, Army Air Forces — modifications. The first was the conditional contract of 17 May. Under its terms, Boeing was asked to build 250 B-29s and 335 additional B-17s, conditional upon the expansion of its facilities at Wichita to meet production goals of 65 B-17s per month by 1 July 1941, and 25 B-29s per month by 1 February 1943. Boeing broke ground at Wichita 25 June 1941, for the expansion around the nucleus of the plant of the Stearman Aircraft Company, which had become a wholly-owned subsidiary of Boeing in 1939. The programme was proceeding at an accelerated pace when all hell broke loose at a remote Navy base called

Pearl Harbor, and the United States was at war.

In the days that followed, the Air Forces moved fast on all their programmes. On 31 January 1942, the Air Staff ordered 500 B-29s and $53 million worth of spare parts for the planes. The final production programme for the B-29s came from a meeting of military and industrial representatives in February. Boeing-Wichita would have the responsibility for production and assembly of the B-29s. Bell Aircraft Company would build B-29s at a plant yet to be erected at Marietta, Georgia (now the Lockheed-Georgia factory). North American Aviation, then a division of General Motors, was to build the bombers at its Kansas City plant. General Motors' Fisher Body Division would produce B-29s at a Cleveland, Ohio, plant then unbuilt.

In April, the Wright Aeronautical Corporation was ordered to triple the quantity of the original order for the big, new R-3350 engines for the B-29s. And in August, after the Battle of Midway and the planning changes it forced, the Army and the Navy shuffled their plants and projects at two locations: Boeing at Renton, Washington, and North American Aviation, at Kansas City. The Navy took over the Kansas City plant; the Army got Renton. The Boeing Sea Ranger, a prototype Navy flying boat, was cancelled to free the Renton factory. North American built B-25 bombers at Kansas City and some of them went to the Navy to meet their urgent need for medium bombers. Fisher Body was pulled out of B-29 production plans to concentrate on the P-75 fighter, and the Glenn L. Martin Company got the job of building B-29s at its huge Omaha, Nebraska, plant.

In early September, Boeing workmen hauled the first XB-29 out of the assembly shed with tractors, and the flight crew ran up the engines and made the first taxi tests. A few days later, the XB-29 taxied fast and hopped — maybe 15 feet into the air — three times, touching down on the long runway at the Seattle plant.

Then, on 21 September 1942, the flight test crew headed by Eddie (Edmund T.) Allen climbed aboard, fired up the engines, taxied out and flew. They came back one hour and 15 minutes later, with generally good impressions and a few gripes.

The second XB-29 made its first flight 30 December 1942. Less than two months later, it was a heap of burning wreckage that killed Allen and the flight test crew. A fire had begun in the number one engine — the first of many that were to plague the programme — and had burned through the wing structure.

Bomb bay doors yawning wide, a Renton-built Boeing B-29A-5-BN (serial 42-93844) poses in the cloudless skies over Washington. Superfortresses had two bomb bays, one forward and one aft of the wing carrythrough structure, and could lift a variety of bomb loads to a maximum of about 20,000lbs. Early production B-29s had electrically driven bomb-bay doors that took many seconds to open and close. Later models had pneumatic actuators that snapped the doors open and closed in a fraction of a second. / *Boeing*

The third prototype XB-29 made its first flight 16 June 1943, and during July, Boeing made its first delivery to the USAAF, which accepted seven of the YB-29 service test series from Wichita.

Only three experimental prototypes were built at Boeing's Seattle plant. All production aircraft came from four sources: Boeing's new facilities at Renton, Washington, and Wichita; Bell's Marietta plant; and the Martin plant at Omaha.

Boeing-Wichita delivered the first 175 B-29s by 1 March 1944. This was the initial batch of aircraft to equip the 58th Bombardment Wing (Very Heavy), the first unit to receive and operate B-29s. But these aircraft were not combat-ready right off the line; they had to be modified extensively. The 1,000th B-29 was delivered in February 1945, and by the following month, production schedules had stabilised at 100 B-29s per month at the Wichita plant alone. In July 1945, Wichita workers were turning out an average of more than four B-29s each working day.

The contracts for the big bomber called for a total of 6,289 Superfortresses to be produced, with deliveries to continue well into 1947. The total actually produced and accepted by the AAF was 3,960 B-29s.

Production was not all of the B-29 story. The modification programme accounted for an enormous number of workers and time. During the latter half of the war, the B-29 modification programme took over a major share of the country's total modification capacity. At the AAF modification centre in Birmingham, Alabama, almost 9,000 employees were assigned to work on the Superfortresses.

### Describing the B-29

On the ground, the Superfortress spanned 141 feet 3 inches, and stretched 99 feet from nose to tail turret. Its tall tail towered 27 feet 9 inches into the air, or — as Boeing publicists were fond of saying — as high as a three-story house. It was designed to operate at a gross weight of about 120,000lb, and at a maximum overload of about 135,000lb. But B-29s were operated at weights as high as 142,000lb, and probably heavier at times.

There were three basic B-29 models, differing only in detail. The standard B-29, built at Wichita, Marietta and Omaha, had a continuous wing centre section to which the outer panels attached. The B-29A models, produced at Renton only, featured a five-piece wing, with a separate centre section, outboard and inboard panels. The fuel capacity of the B-29 was 9,363 gallons; on the B-29A it was 9,150 gallons (or 213 gallons of wing joints, as one engineer observed).

The B-29B was a special model for night precision attacks using radar bombing techniques. It had only a tail turret for defence, all other armament having been removed. It carried the AN/APQ-7 Eagle radar, updated Loran equipment for more precise navigation, and the AN/APG-15B

*Top right:* Before there were transistors, there were vacuum tubes, and the black boxes in the radio operator's position in the B-29 housed dozens of tubes. The primary radio receiver is mounted at the back of the table (centre) with the antenna switching unit above it. The transmitter is mounted at the right, as are the oxygen system controls, the interphone controls, the trailing antenna reel drive and controls, and a rat's nest of miscellaneous knobs and dials. / *Boeing 55703-B*

*Bottom right:* Contrast this combat cockpit that has, literally, been through the war with the pristine production cockpit shown in Boeing photo P-38536. This one has signs of wear, chipped paint, taped-on calibrations, instructions and warnings, including one not to exceed 300mph indicated airspeed. Radio call is 69760, indicating the aircraft is a Wichita-built B-29-60-BW (serial 44-69760). / *Dr Lyman C. Perkins*

*Below:* Aircraft commander (left) and pilot (right) of a Superfortress had excellent forward and upward visibility through the greenhouse nose of the B-29. The then super-secret Norden bombsight can be seen, uncovered, forward of the gap between the two flight instrument panels. / *Boeing P-38536*

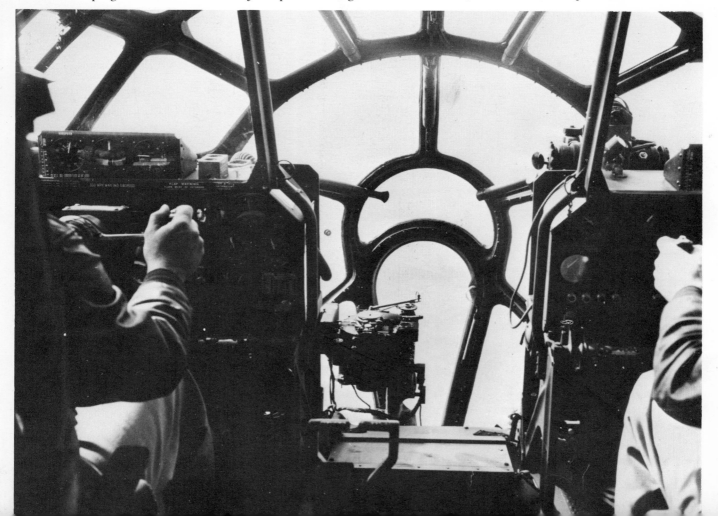

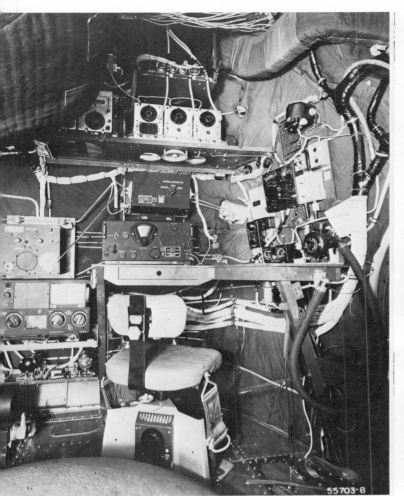

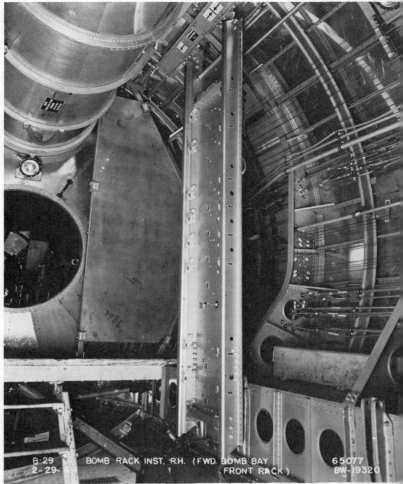

B-29
2-29-
BOMB RACK INST. R.H. (FWD. BOMB BAY
FRONT RACK )
65077
BW-19320

55703-B

*Above:* The Superfortress bomb-bay structure was forthright: Horizontal beams fore and aft to carry the loads across the gaps of the bays, and vertical bomb racks from which to sling the shackles that held the various combinations of bomb loads. But this photograph also shows the vulnerability of the B-29 at this section: Note the hydraulic lines (11 of them), electrical wiring bundles (3) and control cables (20) running along the side of the fuselage. The forward pressure bulkhead is at the left; its centre is pierced with an access door to the bomb bay. Above it is the long cylindrical pressurised tunnel connecting the forward and aft pressure cabins. / *Boeing BW-19320*

17

*Right:* Early models of the B-29 had provisions for crew bunks for relief, as well as provisions for troop carrying. These features soon were abandoned, as the fuselage space was taken over by radar operators and 'Ravens' who ran the complicated electronic countermeasures equipment. / *Boeing X-711*

radar for night sighting of the tail guns. Its fuel capacity was the same as standard B-29s.

The powerplant of the B-29 was a quartette of R-3350 engines — the number refers to the total displacement in cubic inches — a team of powerful, untried engines developed by the Wright Aeronautical Corporation. They were twin-row radials, with 18 cylinders, and their exhaust was directed through ducting to drive a pair of General Electric Co B-11 turbosuperchargers for improved high-altitude performance. The turbos were automatically regulated by a Minneapolis-Honeywell electronic system. Under the engine were slung two oil coolers and the intercooler for the turbosupercharger operation.

Engines were rated at sea level at 2,200 brake horsepower for takeoff, and at 2,000bhp for maximum continuous operation. The superchargers held the sea-level power rating up to an altitude of 33,000 feet.

The Wright engines were called everything from the Wrong engines to flamethrowers. They ran hot on the ground, and required redesign of the cylinder baffling and reworked cowl flaps before they would even approach reasonable cylinder head temperatures. They also were prone to swallow valves. In later years, the engines became reliable and much less troublesome. But in World War 2, they were nothing but trouble. Ask any pilot, any flight engineer, any mechanic.

'Engine fires were one hell of a problem. When the magnesium caught, there was no stopping them. One night we had a crash at Pratt during training, and the fire tender came up and poured on a whole load of foam. I swear it didn't change the intensity of the fire one bit.

'We were sitting on Saipan one night, looking across the water watching the 313th and the 58th take off from Tinian. Five B-29s caught fire, either on the runway or over the water between Tinian and Saipan.

'There's a story that the very last plane off Saipan, after the war had long since ended, just got into the air and the number four engine burst into flames.' — *H. W. Douglas, 869 Bomb Sqn, 497 Bomb Group*

The XB-29s were powered by the R-3350-13 model, and the YB-29s got -21 engines. Production B-29 aircraft had the R-3350-23 engines installed, and the B-29A got -57 engines.

They turned three-bladed, 17-foot diameter propellers on the experimental ships, and four-bladed props with a diameter of 16 feet 7 inches on the production airplanes. They were Hamilton Standard Hydromatic propellers, with constant-speed governors and hydraulic operation for pitch change and feathering. The engine gear ratio was 0.35, which meant that the propeller turned a little more than one-third of the engine revolutions per minute. At takeoff, with 2,800 engine rpm, the prop was turning at 980rpm, and at minimum cruise setting of 1,400 engine rpm, it was just ticking over at 490rpm.

Toward the end of the war, some B-29s particularly those acquired by the 509th Composite Group, were equipped with Curtiss electric propellers, which had reversible pitch for added braking effect. They also were fitted with blade cuffs near the root of each blade, to increase the airflow

*Above:* Boeing's Wichita plant turned out B-29s by the dozen. In this spectacular rainy night shot, there are 24 B-29s — the -45-BW version — complete or nearly so. Three huge bays of this plant each had two parallel production lines, and each of them had four final assembly positions, judging by this photograph. / *Boeing BW-23991*

*Bottom left:* B-29 wings built at Wichita, and at all sub-contractors' plants, had a continuous centre section, with the wing roots meeting on the airplane centreline and the fuselage half-shells bolted on top and bottom. The B-29A models built at Boeing's Renton plant had a short cylindrical fuselage centre section with stub wing attachments, plus two outer panel sections to make up a five-piece wing. Here B-29 wing centre sections are being produced at Wichita, at aft stations on the production line. / *Boeing BW-23591*

*Above:* The last Renton-built Superfortress off the line (serial 44-62327) shows a couple of late-model changes to the airplane. Curtiss reversible-pitch electric propellers have replaced the Hamilton Standard Hydromatic units, and a streamlined, four-gun turret housing has replaced the earlier flattened hemispherical shape. / *Gordon S. Williams*

*Right:* The 'wing' underneath this B-29's belly is the radome of the AN/APQ-7 'Eagle' radar, a precision bombing radar system. It was installed on B-29B models only in service, and is here shown in an experimental installation on a standard Boeing B-29 identified as a Martin-built aircraft. / *Gordon S. Williams*

in that area and drive it through the engine cowling for improved cooling.

The B-29 sported a variety of new electronic equipment. As tactics evolved, additional pieces of radio and radar gear were developed to aid detection, or evasion, of enemy defences. Other equipment was designed to improve the performance of the B-29's bombing systems, or to enable the navigators to plot positions and find targets more accurately.

Early model B-29s used the AN/APN-4 Loran system, a long-range navigation aid based on the detection of a broadcast 'grid' of Loran lines of known position. Late model aircraft carried the APN-9 equipment. Philco built the -4, and RCA built the -9 Loran equipment.

The major radar bombing-navigational aid was the AN/APQ-13 equipment, developed by the Bell Telephone Laboratories and the Massachusetts Institute of Technology Radiation Laboratory. It used a 30-inch radar antenna mounted in a hemispherical radome installed between the bomb bays. It was often retouched out of photos released during the war, but it was standard equipment on B-29s in the Marianas.

The AN/APQ-7 Eagle bombing-navigation radar was developed at MIT's Radiation Lab and at Bell Telephone, and built — as was the APQ-13 — by Western Electric Co. It saw service on the B-29s of the

315th Bombardment Wing (VH) in their campaign of precision attacks on radar-located targets at night.

The Eagle radar was installed in a wing-shaped housing slung underneath the belly of the B-29s. It spanned 17 feet, had a 31-inch chord, and was just under eight inches thick. As built, the forward section was a white plastic radome and the aft section was conventional aluminium alloy. As used in the field, the entire unit was painted black along with the rest of the B-29 belly area.

Late in the war, and too late to have any real operational significance, a gun-laying radar was installed on the B-29s of the 315th BW. Built by General Electric, this radar solved the relatively simple problems of tail gunnery: No lead angle, point-blank range, straight-in attack. It was mounted in a ball-shaped radome below and completely outside the tail turret.

The SCR-729 radar interrogator system had paired antenna, one a double dipole type and the other a whip, mounted on each side of the B-29 nose near the navigator's and flight engineer's positions. This Philco system was used to determine the range and bearing of any aircraft it interrogated by radar.

The SCR-718C radio altimeter, built by RCA, was used primarily to determine the absolute altitude above the ground for the bomb run. Its output could be used with data

The radome covering the AN/APQ-13 radar shows clearly under the wings of these B-29s from the 873rd BS, 498th BG, on a combat mission out of their Saipan base late in the war. / Collection of Mrs Thomas Isley

One anticipated problem — ditching a B-29 in the open seas — was investigated in a number of model tests in a towing tank operated by the then National Advisory Committee for Aeronautics at its Langley Memorial Laboratory, Langley Field, Virginia. Scaled, dynamically similar models were suspended on the instrumented carriage shown, which moved above the surface near scale stalling speed and released the model to strike the surface in a simulation of the actual full-scale ditching. / *NACA LMAL 46809*

from the drift meter to get an indication of ground speed and track.

The B-29 carried the usual complement of radio equipment for communications with ground stations and other aircraft. The state of the art of those days produced radios with tubes, and the sets were bulky, heavy, fragile, unreliable and limited in capability. And, since it was before the days of jet speeds, the B-29s carried a number of external antennas, including a long single wire that stretched from the fuselage to the vertical tail.

'When we took delivery of our new B-29, she wasn't complete in every detail, as we had expected. Some fairings and small trim items were missing. But we scrounged the parts and put a beautiful ship together. The guys even waxed the leading edge.

'I fitted a picture of my wife behind the plastic piece in the centre of the wheel, under the impression B-29. (I still have this piece today; it flew every hour with me.)

'When I first went up to the cockpit, I had to remove the bill of sale from the pilot's seat before I could sit down. The bill was from Boeing to the US Army, for one each B-29 aircraft, price $1,000,203.50.

'We flew it out to Guam, and immediately upon landing our airplane was confiscated for another crew to fly a mission that night. The next day we were waiting for them to bring our bird back, and we spotted this lame B-29 in the pattern, shot full of holes, bomb-bay doors flapping. Right; it was ours. We never flew that machine again.

'I had been in the Air Force since 1941, and had flown a lot of different aircraft, but none was more exciting or challenging than the

B-29. I hated it and I loved it. We had great admiration for its advanced — and untested — technology, its speed, comfort, defensive weapons. She was extremely rugged, but always unpredictable. Every flight or mission had its problems. Forced landings were common occurrences. Sometimes we wondered whether the battle was with the Japanese or the B-29.

'People have this stereotyped image of the heavy bomber pilot; you know, the dogmatic, by-the-book, straight-and-level type. But we were flying the greatest fighter plane in the air at the time. We had the manoeuvrability when we were light, and my gunners and their equipment were so good they could make a Japanese fighter pilot change his mind and his course 1,200 yards off.

'We flew tight formation when we had to, and we flew straight and level over the target. I never left the formation on the run in, of course, but it was frustrating not to be able to break loose and tangle with a Japanese fighter.

'When we were on individual missions, operating independently of any formation — say on a 'porcupine' mission — we'd fly to the target as briefed. We were flying on what we called 'government time'. Coming off the target, we said we were on our own time, and that's when you'd see some fast and fancy flying, even some aerobatics.

'Let me tell you, she could fly like a fighter. When we were light, we could go fast on the level and very fast downhill. We saw a couple of Navy Grumman Hellcats once when we were light and on a test flight, and we bounced them. I must have surprised the

hell out of them when they saw this big four-engined bird do a wingover and roar past them. She did beautiful wingovers for such a giant airplane, and everything stayed right in place inside.' *Charles B. Hawks, Jr, aircraft commander, 43rd BS, 29th BG*

When the crews trained on the B-29s, they learned all the limitations the airplane had. They learned that the power settings were not to be exceeded, that landing weight limitations were to be taken seriously, and that speed and manoeuvrability parameters were to be respected.

When they got to war with the airplanes, they learned differently. B-29s that weren't supposed to be thrown around by their pilots were thrown around violently by turbulence in the thick of fire raids. Engine power was pushed to the utmost, and airframes were asked to take strains that would have made the Boeing designers shudder. But the B-29 had the ability to do more than the designers had intended, and her rugged airframe got the crews back home, time after time. It also enabled the pilots to do things with the airplane that they had learned not to do in training.

'Soon after the B-29s had left, one was back in the pattern. The pilot — who was a Lieutenant Colonel, and I wish I knew his name — made a beautiful landing, and taxied over to the hardstand area. He called the crew chief over and asked him to fix some item on the airplane, right away. When the crew chief asked him why right now, the Colonel said that he wanted to take off again and catch up with the group.

'The crew chief said, well, Colonel, you know we'll have to refuel and reload the bombs, and that's going to take some time to do all that. "It's all still in the plane," said the Colonel.

'Damned if he hadn't landed a fully loaded B-29!' *H. W. Douglas*

'Major Joe Kramp, who always followed his signature with three letters — WGA, for World's Greatest Aviator — may have been just that. He flew a stretch of five missions in three days with green crews each time, which could not have been a picnic.

'The pilots all took advantage of the height of the cliff at Saipan to gain a little extra airspeed. They'd lift off just before the cliff and then put the nose down to gain a bit on the speed. Kramp used to use every foot of that height, and once he cut it so close that the plane actually skipped off the water, like you'd skip a stone across a pond. The waist gunners reported that water came into their compartment. The impact cleaned off the radome, bent the bomb bay doors and the tips of the two inboard props.

'That didn't stop Major Joe Kramp, the World's Greatest Aviator. He flew the mission, 3,000 miles round trip, and in his post-flight report he said the airplane felt a little rough.' *Don Miller, tail gunner, 874 BS, 498 BG*

'I rode along on a test flight to check out the APQ-13 radar, and I sat in the CFC (Central Fire Control) gunner's seat for a while. We were bounced by four camouflaged P-47s, and they got pretty close. Our pilot waved them off, but they continued to buzz us. So

Engine-out performance was critical on the B-29s, and a combat situation was very different from this controlled test flight done over the friendlier environment of the Arizona desert. Here, only the number one engine is running; two, three and four have been shut down and their props feathered. The airplane is a B-29-35-MO (44-27274), built by Martin at Omaha. In combat, you could get back on three engines, and occasionally on two. But on one ... unheard of. / *Boeing X-1241*

The Challenger was a stripped B-29B assigned to Lt Gen James H. Doolittle, commanding the Eighth Air Force on Okinawa after mid-July 1945. Like all standard B-29B models, this aircraft did not have gun turrets on the upper and lower fuselage. / *Boeing P-6024*

our pilot got fed up, put the nose down a little and asked for full power. We left the first two fighters behind fairly soon, then the third and finally the fourth. We were in a shallow dive, with full power, down to about 22,000 feet.

'The pilot asked the navigator for the maximum speed during the dive, and the navigator said we were doing 475 miles per hour.' *H. W. Douglas*

### Defensive Armament

Range and pressurisation dictated development of the remotely controlled defensive gunnery system on the B-29s. The great range of the aircraft eliminated all-the-way fighter escort and created a need for an effective defence with heavy firepower. Its pressurisation meant that men could not ride in the turrets as they did in other bombers.

A remote system, however, would allow the gunners to sit inside the pressurised fuselage of the B-29, and the turret assembly could be sealed in an enclosure to maintain the pressurisation integrity of the aircraft.

Bendix, General Electric, Sperry and Westinghouse competed for the defensive system, and Sperry won the initial contracts. The first three prototype XB-29s had the Sperry system, with retractable turrets and periscope sights, but all production aircraft were armed by the General Electric system.

There were five gun positions — upper forward, upper aft, lower forward, lower aft, and tail — and five gunnery positions, manned by four gunners and the bombardier. On early model B-29s, the upper and lower turrets mounted a pair of .50-calibre machine guns. The tail turret had the same pair, plus a 20mm cannon. But combat experience — the Japanese made head-on attacks on B-29 formations — caused a change to a four-gun upper forward turret, and the removal of the 20mm cannon because of problems with the feed mechanism and because its shells followed a different trajectory from that of the .50-cal machine gun bullets.

Originally, the Air Forces* decided to produce the system without a computer for solving the ballistics equations, hoping that the gunners would be able to solve them by visually compensating for lead, lag and windage. That was asking a bit much, because if a gunner were to have control of two turrets simultaneously, as was the plan, two different sets of ballistic equations would have to be solved visually, and even the most expert gunners could not handle that.

So the B-29 system ended as a computerised and flexible system that gave control of the turrets to more than one gunner, in case another gunner was wounded and could not handle his primary assignment.

The key man in the system was the Central Fire Control (CFC) gunner, who perched on an elevated seat known sometimes as the barber's chair under a transparent sighting blister just forward of the upper aft turret. He controlled the master gunnery panel, which assigned turrets to each gunner. The upper forward turret was primarily for the bombardier, and secondarily for the CFC gunner. The upper aft turret was primarily for the CFC gunner. The lower forward and lower aft turrets were assigned to the side gunners, and either could fire one or both turrets to meet attacks from his side. The lower forward turret could be taken over by the bombardier as a secondary assignment. The tail turret was primarily the tail gunner's responsibility; but it also could be fired by either of the side gunners.

The gun sights included a dead-man's switch; if a gunner were knocked out of action, his turret automatically was assigned to the gunner with secondary control. It was a reflector sight, with the optics focussed on infinity so that the gunner could use it with both eyes open. What they saw in the sight was a circle of orange dots around a central pip. They selected a wingspan dimension, and adjusted the sight manually to that number. When an enemy fighter came into view, the

trick was to set the orange circle with the right-hand range knob on the sight, so that the circle just enclosed the wingspan. Then the gunner had to continue to change the diameter of the orange circle while the fighter bored in, holding the pip on him at the same time, and firing the guns with thumb triggers when the aim and range permitted.

Computation of all the geometry and the ballistics involved was done electro-mechanically by analog computers in 'black boxes' under the cabin floor, protected by armour.

'By World War 2 standards, the B-29 had an extremely sophisticated self-defence system. And I recall the horror in the eyes of an Air Forces general when he learned that each gun turret had six vacuum tubes, and failure of any one would cause the loss of that turret's protection.

*Above:* Twin .50-cal machine guns point skyward under the control of the top gunner, whose head can be seen in the upper sighting blister, partially hidden by his gunsight. / *Boeing X-379*

*Right:* The tail turret guns — one 20mm cannon and a pair of .50-cal machine guns — are protected by covers while this B-29A-1-BN (42-93838) stands in the open on the ramp at Boeing's Renton, Washington, plant. The tail gunner's escape hatch is just above the small fairing between the inboard end of the elevators and the fuselage. / *Boeing X-258*

'The decision was made to rush into production of the analog computers roughly 12 to 18 months after the production decision on the turret system itself. So the first computers were installed at a modification centre at Birmingham, Alabama, and I was GE tech rep there.

'When the Air Forces were rushing to get the first wing of B-29s off to India, it was pretty apparent that a lot of the systems were in bad shape. So General K. B. Wolfe called the president of each company involved, at 3.00am as I recall, to emphasise the gravity of the situation, and asked them to send out a team of experts to get their particular systems in shape to go overseas.

'I was sent from Birmingham in a chilling ride in a B-24 when the pilot got lost and descended to read the name of a town off a sign on the post office. Teams were sent to four towns in Kansas where the B-29s stood at nearby airfields.

*Above:* The initial armament of the B-29 tail turret was the trio shown: One 20mm cannon, two .50-cal machine guns. But the unmatched trajectories of the two types of projectiles, and problems with the feed mechanism for the cannon, led to its removal in war zones, and reliance on the paired machine guns for defending the tail. / *Boeing X-385*

*Right:* The 'barber's chair' was the position of the top, or CFC (Central Fire Control) gunner. The seat was directly opposite the entrance to the pressurised tunnel between the forward and aft cabins of the B-29. The top gunner operated the switching system that allocated specific turrets to specific gunners, and additionally operated his own gun sight controlling the upper aft turret as a primary responsibility. / *Boeing X-321*

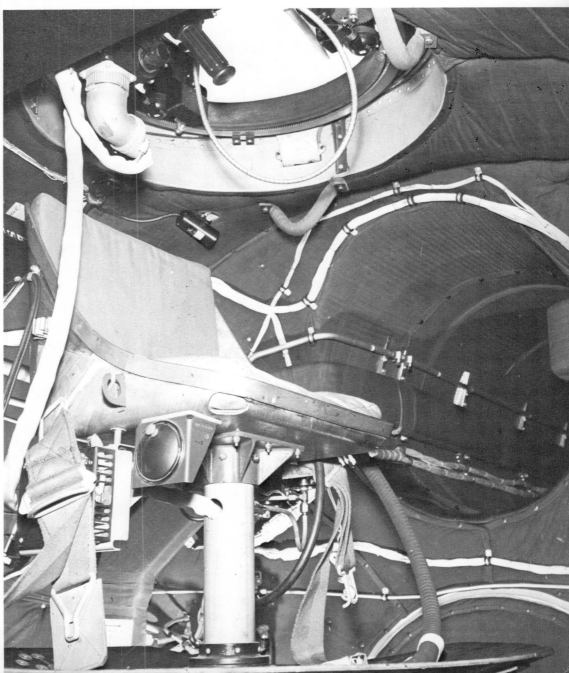

Alternate armament schemes were devised and even tested on the B-29, and this combination of Emerson, Martin and Sperry turrets was one such programme. The nose installation was a pair of Emerson barbette turrets, remotely controlled, each mounting a single .50-cal machine gun. The General Electric turrets were replaced by Martin manned turrets on the upper fuselage, forward and aft, and by Sperry ball turrets on the lower fuselage, fore and aft. Additionally, the side gunners' sighting blisters were replaced with installations for a single flexible mount .50-cal machine gun. These installations were made on the 72nd production B-29 off the line at Wichita, a B-29-29-BW model, serial 42-24441. The photographs were taken on 7 October 1944.
/ *Boeing*

*Right:* 'Hey, don't watch me! Watch what you're doing!' And what they are doing is loading the four .50-cal guns of the upper forward turret on *Thumper*, a Wichita-built B-29-41-BW (42-24623). The protective fairing has been removed for the job, and — with the guns fully loaded — is now about to be replaced. / *A. F. Migliaccio Collection*

*Below:* Technicians check the mechanisms of the tail guns and load the 20mm cannon feed drum on this B-29 operated by the 500th BG on Saipan / *Ingram T. Hermanson Collection*

'We worked 16-hour, sometimes 24-hour shifts. When we got too tired to carry on, we would return to the tiny hotel, wake up our replacement, and climb into the still warm bed.

'It was freezing cold at the time with blizzards and high winds. I recall sitting in the tail of a B-29, trying to resolder a bad connection, and having to cup the soldering iron in my gloved hands to get it warm enough to do the job. Aircraft sat out in the open, heated by external engine-driven gas heaters and with the power supply coming from a separate engine-driven generator. One or the other was always running out of fuel, halting our operations until we could hike a half-mile to get more gas.

'The condition of the GE system was pretty horrible, and I assume that was true for many others. Wires interconnecting aircraft cables made by newly trained workers sometimes ran to the wrong pins on connectors. Whoever stripped the insulation off sometimes nicked four or five of the seven strands of wire, and left the connection hanging by only a couple. There were blobs of solder shorting out adjacent pins or sockets in the connectors. We did the best we could to assure that the turret system was operable, but we lacked the time to inspect every wire and every connector, and we could only hope they would hang together.

'In late 1944, after the B-29 was already operational, Eglin Field started its "operational suitability" tests, and I was sent down there when we got reports that the system was doing badly in the tests. When I arrived at Eglin, I discovered two reasons why the system was doing so badly. First, Eglin was short of competent engineers to run the test on the GE system, so our competitor thoughtfully volunteered to supply one of their engineers, already stationed there, to supervise the tests on the GE system at no cost. Second, nobody had bothered to check out the GE equipment before tests to see if it was in operating condition. I discovered that a rat had built a nest in one of the computers.' *Philip J. Klass, technical representative, General Electric Company*

'We got a specialised briefing, just for gunners, after the main briefing. They told us the usual thing: how many and how good the fighters were going to be, what their tactics might be like, things like that. Then we'd go and clean and load our own guns and check the ammo. The ammo came out from ordnance in belts and boxes, and we'd lay them out and check them for rounds that were out of alignment in the belts.

'When it came time to board the airplane, I'd go in the aft entrance door, crawl through the tail section and into the tail turret, close the door and adjust the seat. You had to sit up straight, there was no relaxing back there. Not that you'd want to, anyway . . .

'We gunners used a lap belt only, wore soft helmets with oxygen masks, a flak helmet over that, and a full suit of flak armour. The chest chute was stowed on the floor, and you generally hooked it on at the start of combat. If you had to bail out, you were supposed to take the flak suit off first, over the chute and over your shoulders. There was a rip cord on the flak suit that unfastened the thing, supposedly.

'It was cramped, but there was sufficient space for the job. I first flew the tail turret when there were three guns: one 20mm cannon and two .50-cal machine guns. But we could only get about 20 rounds out of the cannon before it jammed, and there was so much trouble with the feed mechanism that they removed the cannon. We carried 120 rounds for the cannon and 1,200 round per machine gun. We came home empty.

'Some time after takeoff we'd test-fire the guns by triggering a couple of short bursts. If we had minor troubles, there was a pretty good chance we could fix them in the air on the way to the target and before we had to pressurise the airplane for the climb to altitude. We kept the gun heaters on all the time and we did not lubricate the guns with oil, because the oil would freeze at the high altitudes we flew.

'The tail guns would cover a volume of plus or minus 30 degrees in both azimuth and elevation. The sight was the same as the side gunners' sights. The left hand gripped a deadman's switch, which you had to hold down in order to fire. The right hand you used to work the ranging control. It was the job of the flight engineer to set the airplane altitude, airspeed and temperature to get true air data

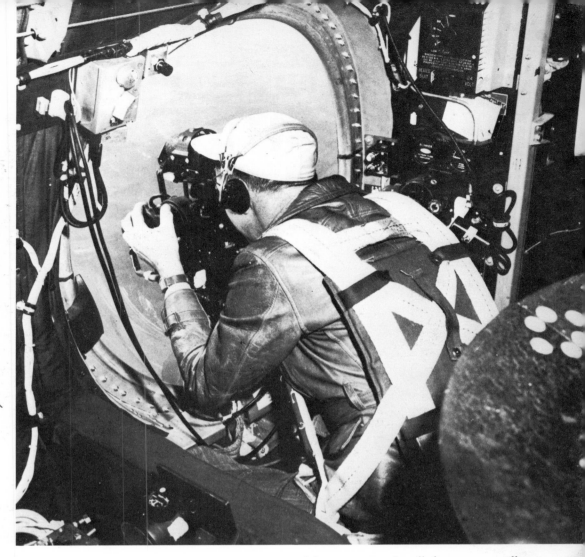

*Left:* Sgts William F. Dawson (left) and W. R. Lambert load the four .50-cal machine guns of the forward upper turret on their B-29 during the Korean war.
/ *William F. Dawson Collection*

*Below left:* The tail gunner had adequate, although somewhat cramped space. 'There wasn't room to spread out back there', said one of them. Isolated from the rest of the crew during combat, he was lonely as well as apprehensive. His guns, gunsight and bullet-proof glass windshield protected him in front; he leaned against a piece of armour plate to shield his back.
/ *Boeing Wichita BW-24594*

*Right:* The side gunners worked in large hemispherical blisters that blew out from time to time, adding some uncertainties to their combat experience. On the bulkhead to his right are oxygen and electrically heated suit controls; above and to his left is the rotating switch for the intercom system.
/ *Boeing Wichita*

*Below:* Among the four .50-cal machine guns of the forward upper turret is the cam follower, a simple mechanical insurance policy to keep gunners from shooting off parts of the aircraft.
/ *Boeing Wichita BW-29382*

out of the computers for all the gunners. All we had to do was to sight, adjust the ranging control for the wingspan of the fighters, and thumb the triggers.

'You could hear your own guns when you fired them, of course. And you felt the shock, the recoil, of the other guns when they were fired, even though you couldn't hear them. The belt links and spent cases from the tail turret and the two lower turrets were ejected overboard; the rest of the cases and links fell into the fuselage. Our first bombing formation was a diamond, and the tail-end plane flew above the lead, high enough to clear his wake and still low enough to see the tip of the tail of the lead aircraft. They did that to avoid getting the links and cases of the airplane ahead through their own windshield. There was one crew that got a little too low in the formation, and got a face full of links and cases. When they got back, the pilot and co-pilot were ordered to change the windshield glass themselves, to remind them not to get too low in the formation the next time.

'After we got back to base, we cleared all the guns before we left the airplane, swabbed them with gun oil, and went to the debriefing.' — *Don Miller*

# Eleven Men

The crew complement standardised for early operations of the B-29 consisted of 11 men. Five were officers: the aircraft commander, pilot, bombardier, navigator, and flight engineer. Six were enlisted men: radio operator, radar operator, central fire control gunner, left and right gunners, and the tail gunner.

Later in the war, one or two additional officers, known as 'Ravens', flew with the crews to operate the highly specialised and highly classified electronic countermeasures equipment.

By mid-1944, the flight engineer ranks had been opened to enlisted men, and they took over that position toward the end of the war and subsequently.

The crew concept was the cornerstone of the B-29 operations. Crews were selected to be a permanent team, to be changed only in the event of the wounding or the death of one or more members. They trained together, after completing the individual specialist trainings that each crewman received. That required some juggling of the standardised cirricula and schedules that were then in existence.

Training programmes were fluid during the war, in response to the changing needs and the demands of new tactics and new equipment. Pilots at first spent nine weeks in each stage of their training — primary, basic and advanced — and later the course was lengthened to ten weeks per phase. Navigators started with 15-week courses, later increased to 18 and then to 20. Gunners took a 12-week course that later shrank to six weeks. Bombardiers also took a course in flexible gunnery — non-turreted machine guns — either before or after their specialist courses.

The first of the B-29 crews were drawn from among combat crews with previous experience on four-engined aircraft. One nucleus came from anti-submarine operations in Europe and North Africa, and had flown Consolidated B-24 bombers. Other pilots were taken from among the instructors in multi-engine flight schools. Then, as the war progressed, raw aviation cadets were moved through primary, basic and advanced to transition training and the co-pilot's seat of a B-29.

Training Command had the responsibility for all the specialist training courses for aircrew classes. But all B-29 crew training and unit training was the responsibility of the Second Air Force.

The B-29 was a special airplane, and it required a new approach to training. It was, of course, bigger than the standard heavy bombers. Further, the intended B-29 operations emphasised high-altitude, long-range navigation and the use of radar for both navigation and bombing. It demanded much closer integration of the crew, whose functions overlapped and became interdependent during the flight.

The aircraft commander, pilot and flight engineer were one such team. Their ability to think and to react as a single individual was most important during critical portions of the flight, such as the takeoff, where a slight hesitation in recognising the problem and taking corrective action could mean a fiery and sudden death.

The bomb run tied together the efforts of the aircraft commander, the navigator, the bombardier, and the radar operator. Navigation also required the assistance of the radar operator and the pilots as well as the work of the navigator himself. The left and right gunners also were scanners of the airplane, whose duties included watching the engines for signs of trouble, calling out flap deflections and the condition of the landing gear. By reporting attacks, the gunners often gave indirect steering information to the pilots.

For five weeks prior to their crew assignments, the pilots, co-pilots and flight engineers went through a special course designed to emphasise the teamwork they would need in operations. Then they were assigned to the Second Air Force units that would give them their full crew training.

This specialised training plan, modified specifically for the requirements of B-29 operations, began in the fall of 1943, and turned out a total of 2,350 crews before the end of the war.

'The available flying time in the B-29 was very limited in training; there was a shortage of aircraft. Most of the early crew training was done in B-17s. I had come to B-29s from a tour with an anti-submarine squadron in England and I had 450 hours in B-24s. I was one of two pilots with combat experience in the squadron.

'My first flight in the B-29 was on 18 May 1944. I logged six hours, 20 minutes, and shot 14 landings in that time period. I didn't fly a B-29 again until 7 June, when I made 10 landings on a five hour 20 minute flight. On 11 June I was checked out as pilot of B-29s, with a final flight of one hour 40 minutes with three landings.

'Co-pilots of B-29s seldom made landings; yet the co-pilots of later replacement crews arriving on Saipan had more landings than I had recorded in the B-29s, and bear in mind that we were an original combat crew out there and a lead crew as well, which meant that we could fly extra training flights.

'My last B-29 training flight was a simulated group combat mission that lasted 14 hours 25 minutes. By then we had 20 trained crews — two per airplane — and we moved to a staging area at Kearney, Nebraska, to wait for 10 B-29s to come off the production line so that we could deploy to Saipan. I had a grand total of 105 hours in the B-29 at that point.' *Ferd J. Curtis, aircraft commander, 881st BS, 500th BG*

Havana, Cuba, was the target for the first long-range missions many of the B-29 crews ever flew. It was, of course, a training flight. The distance was representative of the trip to Japan from the Marianas, and the approach to Havana was over water, similar to the approaches to Japan.

The missions began in late August 1944. The B-29s would lift off training fields in Kansas, and head generally southeast for Cuba. They landed all over the southeastern United States, out of fuel. Crews still hadn't learned the secrets of cruise control on the B-29.

It was a serious situation. The B-29s were expected to start striking the home islands of Japan from Saipan in November 1944, and — with only three months to go — they weren't able to be flown on an equivalent mission without bomb loads, with good communications and meteorological information, and with no enemy fighters or flak.

Training began to tighten. Flight engineers quickly learned about cruise control. The secret was simple: run the manifold pressure way up, and keep the rpm low. Down went the fuel consumption.

'The 58th Bomb Wing had taken just about all the serviceable B-29s with them when they left for the CBI theatre, and we were left with some very tired B-17s for training. It seemed that every one of these planes had some part that didn't work. It's a tribute to the long-suffering ground crews that they were able to fly at all. We had to scratch training missions because of some malfunction, time after time.

'Finally we began to get some B-29s. What a giant of an airplane this 50-ton machine seemed to be! I was awed by the power they represented, and remained so throughout my service in them.

'The first phases of training accelerated after the big birds became available. We shot endless takeoffs and landings, flew bomb runs over three local ranges dropping flour bombs. We gunners had to learn to adapt from the Sperry manned turrets we had trained in to the more complicated General Electric remote control types on the B-29. Malfunctions were commonplace. Guns would jam, overheated barrels would "cook-off" rounds, electrical systems would burn out. But as time passed, these irritations were overcome.

'On gunnery-training missions, we kept busy in simulated attacks made against us by fighter aircraft. The next day, we'd view the gun-camera films to see which crew had the best score. One time the fighter — we trained against one, coming from one angle, but the Japanese had other procedures — failed to show. We didn't want to scrub the mission, so the B-29s took turns making passes at each other. The films next day caused some lifted eyebrows, because they showed four-engined bombers flying in on tight pursuit curves!

'Kansas thunderstorms are legendary, and we had our share, which complicated the training missions. One time we were coming back from a long-range bombing mission in the Gulf of Mexico near Galveston, and we were caught in a severe storm. We were tossed around like a feather, and finally spit out clear of the clouds, upside down. Another time we had turned on final and had just broken out of the overcast when a B-29 broke through the same overcast just ahead of us on a collision course. If his wheels had been down, as ours were, he would have hit us. Never did find out who he was.

'These training programmes, however dangerous, were taken as a matter of course as the programme rolled along. Personally, I always felt safer in the air than I did in the buses that served the base.

'As more B-29s became available, they had us in the air sometimes for two missions per day, which played hell with our love life in town. Missions became longer with bomb runs on Gulf targets, and non-stop missions to Florida and back. We always took a Class A uniform along on those flights just in case we had engine trouble over Florida. Several times we did have such trouble, however suspect. It turned out that those missions were approximately the same length as those we would later fly from Saipan. And let's not forget the "booze runs" to Chicago and Peoria, to pick up a cargo rack filled with the snakebite medicine that couldn't be bought in dry Kansas!' *George S. Gray, CFC gunner, 883rd BS, 500th BG*

Candidates for flight engineer training were expected to be officer graduates of maintenance engineering courses or, later, experienced mechanics. They were to become much more than throttle jockeys. They were expected to know all about the airplane and its systems, and their tasks ran the gamut from providing and setting input data for the central fire control system to adjusting the pressurising in the cabin. In emergencies, they were expected to repair these systems, if necessary.

Their training began with the standard pre-flight aircrew school. It was followed by 19 weeks in a study of first- and second-echelon maintenance of the B-29s. For their advanced training, engineer candidates spent ten weeks in a three-phased course geared to the many real problems of the B-29s. First, they learned how to be excellent mechanics, so that they could handle in-flight malfunctions and emergencies. Second, they learned the operation of the powerplants for best cruise control. Third, they had four weeks of flight training. Most of that time was flown in B-24 bombers that had been modified to carry several flight engineers at separate stations. It wasn't exactly like the B-29, but it was the best that could be done under the circumstances. It was well into 1944 before the very first B-29 became available for ground instruction of flight engineers.

By the time of the Korean war, the B-29s had settled down a bit. Being a flight engineer was no easier then than it had been five years and more earlier, but at least by then, almost everything that might happen had happened, and the proper preventive or corrective actions were fairly well defined. But there was always the unexpected:

'B-29 combat crew training for the Korean war was rough on young teenage engineers, and on retread pilots who didn't want to be there in the first place. And it didn't help matters to know that after the training at Randolph (AFB, Texas), there was Korea waiting. Check rides, standboard exams, and flight checks were things to be despised, but we all knew the best thing to do was pass and get the hell out of Randolph anyway.

'On one particular day our crew was getting a check ride from a major who occupied the co-pilot's seat for the flight. He was a stickler for detail, and he demanded instant response and perfection from the crew. After minor skirmishes on pre-flight, takeoff and climb-out, we settled down for the rest of the routine.

'Our aircraft commander was a retread captain who didn't give a damn for anybody or anything, and his nickname was "Tex". We were sitting there, flying straight and level with everything working like a well-oiled watch, when the major yanked number four throttle back to idle, slumped over the control column and yelled, "You just lost number four and I'm dead! What are you going to do about it, Captain?"

'Old Tex punched the mike button, and in a cool, couldn't-care-less tone said, "Engineer! Come up here and drag this dead bastard out and help me fly this son-of-a-bitchin' airplane!"

'We passed the check ride.' *Eugene L. Davis, flight engineer, 370th BS, 307th BW, Korea*

And training never stopped. Even after flight crews were flying combat missions on a regular basis, there were often special training flights to accomplish.

'Would you believe flying a 3,000-mile mission only to land, refuel and then practice formation flying? We did. Our CO was unhappy with our daylight bombing patterns, because he believed — and he was probably right — that the Japanese fighter defence picked on loose formations. And let me tell you, tight formation flying in the B-29 — the only kind our CO would allow — took lots of muscle and sweat.

'During our next daylight raid we flew so tight that one flak burst nearly took out two aircraft. We got punctured, and our wing man got punctured.' *Charles B. Hawks*

'Our crew was designated as a lead crew and it was regarded by some as a dubious honour, because the attrition rate of lead crews was high. The Japanese fighters had found that their most effective attack was a direct frontal approach, because from more conventional fighter approaches the B-29 had very effective defensive firepower. B-29 formations were staggered vertically to make full use of that firepower.

'The Japanese fighters would attack from the front of the formation and, rather than break away within our firing range, they would continue right on through the formation and be in position to attack the next formation in trail behind. The lead aircraft was the prime target for this type of attack.

'Initial selection of lead crews was from the three flight leaders in each squadron, and that was based on rank. We lost our initial flight leaders rapidly. Major Bob Goldsworthy was shot down by fighters over Tokyo in December 1944. The deputy flight leader on that mission, Captain Joe Irvin, had to ditch on the way back with a damaged B-29, and didn't survive. Captain Hod Hatch replaced the operations officer in January, which left only Captain Bob Fitzgerald as a flight leader and he was shot down over Nagoya later.

'The selection of my crew for lead training was not by my rank or record, because I was a junior captain and had not led a single mission. I think that greater consideration was given about then to the performance of the crew as a whole. My navigator, bombardier and radar operator had worked with good co-ordination since our early training. I had done an earlier combat tour, in an anti-submarine squadron based in England, flying Consolidated B-24s, and that was a factor. Anyway, my crew was selected as a lead crew in January 1945.

'That meant additional training, and it had not been anticipated that there would be any need for training in the theatre. There was no bombing range. Later, replacement crews bombed the island of Truk for shakedown purposes, but that practice was discarded because of the poor ratio of aircraft flight time to the training time over the target on the bomb run. So we used nearby islands for simulated, dry-run bombing.

'A typical training mission would start with a crew briefing given by the squadron staff including a flight plan and a target bomb plan. We followed standard combat procedures except for the bomb and ammunition loading. A shortened low-level flight was made to the point where we began the climb to bombing altitude. We reached that height just prior to the departure point for the run. A radar run was made to the initial point (IP) where the bombardier took over and made a visual bombsight run on the primary target. We continued to follow the flight plan with a complete radar run to another departure point, initial point and the secondary target. Return to base was normal and the debriefing was done by the squadron staff.' *Ferd J. Curtis*

In retrospect, the training time available for B-29 crews was terribly limited. Crews were sent into combat with a minimum of time in the very weapon they were expected to use well. It was a situation that held throughout the war, because of the shortage of B-29s for training, because of the accelerating needs for combat crews in the Pacific, and — ultimately — because wars are like that.

Bombardier Del Shaffer arrived at his combat crew training squadron at Clovis Army Air Field, New Mexico, with 186 hours and five minutes of flying time,

most of it in training for his specific crew task. It was September 1944, and the war had less than one year to go, although nobody really thought it would be over that soon.

There was no flying time for him during September, but in October he logged three flights. One of them was a 12 hour 55 minute training flight in a B-17G, the workhorse for the early phases of B-29 combat crew training. His first two B-29 flights were made that month, one of seven hours and the other of seven hours 25 minutes.

In November Shaffer flew on six B-29 training missions, five of them a series of short flights, and the sixth a simulated combat mission lasting 11 hours 40 minutes. In December, he flew five times, four of them in B-29s for about seven hours each, and one in a B-17G lasting a little more than three hours. During the first half of January 1945, Shaffer trained on two B-29 and two B-17 flights, and then he was transferred with the rest of his crew to Kearney, Nebraska, for the staging procedure that would eventually send him to Saipan.

He then had a total of 268 hours 25 minutes in airplanes, and less than ten hours of that time was flown at night. He did no flying at Kearney in January. On 12 February he was on his way to Saipan and a slot in the 874th Bombardment Squadron, 498th Bombardment Group, of the 73rd Bombardment Wing (Very Heavy).

On 16 and 17 February he made two flights out of Saipan in the B-29. The first lasted two hours, 20 minutes; the second took six hours 35 minutes. On 25 February, Del Shaffer went on his first combat mission, a daylight raid on Tokyo. The mission lasted 15 hours 30 minutes, and included nine hours in instrument conditions and three hours of night flying.

The night incendiary raids began in March and, by the end of that month, Shaffer had spent nearly 44 combat hours under night conditions. That was more than four times as much night flying time as he had acquired in five months of training.

All of the pre-deployment training was done at a network of bases scattered around the midwestern and southwestern United States, where the weather was generally more co-operative than it was along the eastern seaboard or around the Great Lakes region. Many of the young airmen were married, and their wives — if they weren't working — made the trek from base to base to be with their husbands. Their constant moves from station to station, their need to find temporary housing near the base, their youth and inexperience and often their naivete, made them vulnerable. That they put up with so much, and that so many marriages survived it all, is remarkable.

'Tom graduated in the pilot class of 42-F at Phoenix, Arizona, and we were married the day he pinned on his wings. He was ordered to Salt Lake City, Utah, for assignment, so we boarded a troop train in the June heat. It was probably 110 degrees, but Tom proudly sweltered in his brand-new Second Lieutenant's uniform, the "greens and pinks". We rode all the way to Salt Lake City via Los Angeles and rode right back again. Tom's orders were for Tucson, Arizona, which may be 100 miles or so from where we started out. We must have spent a week on trains.

'Tom was a B-24 instructor pilot there, but after a couple of months changed to crew training and we were moved to El Paso, Texas, where the crews had to live on base under simulated combat conditions. That meant I lived in the YWCA in town, and got to see Tom on his one day off each week.

'Juarez, Mexico, was right across the river, just a short streetcar ride away, and every crew member who wanted to get liquor would come to the YWCA, ask for me, and take me to Juarez where I would get "my" allotment and carry it back for the crew. One day Tom got an extra day off and came in for me, but I had already headed for Juarez with the officer who was the best man at our wedding. We had a rather prim lady at the YWCA desk, and when Tom asked for me, she told him that Mrs Isley had left. Tom asked where, and she said, "I don't know; but she had pants on!" Tom's retort: "Well, I certainly hope so!" Women didn't wear slacks as much in public those days. I had been in the fashion business, and in Hollywood at that, so I was probably a little far out for my fellow YWCA inhabitants.

'When we were ordered to Salina, Kansas, the people there were willing to make sacrifices, saying they wanted to take good care of "their boys". We, along with another couple, were able to rent a bedroom apiece in a Salina home. One of us paid $40 and the other $50 per month rent. Our landlords slept in the basement. (Note: For comparison, a three-room luxury garden apartment in the New York suburban area was renting for as much as $60 per month at that time.)

'One night they invited us for dinner at a local restaurant. Fine; we thought we'd earned that. So we all went out, and the husband picked up the check while giving us the "everything-for-the-boys" routine. The next day the lady of the house came to us girls and said, "Well, we don't know how it is where you come from, but when we go out to dinner, we always share the check, so would you please pay for your dinners?" And, of course, we forked over the money.

'After Tom had served a year in North Africa and England in an anti-submarine outfit, he came home and went into B-29

transition training at Clovis (New Mexico), and we were house-hunting again. Clovis was full, but we finally located a backyard shack in a neighbouring town. It was about 12 feet by 12 feet, made into a living-bedroom, kitchen and bath. The outside was painted purple and it was trimmed in orange. I forget what we paid, but I know it was a horrendous amount for a brightly coloured shack out back.

'In Great Bend (Kansas), we couldn't find a place there either, and again settled in a neighbouring town where some people rented us their basement. Our shower facilities were a water pipe with a nozzle at the end, suspended over a storm drain. No lavatory, but a kitchen-type sink in the corner that we shared with a congress of cockroaches. It was Tom's duty the first thing every morning to wash them down the drain before I'd put my feet to the floor — one time into six inches of water, I well remember.

'We were young, we were in love, and it was wartime. We kept saying that, and thinking that, like a litany, perhaps to avoid the thought that we were being used, that "nothing's too good for our boys" usually carried a hefty price tag and wasn't too good anyway.' *Mrs Thomas Isley*

Capt James J. Garrity was the Adjutant of the 883rd Bomb Squadron, 500th Bomb Group, 73rd Bomb Wing when that unit moved to Saipan to begin the aerial assault against the Japanese home islands with other units of the 73rd Wing. He put together a photo album which included these pictures (*right*) of the first crews to fly with the 883rd, and added his own personal comments about each crew. They constitute a remarkable documentation of one group of men at one stage in time, and they are presented here exactly as Garrity showed them in his album.

LT. COL WILLIAM L. M°DOWELL

LT. COL WILLIAM L. M°DOWELL (COMMANDING)
WEST POINT CLASS OF 1939
SECOND TOUR OF DUTY OVER SEAS AFTER SUB-PATROL IN CARRIBEAN
SQUADRON "C.O'S" REQUIRED TO FLY ABOUT 8 MISSIONS, COL MAC
FLEW ABOUT 20+. A REGULAR "JOE" AND "A MANS MAN."

REQUIESCANT IN PACE

LT COOPER'S CREW CRASHED INTO FARM HOUSE AND WHEAT
BARN IN COPELAND, KAN. DURING TRAINING, ALL MEMBERS, EXCEPT
THE OFFICER IN CENTER (HANK) WERE KILLED, HE WAS ON THE FLIGHT
BUT THEY LANDED BECAUSE HE WAS SICK, AND CRASHED ½ HR LATER.

351 HANSEN ('B' FLIGHT LEADER)
REQUIESCANT IN PACE

MAJ. HANSENS CREW DEPARTED SAIPAN ON THEIR FIRST
MISSION, AT NIGHT, ON NUISANCE RAID OF ONE EVERY HALF HOUR. JOE AMOS (SEE LATER)
AND I WERE ON THE END OF RUNWAY AND WERE LAST TO SEE THE PLANE AIR BORNE.
TO THIS DAY THERE IS NO REPORT. THEY JUST VANISHED.

363 AMOS
REQUIESCANT IN PACE

JOE'S PLANE WAS CRIPPLED OVER THE TARGET AND HE NURSED IT BACK TO THE
JIMA ISLANDS (NIP HELD). LANDED AT SEA AND TOOK TO DINGHIES. OUR GANG FOUND HIM
AND NURSED A U.S.SUB. UP TO ABOUT 2 MILES. THE SUB DID NOT GET THEM, AND CONTACT
WAS LOST AT DUSK. NO FURTHER REPORTS.

**357 CHARTERS**
REQUIESCANT IN PACE

THIS WAS CHARTERS 2ND TOUR AGAINST THE NIPS. HE FLEW WITH THE OLD 19th BOMB GP.
THEY LANDED AT SEA, AFTER DAMAGE OVER TARGET. HIS "BUDDY" PLANE TOOK HIM
DOWN, BUT CONTACT WAS MADE AT NIGHT. NO FURTHER INFORMATION.

## "RESTRICTED"

**354 HOLMES**
REQUIESCANT IN PACE.

THIS WAS HOLMES 2ND TOUR AFTER ONE AGAINST GERMANY. THEY LANDED AT SEA ABOUT
200 MI. FROM SAIPAN NEAR A U.S. DESTROYER. MAJ GAY, OPERATIONS OFF. AND LT. SPARKS WERE
BURIED AT SAIPAN. THE PERSONNEL INDICATED WENT DOWN WITH THE PLANE. OTHER PERSONNEL
CAME BACK ON THE DESTROYER WITH SEVERE FRACTURES. LT. POPE AND SGT. COLLINS RECEIVED
MINOR SHOCK AND REMAINED IN THE COMMAND.

## "RESTRICTED"

343 ASHLEY ("A" FLIGHT LEADER)

CAPT. ASHLEY, AIRLINE PILOT, WAS SUCCEDED BY LT. BARRON, AFTER 5 MISSIONS.
THEIR PLANE WAS NAMED "THE BARRONESS". THEY FLEW 35 MISSIONS, ALL WERE
RETURNED SAFE TO THE U.S.

SGT. DIETZ
A TOP TAIL
GUNNER IN
EACH THEATRE. →

THIS LT. DID
NOT COME WITH
US. HIS BROTHER
WAS SHOT DOWN
A WEEK BEFORE
THEY DEPARTED.

The Crew of "Supine Sue"

344 MORELAND

ONE OF THE BEST B-29 CREWS IN COMBAT. OUR "LEAD CREW" AND EVENTUALLY ONE
OF THE LEAD CREWS FOR THE AIRFORCE. COL. MAC FLEW THIS CREW OUT FROM 20 TO 30
MISSIONS. MORELAND WAS ORDERED TO U.S. TO SET UP "LEAD CREW" SCHOOL AT MUROC.

346 SETTERICH

SGT. DALEY
RADIO OPERATOR
HELPED CONTACT
THE SUB.

A SCRAPPY CREW OF THE FIRST ORDER. THIS WAS THE CREW FOUND (AMOS)
AND FLEW COVER TO GET THE SUB IN FOR A PICK UP. THEY POWER DIVED ON, AND
SHOT DOWN, A NIP SEA PLANE WHICH WAS SNOOPING AROUND. THEY FINISHED ALL
MISSIONS SAFELY.

"RESTRICTED"

347 RYAN

RYAN FLEW THEM ALL AND THE CREW CAME BACK O.K. OVER THE TARGET
ON ONE MISSION THE FUEL CONTROL CABLES, FOR TWO ENGINES, WERE SEVERED. LT. LOGAN, HELD
THE ENDS OF THE CABLES AND FED GAS, BY DIRECTION, ON THE RETURN 7 HR TRIP TO
SAIPAN HE WAS AWARDED THE D.S.C. THEY SELDOM STAY AIR BORNE WITH TWO OUT ON
THE SAME SIDE.

**"RESTRICTED"**

348 CHENEY

BILL FLEW A SNOOPER MISSION ON THE ISLAND OF TRUK, MAST HIGH. THE AIRPLANE LOOKED LIKE A SIEVE WHEN HE RETURNED. A GOOD CREW AND THEY FINISHED ALL MISSIONS.

THIS CREW HELPED ME CONSTRUCT THE EM. CLUB-HOUSE

(3RD FROM RIGHT)
SGT. GLOCKNER 2ND TOUR 81 TOTAL MISSIONS. AND TIED AS TOP GUNNER IN OUR AIR FORCE.

350 CLINKSCALES

THE SCRAPPING GAME-COCK FROM SO. CAROLINA. ONE OF THE ROUGHEST CREWS IN THE SQUADRON. MAN FOR MAN "CLINK" FINISHED THEM ALL AND WAS MOTHER TO THE FIGHTERS FROM IWO, FOR NAVIGATING THEM HOME.

## "RESTRICTED"

352 ▬

A DAM GOOD CROWD OF FELLOWS, BUT THE ORIGINAL (CAPT) AIRPLANE
COMMANDER DOES NOT DESERVE TO BE EXHIBITED IN THIS COMPANY.

← SGT. RENNER
2ND FROM RIGHT.

353 McCLANAHAN

MAC STARTED WITH THE R.C.A.F. IN EUROPE AND HE HAD A SCRAPPY CREW. HE RETURNED
ONE NIGHT WITHOUT SGT. RENNER, OUR FIRST CASUALTY. A GUNNERS GLASS BLISTER BLEW OVER
TOKIO AND RENNER PLUMMETED INTO SPACE. MAC DOVE THE PLANE TO SAVE THE CREW IN REAR.
ALSO, HE SAT ON BRADENS BACK (SEE LATER) WHEN THE FORMERS GUNS WENT OUT AND FOUGHT
THE NIPS OFF FOR SEVERAL MINUTES. THEY ALL CAME HOME EXCEPT RENNER

355 GREGG

A HARD LUCK CREW BUT THEY FINISHED ALL MISSIONS.
IT SEEMED THEIR PLANE ALWAYS RETURNED WITH FLAK DAMAGE.

356 SCHMIDT

THE FLYING DUTCHMAN AND THE LIFE OF ANY PARTY. SECOND TOUR
OF DUTY AFTER EUROPE. THEY CAUGHT A LOT OF FLAK AND ALSO PURPLE HEARTS.

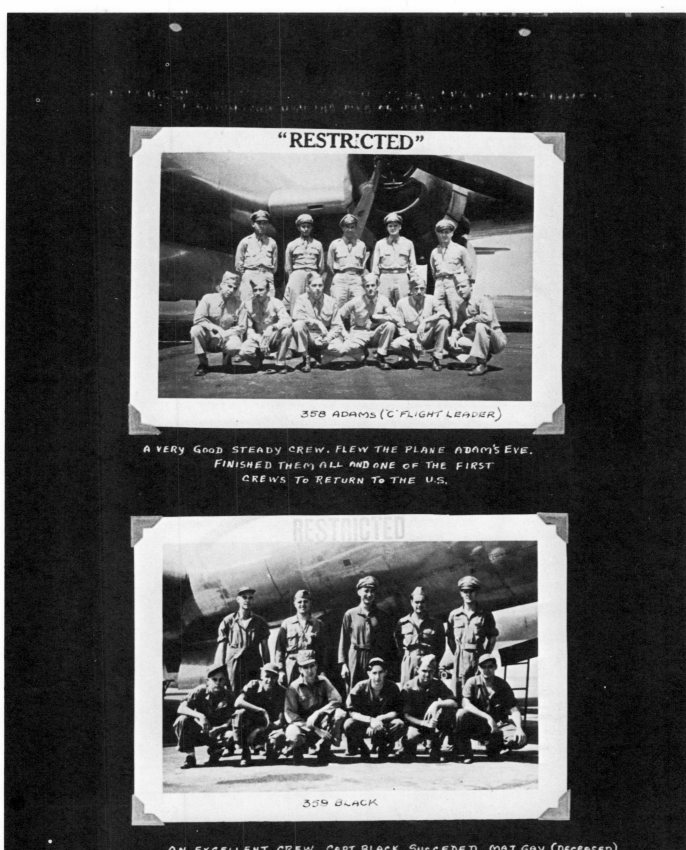

"RESTRICTED"

358 ADAMS ('C' FLIGHT LEADER)

A VERY GOOD STEADY CREW. FLEW THE PLANE ADAM'S EVE.
FINISHED THEM ALL AND ONE OF THE FIRST
CREWS TO RETURN TO THE U.S.

RESTRICTED

359 BLACK

AN EXCELLENT CREW. CAPT. BLACK SUCCEDED MAJ. GAY (DECEASED)
AS OPERATIONS OFFICER.

SGT. POWERS
TAIL GUNNER,
RECEIVED
BROKEN BACK
WHEN PLANE
FLEW OVER
THERMAL UP-
DRAFT ON A
BURN RAID

360 FEATHERS

THE TENNESSEE SCHOOL TEACHER. THIS GANG LIVED ON BORROWED TIME!
FIRST A.C.COMM TO FLY A B29 BACK FROM THE TARGET WITH TWO ENGINES KNOCKED
OUT ON SAME SIDE. IT WAS A "HAT TRICK" WE SWEAT THEM IN ONE HOUR AFTER
REGULAR TIME. THEY DID IT THE 2ND TIME AND LANDED AT IWO. THE LORD WAS
WITH THEM AND THEY FINISHED ALL MISSIONS. A LOT OF PURPLE HEARTS.

## "RESTRICTED"

361 IRBY

THE QUIET CREW OF THE LOT! VERY EFFICIENT AND METHODICAL.
THEY FLEW 32 STRAIGHT MISSIONS WITHOUT AN ABORTION. THE CREW
CHIEF HELD THE RECORD OF THE FIELD, ON MAINTENANCE, FOR A LONG
WHILE. A SWELL CROWD OF OFFICERS AND E.M. THEY FINISHED 35!

# Going to Guam

Four-engined Douglas C-54 transports, carrying the markings of the Air Transport Command, sit in the bright sun on the ramp at Hamilton Field, California. Hamilton is the port of embarkation for the Pacific; specifically, this day, for the Marianas and assignment to the XXI Bomber Command.

Officially, the officers and men waiting in small groups with their B-4 bags and manila envelopes do not know where they are going. There have been rumours, and some, more certain than others, have spread the word.

The orders come down the line and the groups break into single file, climb the ladders to the open doors of the C-54s, and find seats.

One by one, the engines are started and the long line of transports taxies out to the runway. Each holds for engine run-up, then turns on to the runway, accelerates, heads out over the Pacific.

One hour out the question is answered. Before departure, each man had been handed a single letter-sized envelope, with his name neatly typed on the front: Rank, name and serial number. Across the bottom of the envelope is a rubber-stamped impression: DO NOT OPEN UNTIL ONE HOUR AFTER DEPARTURE.

The envelopes are ripped open, the orders extracted. Stapled to the order is a small mimeographed slip, typed in capital letters:

YOU ARE DIRECTED TO TAKE EVERY PRECAUTION TO SAFEGUARD THESE ORDERS. THESE ORDERS *WILL NOT* BE PLACED IN THE SAME CONTAINER WITH OTHER ORDERS AND RECORDS. EXCEPT AS MAY BE NECESSARY IN THE TRANSACTION OF OFFICIAL BUSINESS, YOU ARE PROHIBITED FROM DISCUSSING YOUR OVERSEAS DESTINATION EVEN BY SHIPMENT NUMBER OR SHIPPING DESIGNATOR.

IN CASE OF EMERGENCY THESE ORDERS WILL BE DESTROYED.

THESE ORDERS MUST BE TURNED IN TO THE COMMANDING OFFICER AT YOUR OVERSEAS DESTINATION.

Full of the standardised abbreviation and couched in that special language spoken only by the military, the orders read:

'The fol named AC pers (W) of Shipment FH---AE, HRT PAE ICW par 2, SO ♯28, Hq Kearney AAFld, Kearney, Neb, dated 28 Jan 1945, WP at the proper time by MNOCA (Auth: AR 55-120, par 3b (2) as amended) (APR UST 2-1990-S-JAN) fr Hamilton Fld, Calif to Mariana Islands (Guam), reporting upon arrival thereat to the Commanding General, XXI Bomber Command for asgmt.

'Pers will be clothed and equipped in accordance with List B, Indiv Clothing and Equip Lists A to K, 15 Nov 1943, as amended. Clothing and Equip to be transported by air will not exceed 86lbs for Pilots and EM, 120lbs for Bmbdrs, 160lbs for Navs and 94lbs for Engrs.

'This shpmt will use temp APO 19037-AE (suffixed by indiv crew no. to which asgd ie 19037-AE-8) c/o Postmaster, San Francisco, Calif, until arrival at destination.'

Down below the substance of the order is the long list of names in this shipment. You know your own name is there, under Crew No. FH---AE-9, but you check to make sure. Yep, there it is.

Jesus! You're going to Guam! Island paradise . . . palm trees . . . long coral beaches . . . native girls . . .

Dream on, Shipment FH---AE; it isn't going to be like that at all.

# Towards Command and Control

One of the key figures in Superfortress operations was Brig Gen Haywood S. Hansell, Jr, an outstanding pilot, combat commander and brilliant planner. Hansell was the first commander of the XXI Bomber Command when it deployed to the Marianas. He has drawn on that experience, and his earlier planning studies, to summarise the background of the organisation that eventually commanded and controlled the B-29 operations.

'The grand strategy of World War 2 called for the defeat of Hitler first. To help in that battle, the B-29s were planned for deployment first against Germany, with 12 groups to be based in Northern Ireland and 12 near Cairo, Egypt. When the time had come when we were sure that the defeat of Hitler could be accomplished, we would turn to the offensive in the Pacific. And that time came in August 1943 at the Quadrant meeting of the United Nations in Quebec.

'At that time, the strategy for the offensive operations in the Pacific was laid down. The Joint Plans Committee strategy called for a surface operation across the Central Pacific, terminating somewhere on the east coast of China, and another one coming up through the southwest Pacific with the same objective. For the final victory over Japan, there was to be an invasion. There was no mention of any air offensive or of any strategic air warfare in these plans.

'At the conclusion of the meeting, Gen H. H. Arnold tabled a plan for airpower operations. He was determined that the B-29s should be used directly against Japan, rather than in support of a surface invasion by surface commanders. It was very difficult to rationalise, however, because we didn't have the bases. There was no way of getting to the Japanese islands at that time.

'Arnold proposed basing B-29s in India, and at advanced bases in China, and of attacking the Japanese homeland from those bases. The plan was immediately thrown out by the Joint Plans Committee and the Joint Logistics Committee as being completely infeasible. And it was a horrendous plan, but it was the only plan that would permit the use of the B-29s against Japan.

'It was brought up again at the Cairo Conference in December. Chiang Kai-Shek

Marpi Point, the northern tip of Saipan, was the site of a Japanese fighter strip, Banadaru field. It was converted, as were the other Japanese airfields on the island, into an operational strip for US aircraft.
/ Dr Lyman C. Perkins

*Left:* Kobler Field, a fighter strip adjacent to the B-29 base at Isley Field, was at the southwestern tip of Saipan. Isley is out of the picture on the right. The prominent mountain (left centre) is Mount Topatchau. Magicienne Bay and Kagman Point lie beyond the runway. Saipan was blocked on the West by an almost continuous reef, which can be seen in this picture. Anchored ships lie outside the reef. Saipan was, and remains, a beautiful island, with a moderate temperature range, and glistening white beaches behind the reefs. / *Dr Lyman C. Perkins*

*Below:* The operations shack on Isley Field was converted from the Japanese operations building at the field. The B-29 base was named after Navy Commander Robert H. Isely — the correct spelling — who was shot down during an attack on Aslito field. Somewhere along the line, his name went into the official records as Isley, and that's the spelling that was used. Notice the sign. It originally spelled the name correctly, and later the letters 'E' and 'L' were reversed. / *A. F. Migliaccio Collection*

was at the conference and he agreed to build the bases. The President approved it; we had abrogated a number of agreements with China, and this looked like an opportunity to do something that would recognise the importance of China. It was approved in spite of its very bad logistics.

'There were three very important things accomplished at Cairo, from our point of view. One of them was the recognition of a strategic air offensive. The plans from Cairo on recognised the strategic air operation as one of the vital elements of the overall strategy. The second thing was the approval of the bases in China, and the agreement of the British that they would build bases in India, in order to launch the B-29 operations. The third was the agreement of the Joint Chiefs of Staff (JCS) to capture the Marianas islands as bases for B-29 operations, and that of course was a basic strategic step.

'When we got back from Cairo, we began to run into an extremely difficult command and control problem. The B-29s that were operating in the China-Burma-India (CBI) theatre would be under the control of Lt Gen Joseph W. Stilwell. This was also a political agreement of Quebec. There had been a lot of argument about American forces being commanded by British commanders, and the American position had insisted that all forces in the CBI theatre be under an American commander, who was Gen. Stilwell.

*Above:* The control tower at Isley Field performed only a secondary function in regulating the flow of aircraft on and off the field. Radio silence was maintained for all strikes, and so aircraft took off on a timetable, with flagmen to send each aircraft on its way.
/ *Collection of Mrs Thomas Isley*

*Left:* The roads on Saipan required some care in driving. Good safety practices demanded some reminders to drivers, and this billboard — one of many done around a similar theme — was one of the more striking eyecatchers.
/ *Dr Lyman C. Perkins*

'CURVES ON ME MAY LOOK SWELL....... BUT ON THIS ROAD THEY CAN BE HELL_'

DRIVE CAREFULLY_

SAIPAN

*Left:* Over the tail of V–45 is the panorama of the hardstand area of the 499th Bomb Group, 73rd Bomb Wing, at Isley Field on Saipan. Quonset huts and tents dot the spaces between the aircraft. The aircraft are standing quietly now, waiting for the crowds of armourers, mechanics, technicians and ground crews to arrive and prepare them for the next mission.
*/ AAF Pacific via Boeing-Wichita*

*Below:* Later in the war, the hardstand area of the 497th Bomb Group, 73rd Bomb Wing, looked like this. Same planes, same tents and Quonsets, same feeling of quiet waiting. Only the tail markings have changed, the A above the 73rd Wing's square symbol was replaced by the single large A on the vertical tail.
*/ Dr Lyman C. Perkins*

'But Stilwell had ideas of his own about using the B-29s, and for using them in Southeast Asia. The Marianas, when we got them would be in Admiral Chester W. Nimitz' command area; he naturally assumed that he would have control of all forces in the area. Gen Douglas A. MacArthur was screaming to high heaven for B-29s for the Southwest Pacific, prompted by Lt Gen George C. Kenney. Kenney had been in on the inception of the B-29s at the Materiel Division. He had a great desire to get them. Gen MacArthur had a great deal of influence, and great pressure was brought to bear to get the B-29s to the Southwest Pacific. In addition, if we built a base in the Aleutian chain as once suggested, that base would be under still another commander.

'What we needed was centralised control at the target, not the base area, but it's very difficult to do that properly. We found a way, however, through — of all the people in the world — Admiral Ernest J. King, Chief of Naval Operations (CNO). With Gen Arnold's agreement I went to him and told him that we had a problem very much like the Navy problem. Their fleets were based at various bases in many theatres of operation, but the control of these forces was retained through Navy channels all the way up to Admiral King. The theatre commanders who controlled the bases had no control over Admiral King's forces.

'We had a similar problem. We had strategic air forces based in many separate theatres, but the critical issue was to control them at the target area: Japan. This was going to require centralised control similar to that

exercised by the Navy, and actually similar to that exercised by Admiral King. He was not only CNO and Navy member of the JCS, he was also Commander in Chief, US Fleets, and he commanded and controlled Naval fleet units wherever they might be.

'We suggested to him that a similar arrangement might be appropriate for the B-29 strategic air forces, and that Gen Arnold might occupy a similar position on the JCS, exercising control over the B-29s wherever they might be. Admiral King agreed to this, Gen George C. Marshall went along with it, and on the basis of this we got the Twentieth Air Force (20 AF) established.' *Haywood S. Hansell, commander, 73rd BW*

### Setting Sun to Matterhorn

The debate on the best employment of the B-29 force was not settled until after the first B-29s had arrived in India, ready to fly combat missions. It had started with an ambitious plan called Setting Sun, which was modified into one called Twilight, which was further modified into a plan called Matterhorn which was argued, changed, augmented, reduced, simplified, complicated, reconsidered and finally informally approved by the JCS in April 1944. In its final form, Matterhorn assigned the first operational unit — the 58th Bombardment Wing (Very Heavy) — to India and advance bases in China, and assigned the second and subsequent wings to the Marianas. Logistics support of the 58th in China was to be by air, using the B-29s themselves.

It took a year to approve Matterhorn from the time that Gen Arnold had named Brig

Gen Kenneth B. Wolfe to organise, equip and train B-29 units. The 58th Bomb Wing was activated 1 June 1943, established at Marietta (Georgia) Army Air Field (AAFld) 15 June and Gen Wolfe moved in as commander 21 June. Training, it had been decided, would be done in the area near Wichita, Kansas, where Boeing had built a new factory to turn out the B-29s. The Second Air Force was given the task, and set up on four fields: Smoky Hill AAFld near Salina; Pratt AAFld, at Pratt; Great Bend AAFld, at Great Bend; and Walker AAFld, near Victoria, Kansas.

Wolfe moved his headquarters to Smoky Hill in mid-September, and took over 27 November as commander of the newly organised XX Bomber Command, which included the 58th Bomb Wing and the newly activated 73rd Bomb Wing, later to be assigned elsewhere.

'I'd been at Langley Field, Virginia, with a Signal Heavy Construction Battalion and was transferred, on 11 August 1943, to Marietta Army Air Field, to be assistant communications officer in the newly formed 58th Bomb Wing. The problem, of course, was to get the 58th ready for deployment overseas and combat in what was no time at all.

'The first B-29 any of us had ever seen arrived during the month and promptly went into the shop for rework. About a week later, it was rolled out on the ramp, ready to go. Somehow, the main landing gear switch was activated, and the B-29 collapsed on the ramp with a great crunch. People were working

*Above:* Inside the Quonset hut you had a bunk, a dresser made of bomb crate wood salvaged from the dump, and a clothesline that served to hang your extensive wardrobe and your laundry. TSgt Anthony F. Migliaccio, CFC gunner on *Thumper*, lived here, his 'room' labelled by the stencil on the side of his B-4 bag at the head of his bunk. His helmet hangs from the left side of the foot of the bunk. */ A. F. Migliaccio Collection*

*Top left:* And this was your home away from home, if you were a combat crew member of the 73rd Wing on Saipan: Standard Quonset huts, with corrugated sheet metal sides and roof to warm in the sun, and some semblance of ventilation from hinged side panels and the roof vent. The hut with the picture-window front was the squadron mess hall. */ Ferd J. Curtis Collection*

*Bottom left:* Let's be frank; the accommodation on Saipan was not de luxe. Sgt Don Hetrick (left) and his buddy stand in front of their living quarters, and the name explains itself. */ Don C. Hetrick Collection*

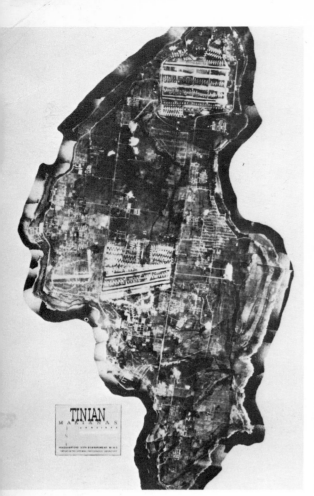

around it at the time, but the only casualty was a civilian engineer who had been standing on a ladder in the rear bomb bay when the gear folded. The medical report was that he had not been touched by any part of the airplane, but had a heart attack and died from that.

'Less than a month after arriving at Marietta, I was transferred to Smoky Hill AAFld for duty with the 58th Bomb Wing Development Detachment, an advance headquarters for the wing until it could be moved from Marietta.

'We were supposed to be ready to fly combat missions in May 1944, and we had yet to see more than one B-29. We had to select four training bases, create bomb groups, find the men to fill the tables of organisation, get the equipment, and complete accelerated service tests on the aircraft. And while we were doing this, thousands of Chinese and Indian labourers were building four fields in China and four in India.

'Well, the service tests were very limited. We wanted to make sure some of the radios worked in the air, and they did.' *Francis B. Morgan, ass't communications officer, 58th BW*

The tables of organisation called for a bomb wing of four groups, each with four squadrons, with seven aircraft per squadron. Eleven-man crews were assigned to the squadrons, two for each airplane. On paper,

*Right:* Parts of three of Tinian's North Field runways can be seen in this picture, taken from about 2,000 feet almost directly over one runway. At left centre, one B-29 picks her way along the taxiway, headed out of her hardstand and toward takeoff. / *Dr Lyman C. Perkins*

*Above:* This overhead photo mosaic of Tinian shows the two major airfields used by American units after the island was captured. North Field, with its four parallel runways, is — logically — at the North end of the island. It was home for the 313th Bomb Wing and later added another tenant: The 509th Composite Group. About midway along the island is West Field, home of B-24 units. / *313th Wing Photographic Laboratory*

*Right:* North Field on Tinian was the world's biggest bomber base, and probably still holds that record. Four parallel runways, each nearly two miles long, handled the movements of the 313th Bomb Wing and the 509th Composite Group. In this picture, B-29s are rolling on three of the runways, and at least 200 more can be counted. / *Dr Lyman C. Perkins*

*Top right:* Northwest Field on Guam was home base for the 315th Bomb Wing and its turretless B-29Bs. Here, aircraft 73 of the 501st Bomb Group shows its clean upper and lower fuselage decking, unbroken by turrets. / *Murray Singer*

*Centre right:* Nine mechanics — and maybe one or two more hidden by the huge nacelles — swarm over the number one and two engines of this 500th Bomb Group B-29. This may show an engine change on number one; the support underneath the nacelle looks like a jacking unit rather than a standard wheeled maintenance stand. Two cowl panels, containing a section of the ducting to carry air to the engine, lie on the ground near the camera.
/ *James J. Garrity Collection*

*Below:* The designers didn't intend that the engine cowling would serve as steps and a perch, but that's the way it turned out in practice. The number four engine of this B-29 gets detailed attention from a trio of mechanics.
/ *Mike Janosko Collection*

it looked good; but the facts were different for aircraft availability and crew experience.

There was only one B-29 available to every 12 crews in training. By the end of 1943, only 67 first pilots had been checked out in the Superfortresses, crews had logged an average of only 18 hours in the planes, and only a half-hour of formation flying in that time. In fact, only one B-29 had even flown a long-range mission.

The 58th was due to ship out, and was nowhere ready to do so. By the end of January 1944, the training programme should have been completed; but less than half had been accomplished. There were three major reasons for shortfalls in the crew training programme. First, delays had occurred in both airframe and engine production. Second, modification programmes were essential to make production aircraft suitable for combat. Third, trained mechanics were lacking, so an abnormally high percentage of Superfortresses were unfit to fly.

Things had gotten critical by the end of February, and Arnold sent out a special team from Washington to break those three bottlenecks. The team had a simple directive: Get the B-29s to India, ready for combat.

One result was the 'Kansas blitz' or 'The Battle of Kansas', as it later became known. Military and civilian employees from the

Army Air Forces, from Boeing and Wright and subcontractors all over, worked on rows of B-29s parked outside in one of the worst Kansas winters in memory. Howling winds could carry a heavy piece of engine cowling a hundred yards along the icy ramp. Snow fell, driven horizontally by frigid blasts, reducing visibility and making working and walking hazardous. Frostbite was a very real danger. Working hours were stretched until people were at the breaking point. Some critical parts were delivered by ambulance.

But when it was over, the B-29s had gone on their way with their crews, late to be sure, and with a whole new job of learning ahead of them.

*Building the Bases*

An existing network of B-24 bases in India, on the plains west of Calcutta, was the starting point for B-29 base construction. They had existing runways, concrete and 6,000 feet long, which could be strengthened and lengthened.

Wolfe set up headquarters at Kharagpur, about 65 miles from Calcutta by rail, and selected four other bases at Dudhkundi, Piardoba, Kalaikunda and Chakulia. The work force included about 6,000 US troops from Engineer Aviation units, augmented by 27,000 Indian civilians. Work began in late

November 1943; they installed a fuel pipeline from Calcutta to the bases, added concrete to strengthen the runways and lengthened them to 7,500 feet.

The schedule was tough, and wasn't met. A British base at Charra, taken over by the US by agreement, received the first B-29s in April 1944.

'Charra was originally a British base for medium bombers and fighters. It consisted of two runways; one 6,000 feet long and the other approximately 4,000 feet long at right angles. The runways sloped with the lay of the land. The land didn't lay too well. When landing, if the back slope or the top of one of the ridges was overshot, half of the runway was automatically unused. We attribute our lack of runway trouble to the conservative statement: we had the best pilots in the Air Force.

'The months spent at Charra were the hot months of the year. The hottest month was June, just before the summer monsoon rains. The sky was generally clear and the scorching wind was from the India desert to the northwest. The only precipitation came from the afternoon thunderstorms and line squalls . . . preceded and accompanied by thick blowing dust and strong gusty winds. The normal maximum temperature was 115

The cowl panels of the B-29 nacelles were held in place by Dzus fasteners, a patented quarter-turn screw with a spring retainer. They were a loose fit in the hole, but could be drawn up very tightly, to secure the cowling even after it had been bent out of shape by continual removal and re-attachment. The mechanic has just begun the task of opening up the engine nacelle preparatory to doing any of a number of things to its complex interior.
/ *Mrs Thomas Isley Collection*

degrees and the normal minimum at night was 85 degrees. Due to the heat the working hours were from 0700 to 1500.

'Because of the decreased lift due to heat and an increasing number of engine fires on takeoff, the times of flying were set at a maximum of 105 degrees, which meant no flying between 0900 and 1700 each day.'
*444th Bomb Group unit history*

Charra was used until July 1944, and the other bases were not completed until September. Kalaikunda became a transport base; the others handled B-29s.

The advance bases in China were built near Chengtu and the villages of Kwanghan, Kiunglai, Hsinching and Pengshan. Local farmers were conscripted for the work, with village quotas being 50 workers per 100 households. By the end of January 1944, about 200,000 had turned out. They started draining the rice paddies on 24 January. Exactly three months later, on 24 April, the first B-29 landed at the first available field, Kwanghan. By 1 May, all four fields were open for traffic, and some of the fields were operationally ready. It was a remarkable task, done by hand by thousands of Chinese labourers.

'On 4 February 1944, I was moved from Smoky Hill to Washington on TDY. The orders were secret, because I had been designated as security officer for a couple of plane loads of cryptographic material. From Washington I went to Miami Beach on the first leg of a long flight via Marrakech, Morocco, and Karachi to Kharagpur, India, Headquarters of XX Bomber Command. I arrived on 1 March with the crypto material and at the end of the month was moved to Hsinching. The base was designated A-1 to distinguish it from three other bases exactly alike and in the same area. A-1, A-2, A-3 and A-4 together formed the forward bases for the four groups of the 58th Wing.

'I was promoted to major and was assigned duty as Communications Officer of Advance Headquarters. That was on 7 April, and A-1 was the advance headquarters of the 40th Bomb Group, but in name only. I arrived there before the base was finished and obviously before any of the B-29s arrived.

'The bases had been rice paddies. They were drained and then excavated to a solid base of earth, and then painstakingly built up to a level about six feet above the surrounding paddies. It was all hand work, done with shovels, wheelbarrows, shoulder-yokes carrying baskets of rocks, and thousands upon thousands of Chinese. There would be up to 90,000 working on any one runway at one time. The final layer of small stones was topped with a slurry of mud —

probably a fairly stiff clay mix — and compacted with huge rollers pulled by dozens of labourers. The runways were 8,500 feet long, and the altitude was about 2,000 feet above sea level at those bases. It would have helped if the runways had been concrete, but you can't have everything.'
*Francis B. Morgan*

The complex of bases in India and China would bring much of Japan's steel industry into target range. But the rich oil fields of Sumatra, a Japanese-held prize, were out of reach. The only way seen to hit them was by staging the B-29s through Ceylon.

The British had developed airfields on that large island, and discussions and negotiations finally settled on one of them, China Bay on the northeast coast. It was expanded to handle two B-29 groups with a total of 56 airplanes. The runway was extended to 7,200 feet, and additional hardstands and a fuel distribution and storage system were completed by mid-July 1944. The field was officially operational on 10 August, when the first mission to use the base staged through there. It was also the only B-29 mission ever to use the China Bay field.

*Preparing for Combat*
The 58th Wing flew its air echelons out to India by way of Gander, Marrakech, Cairo and Karachi. They settled in, with the 58th Headquarters and its 40th Bomb Group taking the base at Chakulia, the 444th Group operating temporarily out of Charra, the 462nd out of Piardoba, and the 468th sharing the field at Kharagpur with the headquarters operations of XX Bomber Command.

Then began a massive effort to move fuel and other supplies to the Chinese bases in quantity, to meet planned dates for combat sorties. Some Consolidated C-87 cargo aircraft were attached to the Command, and they were to be augmented by the B-29s themselves. Some of the bombers had been stripped of all armament except the tail guns, and could lift about seven tons of fuel in auxiliary tanks as against their usual complement of three tons. Air Transport Command also assigned aircraft to the supply task, and flights over the Hump began. They left their bases near Calcutta, flew northeasterly over the Brahmaputra River valley, and turned east at Likiang or Hsichang in China to head for the advance bases. It was a dangerous route, with bad and sudden changes of weather, poor communications, and the danger of interception by Japanese fighters. It counted as combat time for the B-29 crews.

The hauling started early in 1944; it was July before the B-29 operation approached a self-sufficient basis. That month, the

Superfortresses transported about 3,000 tons of supplies, just enough to support the 115 combat sorties they flew during July. But that was the best rate they achieved as cargo craft, and it was less than half of the combat effort they were expected to make.

Under the best conditions, it took two gallons of fuel burned by the B-29s to deliver one gallon to an advance base. Under the worst conditions, it took twelve gallons.

Events were soon to make these advance bases an unneeded asset. A policy shift had resulted in plans to capture the Marianas islands as bases for the B-29s, and that day was near. Further, the operations out of China were so inefficient that Gen Arnold already was weighing alternatives. It was a hopeless cause, and the B-29 effort was redirected to the Marianas.

*The Island Bases*

The Mariana Islands stretch 500 miles along a gentle arc parallel to the Mariana Trench, a deep cleft in the Pacific Ocean that includes the world's deepest spot, sounded 36,198 feet down. They lie between latitudes of 13 and 21 degrees North, and if you fly north-northwest out of Saipan, Tinian, or Guam, you will fly over the home islands of Japan, about 1,800 miles distant.

That distance made the Marianas very important to the B-29 offensive. No other prospective base area offered available flat land at a reasonable remove from the target area, land that could be seized and held against an enemy that was beginning to feel the effects of its over-extended supply lines. And so the Marianas were marked for invasion and capture by American forces. Amphibious units moved into the area, preceded and supported by heavy bombing and shelling by Air Forces and Navy aircraft and Navy battleships.

The first blow was struck against Saipan on 15 June 1944, the same day that B-29s first bombed Japan from bases in China. The Marine 2nd and 4th Divisions hit the beaches at Saipan; by afternoon of the next day they had secured enough of a beachhead for a landing by the Army's 27th Infantry Division. Aslito airfield was captured by the evening of 18 June, and four days later Republic P-47 fighters of the 19th Fighter Squadron were in action, operating from the field against the remaining pockets of resistance on the island. Mopping up continued until the end of the war, but the island was secured for all practical purposes by 9 July.

Guam was next; its capture began 21 July, with a landing by the Marines' 3rd Division and 1st Provisional Brigade, augmented by the 305th Regimental Combat Team of the 77th Infantry Division. By 10 August they had taken the island and organised resistance had ceased.

Tinian was invaded 24 July by the Marine 4th Division, rested a bit after helping to take Saipan. The island was secured by 1 August.

The dust had hardly settled on the coral before the Seabees took over. Seabees — the word was a short way of referring to Naval Construction Brigades, abbreviated NCB or simply CB — filled the bomb craters, regraded the airfields, repaired or replaced buildings, laid out streets, blasted latrines and made the islands not only useful, but habitable, to a greater or lesser degree. In some cases, the schedules were impossible to keep. Saipan's Isley Field — renamed from Aslito when the ownership changed hands — was not really ready for B-29 operations when the first aircraft arrived 12 October 1944.

The Seabees had a little more than 90 days to convert Aslito, a small, bomb-cratered single coral strip, into Isley Field, a huge complex capable of handling the 73rd Bomb Wing: Four bomb groups, 12 bomb squadrons, 240 B-29s and supporting units by the dozens. That they didn't meet the schedule was hardly a surprise; that they came close was a miracle.

The largest bomber base ever built was the one on Tinian, the responsibility of the 6th Naval Construction Brigade (several Seabee battalions made up one brigade). North Field, which handled the 313th Bomb Wing and the 509th Composite Group, had four parallel, paved 8,500-foot long runways, plus their attendant taxiways, hardstands, fuel and bomb dumps, warehouses, shops, housing, roads, sanitation . . . the list is almost endless. The Seabees also built West Field on Tinian for the 58th Bomb Wing, with two parallel 8,500-foot runways.

On Guam, the 5th Naval Construction Brigade built North Field for the 314th Bomb Wing, and Northwest Field for the 315th. On Iwo Jima, the 9th Naval Construction Brigade finished a single, 9,800-foot paved runway, completing it in stages as control of the island gradually passed from the dogged Japanese defenders to the Americans.

Other bases were planned for, and partially constructed, on Okinawa and Ie Shima, as part of the overall concept of basing 20 B-29 groups on those islands.

The Seabees became a legend in their own time, for their brave work under fire. And, in spite of the inter-service rivalry, the airmen respected the Seabees and appreciated what they were doing. They recognised the contribution in a unique way: At least three B-29s were named after Seabee units: The 9th, 18th and 110th Naval Construction Battalions.

*Right:* The most common battle damage done to the B-29s was from anti-aircraft bursts nearby. The shrapnel would riddle the aircraft, making dozens, sometimes hundreds of small to medium-sized holes, all needing repair. This pair of photographs shows typical flak damage to a B-29 of the 500th Bomb Group. */ James J. Garrity Collection*

*Bottom right and below: The Spirit of F.D.R.*, a B-29 from the 504th Bomb Group, 313th Bomb Wing, staggered back to Tinian with most of her vertical tail shot away. Now the engineering officers and staff take over; how much has to be replaced? How soon can she be back in action? Can we patch the tail or does it all have to come off? */ 313th BW*

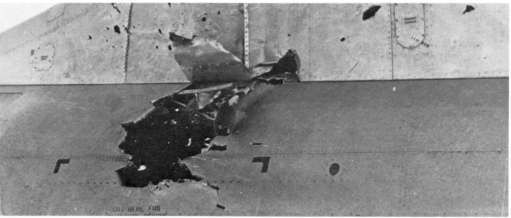

*Keeping Them Flying*

There were very detailed plans for maintenance and support of the B-29s in their combat environment, looking fine on paper, but lacking something when applied to the real world.

Guam Air Depot was to be set up to provide primary support for all B-29s in the Marianas. It was not even organised when the Superfortresses flew their first attack against Japan from Saipan on 24 November 1944, and was not ready to supply fourth-echelon maintenance for the B-29s until February 1945. Some of its facilities, particularly the floating units, didn't arrive until April 1945.

This meant that the service groups attached to XXI Bomber Command units had to perform work that had never been contemplated for them to do. In November 1944, Gen Hansell said, in effect, enough of this, and changed the supply and maintenance procedures to match the needs of the war.

Centralisation was the answer; all supply and maintenance functions came under a deputy chief of staff at Hansell's headquarters. Maintenance at the Group level, which had been the standard procedure planned, was replaced by a pooled operation under the wing maintenance controller. Centralised shops were established and production techniques were adapted quickly. The new system was much more flexible, much more responsive to the conditions of war.

'We were getting about 200 to 250 hours of operation out of an engine initially, before it was time to replace it with another. That meant maybe 15 missions average, assuming the engine wasn't hit by flak or fighters, and that there were no operational problems. Later in the war — by about June 1945 — we got that figure up to 750 hours per engine, which wasn't bad, considering the conditions under which those engines had to perform. One of the reasons was that some of our men figured out a way to add some cooling area to the rear cylinder bank; we fabricated the baffles there, installed them, and dropped the rear cylinder head temperatures by 45C. That change was incorporated in later production engines.

'We made wheeled engine stands for easy handling and the wheels were bogies from the scrapped amphibious landing craft that had littered the beaches at Saipan. We made extra ones for the squadrons, and they could pull an engine, hang it on the stand, and haul it over to our shop for a replacement engine. They got so they could do the whole cycle — pull the old engine, put on a new one — in five and one-half hours. We didn't overhaul engines on the islands; we just weren't equipped for that. They had to go back to the States for overhaul.

'Incoming B-29s brought new engines in for inventory; they could carry a spare R-3350 in the bomb bay. We had to do the engine build-up, because the engines arrived crated with unmounted accessories and carburettors, and we had to install them and build up the complete powerplant with hose connections, coolers, and such. We had an engine build-up line going in the big canvas-

*Top right:* Sgt Don Miller, tail gunner in the 874th Bomb Squadron, 498th Bomb Group, checks out the damage done to the port wing trailing edge of his B-29 after a night raid on Japan. / *Donald L. Miller Collection*

*Centre right:* 'How the Hell did you get back with that hole in her?' This 498th Bomb Group B-29 took a direct flak hit in the bomb bay; it blew a huge hole, peeled back the skin in ribbons, jammed the door partially open. But she came back home, and that was part of what the B-29s were all about. / *Donald L. Miller Collection*

*Below:* The nose of this B-29 from the 881st Bomb Squadron, 500th Bomb Group, sheared off after landing. Capt James Pearson (third from left, standing) and his crew brought the plane back from Tokyo through bad weather and at night with both port engines out of action. The runaway prop from one of them slashed a huge hole in the fuselage. The airplane held together for the return trip and gave up only after the touchdown at Saipan. / *George S. Gray Collection*

topped warehouse we used as a shop. We could handle 275 engines at one time.

'Engine generators were our worst single problem in maintenance, and most of the trouble centred on the brushes. Another trouble area was in the control system for the Hamilton Standard props. It was susceptible to fungus, and the fungus would spread, short out the controls, and the prop would run away in flight.

'Tyres took a hell of a beating, and we got maybe ten to 15 landings per set.

'One of the first problems we had to face was what to do to clear the runway if the gear collapsed on a B-29 during takeoff, for example. It was critical to keep that runway open and handling departures. We didn't want to ruin the airplane completely, as we would if we just bulldozed it off the runway. There was always a shortage of spares and we could repair or cannibalise a ship that wasn't badly damaged. But we did have to consider getting a more-or-less whole B-29 off the runway fast.

'We finally settled on a pair of big "cats" (tractors) with cables that could be slung over each wing root and attached to each "cat". We knew that combination would drag a fully-loaded B-29 off the runway if necessary. Happily, we never had to do that particular job, but the twin "cats" were always on standby near the runway during takeoffs.'
*Alberto R. Pearson, commander, 52nd Eng'g Sqdn, 330th Service Grp*

The statistics bear out the effectiveness of pooled wing maintenance. The abort rate for mechanical failures was almost twentythree

per cent in January 1945, before the wing maintenance concept was in full operation. It dropped to about seventeen per cent in February, ten per cent in March through June, less than seven per cent in July and seven and one-half per cent in August.

There was never any critical problem with parts supplies, even during the maximum-effort raids of March 1945, although there was a chronic shortage of B-29 spare parts until the end of the war. The supply bins and shelves did get very empty at times.

All the parts in the world can be available, and be useless unless they are installed by superior technicians. The B-29 ground crews never got much recognition — although late in the war their names were added to the sides of some B-29s — and few decorations. But the B-29 combat record would have been a sorry one indeed if it had not been for the endless, fatiguing, dirty, often painful work done and done well and continually by the ground crews that truly kept the B-29s flying.

'Before Iwo was taken, the Japanese used to fly over from Iwo and raid Saipan, shoot up the place and drop a few bombs. They'd come in low, part of the time.

'We had some ground crew guys on the airplanes, getting them ready for the first mission to Tokyo. Our lights were on for working around the ships. And here they came — we saw red streaks by the runway and nobody had to tell us it was the Japanese coming in low and trying to knock out our B-29s, and us too. There was one guy

working on top of the fuselage, around one of the top turrets. He saw the Japanese, jumped off the top of that airplane, hit the ground and kept running. And that's a hell of a drop!

'The Betties (Mitsubishi G4M2 bombers) used to come over almost every night we were there, before Iwo was taken.' *Gerald Coke, CFC specialist, 869th BS, 497th BG*

There was a story in *Brief*, the official publication of the Army Air Forces in the Pacific Ocean Area, that told it well. It may be a legend, it may not even be about a B-29, but it has a universal ring of truth and it applies.

The latest report the ground crew had was that their plane had feathered number three engine and number two was throwing oil. The hydraulic system had been shot out, and the engineer had spliced the control cables running to the horizontal and vertical surfaces, hoping they'd hold for the trip back. All equipment had been ditched, and she was managing to hold 3,000 feet altitude.

Then they saw her, one feathered, smoke pouring out of another engine, on final approach. She landed, taxied to the hardstand. The crew chief saw a hole in one cowling, skin rips and tears in the belly. Hydraulic fluid was dribbling down a prop blade. He saw a flak hole just outside an oil line under the cowling of number two engine. Inside, he checked the spliced cables.

The pilot came up to him and said, "Guess she's ready for the graveyard, huh?"

The crew chief looked him straight in the eyes and said, "No, sir! Not *MY* plane!"

Sometimes they just ran off the runway and into the ditch, as did this B-29 of the 505th Bomb Group, 313th Bomb Wing. The props seem to be in low pitch and the partially deflected flaps indicate that the accident probably happened during takeoff. The recovery cranes are already on the job, and will move the stricken aircraft out of the ditch for analysis, repair or the scrap pile. / *313th Bomb Wing*

# Thunder out of China

The first combat mission flown by B-29 Superfortresses in World War 2 was sent against the Makasan railroad shops in Bangkok, Thailand, on 5 June 1944. The big bombers flew from Kharagpur on a round trip of about 2,000 miles. The Japanese defences were expected to be light. It was to be a shakedown mission, but yet one with enough difficulty to introduce the crews and their aircraft to real combat.

In an early morning take-off, 98 B-29s got into the air; 14 of them aborted later. They were supposed to fly in four-plane diamonds, but the weather posed some problems and the formation never solidified. The target was overcast; the formations, such as they were, broke into loose gaggles of single and paired aircraft. Individual planes made their runs over the target, some bombing by radar, some visually, from altitudes between 17,000 and 27,000 feet. The mission had been briefed to drop between 23,000 and 25,000 feet. Seventy-seven planes bombed the target, 48 of them by radar through the overcast.

The trip back was just as disorganised. Five B-29s were lost on the return, 12 landed at B-29 bases not their own, and 30 landed at bases outside the Command. Reconnaissance photos taken a few days later showed that 16 to 18 bombs had fallen in the target area. It was not a great start.

The second strike — a night raid — got off the ground on 15 June, with 68 Superforts headed for the Imperial Iron and Steel Works, in Yawata, Japan. Forty-seven bombed the target, 15 visually and 32 by radar. There was one combat loss, six non-combat losses of aircraft, and a total of 55 crewmen killed or missing. The post-strike photos showed a single hit in the target area, on a powerhouse three-quarters of a mile from the aiming point.

It looked like an impossible situation for the XX Bomber Command. Its resources were strained to the breaking point; the logistics of supplying the advance bases posed nearly insolvable problems. The first two combat missions had done little to impress observers. Wolfe was relieved on 4 July, and sent back to the States with a promotion.

Brig Gen LaVerne G. Saunders was left in temporary command and he continued to order missions against enemy targets. One of them, 10 August, sent 54 Superfortresses agains the oil storage and refinery at Palembang, staging through Ceylon on the trip to and from the distant target. The only damage was done to one small building, and Ceylon was never used again by the B-29s.

On 29 August Maj Gen Curtis E. LeMay arrived to take over the XX Bomber Command. He rode the 8 September strike

Cowl flaps opened wide for maximum available — never enough — cooling on the ground, all four of the big Wright R 3350 engines powering the *Eddie Allen* roar in a full-power run-up. Based at Chakulia, India, *Eddie Allen* carries the four horizontal tail stripes and tip identifying the 40th Bomb Group. The stripes were yellow, the squadron colour of the 45th Bomb Squadron of the 40th BG. *Eddie Allen* was a B-29-40-BW, serial number 42-24579. / Boeing 88806

*Top left:* Chinese labourers, still working on parts of this forward airfield, were responsible for one of the monumental engineering feats of this century: The construction, by hand, of B-29 bases. In the background is *Eileen*, a Wichita-built B-29-10-BW (serial 42-6323) assigned to the 678th Bomb Squadron, 444th Bomb Group, 58th Bomb Wing.
*/ USAF 52306 A.C. via Boeing-Wichita*

*Centre left:* Aircraft 33 of the 678th Bomb Squadron waits on her hardstand at Charra, India, during the early and pioneering days of B-29 operations.
*/ Ron E. Witt Collection*

*Below:* The 676th Bomb Squadron unit establishment included *Shanghai Lil*, parked facing her bomb load for the next mission, still unfinned and unfused. She shows 16 bombing mission markers, eight Hump flights, three photographic missions, and two Purple Hearts for her crew.
*/ Ron E. Witt Collection*

against Anshan, Manchuria, as an observer, and what he learned resulted in an operational revision for the Command. LeMay replaced the four-plane diamond with the 12-plane formation he had used with great success in Europe. He decided to concentrate on daylight precision attacks, and to subordinate night strikes. He suggested that both radar operator and bombardier follow the bomb run, and drop the bombs depending on who had the target in sight at the last critical moment before the triggering. Finally, he asked each group to designate six lead crews, and set up a school to train lead bombardiers.

On 20 September, the Command was streamlined. The 58th Wing was disbanded, along with 16 maintenance squadrons and four B-29 squadrons. Their personnel and aircraft were redistributed in an organisation which had three squadrons of ten airplanes

*Top right:* Rows of fuel drums, jacketed mechanics and the desolate appearance of the place seem to mark this as a forward base in China. The aircraft is from the 40th Bomb Group, possibly from the 25th Bomb Squadron (red tail stripes and tip). / *Ron E. Witt Collection*

*Centre right:* The huge roller in the foreground was used by the Chinese who built this forward base to compact the crushed rock foundations for the runways. The Superfortress with the neatly aligned props carries the yellow tail stripes and tip of the 45th Bomb Squadron. / *Ron E. Witt Collection*

*Below:* This line of Superfortresses, pristine and devoid of any markings except for serial numbers and manufacturer's hull numbers, is parked at a forward base in China waiting to be fuelled and armed for the raid of 15 June 1944, against Yawata and the Imperial Iron and Steel Works. It was to be the second combat mission for the B-29s, and was to produce a single hit on a powerhouse almost one mile from the aiming point. / *USAF 52819 A.C. via Boeing-Wichita*

each, per group, instead of the former complement of four squadrons with seven B-29s each. Maintenance squadrons were merged with bomber squadrons, so that ground personnel increased in number for each squadron.

'Mission by mission the Superfort was proving itself, and the men who flew her had become acquainted with her every whim and foible. These men were now thoroughly indoctrinated in the harsh school of combat and they accomplished their mission with cool precision and deadly "know how". Squadrons hit the target and withdrew in tight defensive formation bristling with cooly manned and accurately fired 50-calibre gun turrets. Flight engineers calculated their gas consumption and established power settings which returned them to base within 50 gallons of the expected 150 gallon reserve. Navigators felt their way across the uncharted and ever changing vastness of China with obscure landmarks and exacting celestial navigation, and terminated their 1,200 mile trip by splitting the home airfield. Letdowns into the mountain-walled Chengtu valley were effected by pilots feeling, timing and guessing their way in the heavy soup and often severe icing on multi-split bent radio-range legs through passes, over low ranges, and within the 20,000 foot west wall until successful contact was accomplished — sometimes a bare 50 feet above the ground. The men of the 20th considered these extreme operational conditions — but continued to carry on.' *444th Bomb Group unit history*

By that time, Arnold was considering the transfer of the XX Bomber Command to a better location. The move was stayed for a few months while the B-29s went after the targets they could reach.

There was a second strike against Anshan on 26 September, staged again through the forward bases near Chengtu, and almost 100 planes bombed the target. But the results were poor.

In October, the Command flew three missions in support of the invasion of Leyte in the Philippines, to hit targets on Formosa that were supplying the major share of aircraft to the Japanese defenders. The 14 October strike, against an aircraft assembly and overhaul plant at Okayama, Formosa, was the first punishing attack the B-29s flew. It had taken them ten missions to learn some of the tricks of the trade. They were to fly less effective missions during the rest of October, all of November and into December.

But in mid-December, they hit Hankow, China, in a raid that has since caused some controversy. Hankow was a major supply base for the Japanese forces in China, storing and moving a large portion of the logistical support for the occupying armies. Maj Gen Claire L. Chennault, commanding the 14th Strike Force in China, had argued loud and long for an air strike against Hankow by the B-29s, but had been denied each request. He had been told that such a raid would dilute the effectiveness of the strategic air war conducted by the B-29s, and that the job was properly the responsibility of the 14th Air Force.

The Japanese kicked off an attack in November that looked as if it were headed straight for Kunming. That city was one end of the strategic air routes over the Hump of the Himalayas, and its loss would have been

*Beter 'n' Nutin* tells an interesting and full combat life story in mission markers and nose art. She was a B-29-36-BW, serial 42-24538, assigned to the 676th BS, 444th BG, 58th BW. When photographed, she had completed 24 Hump flights, 25 bombing missions, acquired eight Purple Hearts for her crew, and shot down one Japanese fighter. In the left background is the tail of aircraft 17, a B-29-35-BW (42-24524) of the 444th BG, 58th BW. / *Ron E. Witt Collection*

critical to a lot of operations in China. This time, Chennault's pleas were heard and acted upon, and LeMay was directed to strike Hankow.

It was to be a joint attack with the 14th Air Force. The B-29s were targeted to strike the docks and warehouses along the Yangtze River by daylight, using loads of incendiary bombs; the heavy bombers from the 14th Air Force were to hit the Japanese-used airfields.

Ninety-four B-29s lifted off the advance bases in China on 18 December, and 84 of them fire-bombed Hankow. The plan had called for a carefully timed sequence of formation flights and drops over the target, but the timing was off and smoke from the fires started by the first formations hampered accurate bombing by the later groups. No matter; the bombs that hit the target burned out about half of the designated area, and ended Hankow's value as a major supply base.

For some time afterward, this single fire raid was cited as 'the reason' for LeMay's later decision to make the fire-bombing of Japan a primary B-29 mission. But such strikes against Japanese cities had been in mind even before Hankow was hit, and before the B-29s had even been committed to combat. Careful and extensive studies had been made at various planning levels. At least two prototype sections of towns, built according to the best intelligence information on Japanese architecture and construction,

*Left:* On the high road, this formation of B-29s from the 44th Bomb Group shows the diamond markings identifying the group. In the centre of the picture is a camouflaged B-29-1-BW, serial number 42-6251, the 37th production aircraft off the line at Wichita. / *Ron E. Witt Collection*

*Below:* Made up attractively and posed prettily, *American Beauty* shows off the slim lines of the Queen of the Skies. She was born in Wichita, a B-29-45-BW, and christened with a number: 42-24703. Her rudder and cowl panels carry her colours, probably the yellow of the 794th BS. The two diagonal stripes on the rudder marked aircraft of the 468th Bomb Group. Names of Group aircraft were painted in the streamer, coming off the nose like the tail of a comet. The radome for the AN/APQ-13 bomb-nav radar juts down between the bomb bays. / *Ron E. Witt Collection*

were erected at bombing ranges and fire-bombed to check the conclusions of the studies. USAAF Headquarters and XX Bomber Command Headquarters had both, independently, considered stripping the B-29s and sending them in low against the Japanese cities, armed with heavy loads of incendiary bombs.

The 18 December raid was further evidence that the concept was sound, and was considered as a 'test' strike. It must have carried some weight in LeMay's mind. But it was not 'the reason' that he made the decision later. That resulted from a much more detailed consideration of the advantages and the disadvantages of B-29 operations against the home islands of Japan.

On 15 January 1945, the B-29s flew their last mission from the advance Chinese bases. It was against Shinchiku, on Formosa, and it was one of several that month sent out to support another invasion of the Philippines, this one against Luzon. Three days later, LeMay was transferred to the Marianas as chief of the XXI Bomber Command.

The B-29s of the XX Bomber Command, now operating only out of their Indian bases, continued to fly against targets in Burma, French Indo-China, Malaya, Singapore and Thailand, but they were generally small shows of force against tactical targets suggested by theatre commanders. In February, the 58th Bomb Wing was deactivated, and the deployment of its forces to the Marianas began.

The last strike by Superfortresses in the China-Burma-India theatre was flown on 29 March 1945. It was a low-level assault against oil storage facilities on the island of Bukum, Singapore. By then, the first air echelons of the 58th Wing had left for the Marianas, and within days, the rest of the B-29s had loaded and flown away.

The XX Bomber Command flew only 49 missions in ten months, putting 3,058 aircraft sorties into the air and dropping 11,477 tons of bombs. It was a poor record: only about two combat sorties per aircraft per month. And of these missions, only a small fraction of them went against Japan.

They did score some notable successes, against Okayama and Hankow, in support of the invasions of Leyte and Luzon, and in their mining of the Shanghai area and its great river mouth, the Yangtze. That experience paid off later in the Marianas.

As a strategic bombing operation, the experience of the XX Bomber Command was of little value. But as a strategic bombing training and shakedown operation, it was of inestimable value. It had taken the B-29 from its fledgling status as an untried weapon of war and had shown the crews and the planners how to operate with it, how to attack with it, and how to cope with many of its technical and operational problems.

# San Antonio and Beyond

The first B-29 combat strike from the Marianas against Japan was scheduled for November 1944. As is so often the case, that decision was made at a very high level of command, motivated by many political and strategic factors, and it was then up to the lower levels of command to carry out the operation. There were many pressures, of time, equipment, training, intelligence, and the availability and capability of the island bases themselves.

Gen Haywood S. Hansell, Jr, describes the background to that first mission:

'The JCS set up the 20th Air Force with Gen Arnold in command, acting as their executive agent, and they issued a directive for operations in the Pacific under the XXI Bomber Command. The first objective was listed as the undermining and defeat of the Japanese air forces through the destruction of engine and aircraft factories.

'It made pretty good sense. But it had some very extensive repercussions. In the first place, we didn't know where any of those engine and aircraft factories were. We knew there were some in the vicinity of Tokyo, some in Nagoya, but there were no photographs, no detailed maps, no target folders. Obviously, we were going to have to find them ourselves.

'In the second place, they were precision targets. We couldn't hit them by night operations, or by radar. So we would have to use daylight optical bombing to do that job. We would have to operate in formation with no fighter escort and against heavy opposition, and operating in formation would cut down the range of our aircraft very seriously.

'So we had to go into an almost convulsive change of tactical operations. In August 1944 we suddenly reversed the whole field of tactics on which the 73rd Wing had been training, abandoned the radar bombing approach, and adopted a new programme for optical bombing. This involved a drastic change, not only in bombing and formation flying, but also in gunnery. We had to learn to use the fire control system, which was very complex, and to select and adopt a bombing formation suitable to the firepower and flying characteristics of the B-29. The effect was to disrupt the whole training programme.

'I got a call to report to Washington just before Jack Catton (Commander, 873rd BS, 498th BG) and I were to go out to Saipan, and I had an interview with Gen Marshall in early October 1944. He said that the joint strategy for the Pacific campaigns had been laid out, and the bombing of Japan was part of that national strategy. He said that the first attack on Tokyo would be a joint operation with the Navy. The Navy would undertake to send a carrier task force up into the Japanese area to divert some of the defending fighters and to provide us with some fighter protection. The idea certainly was welcome from our point of view.

'Gen Marshall wanted to know whether we could carry out our part, which involved an attack on Japan in the month of November, a very short time from then, and he wanted a commitment on that. Obviously I couldn't very well tell him that we couldn't do it, so I told him yes, we could. And I said we not only could, but would. It would involve an attack from bases which were 6,000 miles away, which we had never seen but hoped were ready, against targets whose location we did not know.

'Two days later Jack Catton and I were heading for Saipan. We alternated flying on his airplane, which was called "Joltin' Josie, the Pacific Pioneer" (T Sq 5, 42-24614) and we arrived on Saipan on the twelfth of October after calling on Admiral Nimitz in Honolulu.' *Haywood S. Hansell, Jr*

At this point, let Catton interrupt the story:

'When Gen Hansell and I took the first B-29 out to the Marianas, it was still a classified airplane. So everywhere we went, we created quite a fuss. Would you believe that at Hickam, in Honolulu, we had a white-glove inspection of the airplane by Admiral Nimitz, Commander in Chief, Pacific? And thanks to Master Sergeant Quentin Hancock, my airplane could stand a white-glove inspection.

'When we went through Kwajalein, the island had just been taken in a very severe fight. A lot of blood had been shed to get that stepping-stone for us. We no sooner landed the airplane than a whole bunch of guards cordoned it off, put ropes around it. The folks were a bit upset, and properly so; they wanted to see this new, big airplane, and the Marines had it guarded and nobody could get near it.

'The next day when we came down to take off, there was a B-24 of the 7th Air Force parked next to us. They had a couple of officers standing by a big sign out in front of it, and the sign read, "This is a B-24, a combat airplane. Everybody welcome".' *Jack Catton, commander, 873rd BS, 498th BG*

Hansell, Catton and crew were met by cheering crowds, literally. Thousands of soldiers, sailors, and marines lined the runway, surged after the airplane as it taxied toward a hardstand. Hansell was asked to say a few words, and he did. 'The advance air element of the 73rd Bomb Wing has arrived on Saipan', he stated. 'When we've done some fighting, we'll do some talking'.

A difficult job lay ahead, as Hansell says: 'The situation was pretty bad. We thought we had two bases, with four paved runways, each 8,500 feet long, with shops, warehouses, and storage facilities available. Well, one of the bases couldn't handle B-29s at all because of a hill near one end of the runway. The other base was half-finished, with only one runway, and it was paved for only 6,000 feet. Its second runway was not finished at all.

'Instead of 100 hardstands for each base, we had about 40 all told, and no facilities: no shops, no warehouses, nothing but gasoline

storage and a bomb dump. We had to complete and organise a base, bring in 120 B-29s, and launch an operation in 35 days, and that was going to be very difficult to do.

'We hadn't been there but a short time when we got a big break. Captain Ralph D. Steakley (3rd Photo Reconnaissance Squadron) came in with a photo-recon B-29. He and his crew had been flying constantly, stopping only for refuelling, all the way from Kansas, and he insisted on going at once to Tokyo to get pictures. I tried to discourage him. I even thought of forbidding him, because they were exhausted. But they never faltered, and thank the Lord I did not forbid them, because the next day they fell on one of those rare occasions when the skies were absolutely clear over Japan, and they flew over Honshu for almost three hours and got magnificent pictures. They had pictures of all the aircraft and engine factories that we needed for our first objective. It was a tremendous break.

'But then things began to get a little bad. On 24 October the Japanese fleet started its operations against MacArthur's landings at Leyte Gulf in the Philippines, and there was a major naval engagement. The confusion threw the Navy command in the Pacific into complete disarray. We had only about 20 B-29s on Saipan by then, but I had them armed with 2,000lb bombs and declared our readiness to support the Navy to the best of

The 494th Bomb Group visits Japan and flies past one of its most spectacular tourist attractions. They are about 60 miles out of Tokyo, and all hell is about to break loose in the air and on the ground. Aircraft in the group include T-Square-21, *Lassie Come Home* (left foreground); T-Square-27, *Torchy* (lower right); and T-Square-22 *Bedroom Eyes* (above *Torchy*). / XXI Bomber Command via Boeing-Wichita

our abilities. Admiral Nimitz called off the Tokyo operation for the Navy, requested the JCS to stop the B-29s, and recommended that they ground us until such time as the Navy was able to give us the planned support.

'On top of this setback, Gen Kenney sent a most disturbing letter to Gen Arnold, with a very persuasive argument that we couldn't do the Tokyo operation from Saipan. He contended that we didn't have the range, and couldn't do the mission, and he said the Japanese would shoot us all out of the air anyway.

'The questions of range and defensive firepower were very sensitive. The Air Transport Command had refused to let us fly from California to Hawaii (2,400 miles) in squadron formation, without bomb loads, on the grounds that the airplanes lacked the necessary range. Yet almost immediately after arrival we would have to fly a 3,200-mile mission, with bomb loads, in the face of bitter Japanese fighter defences.

'Gen Arnold forwarded a copy of the letter to me and said that all his senior air commanders agreed with Kenney and that he was inclined to agree with him too. But he concluded, "If you still think you can carry out the mission, good luck."

'Almost at the same time I got a message to the effect that Admiral Nimitz had requested that the entire B-29 operations be devoted to aerial mining. Aerial mining is a fine idea; but the idea of shifting the entire aerial

offensive against Japan to support the Navy's attack on the Japanese transportation system didn't sit very well with us.

'And then "Rosey" O'Donnell (Brig Gen Emmett O'Donnell, commander, 73rd Bomb Wing) came to me with a handwritten letter. We met in privacy, sitting on a log near my headquarters shack. He said frankly he didn't think the 73rd Bomb Wing was in any position to carry out the mission, and he proposed that we change it to a night operation.

'I said, "Rosey", I couldn't agree with you more. A night operation would be much safer, we could pull it much more easily, there is much less risk involved, but the catch is we can't do our job that way. If we have to tell the JCS that on our first mission we have had to give up the job, it will be very serious indeed. It will jeopardise not only the 20th Air Force and the strategic air war against Japan, but the whole future of the Air Force.

'These were the issues that were facing us just before that first operation:

'If we followed the Navy's first request, if we grounded ourselves until the Navy was ready to come along, we would be admitting that we couldn't operate without the support of the Navy, and we didn't want to put ourselves in that position.

'If we changed to the aerial mining operation, as requested by Admiral Nimitz, using the entire XXI Bomber Command, we would be abandoning the air war against the Japanese homeland and devoting ourselves to support of the Navy. This would destroy the basic reasoning for direct command by the JCS and hence would destroy the need for the 20th Air Force.

'If we went to night operations, we would have to abandon the primary target objectives which we had been given. This would also undermine confidence in the 20th Air Force, and raise questions about the need for it.

'If we tried to carry out our daylight attacks on the aircraft factories at Tokyo and failed, we would probably lose the Command as well as a lot of fine people.

'If we tried the daylight attack and succeeded, then the whole future was open to us.

'So at that time and under those conditions, the entire weight of the future was resting on the 73rd Wing: the air offensive against Japan, the future of the 20th Air Force and of air power in the Pacific, and the future of the United States Air Force.

'I took a deep breath and decided to go with the daylight mission as planned. I issued the orders for Mission San Antonio I. You know what happened from then on. It was successful. It did open the way. It did lead to victory over Japan by air power.' *Haywood S. Hansell, Jr*

# Mission from the Marianas

San Antonio I was directed against Tokyo, and specifically against the Musashino plant of the Nakajima Aircraft Co, Ltd, later to be known as the durable, infamous Target 357. The strike was planned to drop a mix of incendiary and 500lb general-purpose bombs, and was scheduled for 17 November.

Bad weather delayed the attack, first for a single 24-hour postponement, then through successive ones. Rain fell on Saipan, and the wind — so necessary as an aid to takeoff of the heavily loaded B-29s — swung around so that the preferred runway direction had to be reversed. Isley Field ran uphill in that direction, and it was obvious that the B-29s would be dangerously marginal in such a situation.

Finally the weather pattern broke, and the morning of 24 November was clear. 'Rosey' O'Donnell climbed aboard the lead B-29, *Dauntless Dotty*. Carrying the tail marking A Sq 1, the aircraft was normally flown by Maj Robert K. Morgan, commander of the 869th Bomb Squadron, but 'Rosey' bumped him to co-pilot for this mission. At 0615 *Dauntless Dotty* began to roll. One after the other, 111 B-29s took off that morning. Several Boeing F-13As (reconnaissance versions of the B-29) from the 3rd Photo Reconnaissance Sqdn, also left Saipan to feint at Tokyo from the southeast, to drop 'rope' to decoy the Japanese radars, and to photograph the strike results.

The weather over Tokyo was miserable. There was a high-altitude wind of about 120 knots — later to be identified as the jet stream — which nudged the Superfortresses' ground speed toward the 450mph mark. An undercast almost hid the target. Already, 17 aircraft had aborted the mission, and six more were not able to bomb because of malfunctions.

The force that hit the primary target was 24 B-29s; the other 64 dropped on the urban areas and docks. Almost half of the striking planes had to bomb by radar. There was a single combat loss, when a B-29 was apparently intentionally rammed by a Japanese fighter and fell, out of control, into the water.

Photo coverage also was hampered by the weather. The post-strike photos showed that 48 bombs had hit in the factory area. Postwar studies showed how little damage had been done and that the casualties were 57 killed, 75 injured. Two B-29s had been lost, one to the fighter, and one when its fuel ran out and it had to be ditched. Eight Superforts were damaged by the enemy, and three by B-29 gunners who got carried away in the heat of their first engagement. One man was killed, a whole crew of 11 was missing and presumed dead, and four were wounded.

But the real value of that first raid lay in two intangibles. First, the B-29s had hit a very important and very heavily defended target area in bad weather and had come through their trial almost unscathed. Second, the attack served the first notice to the Japanese population that their home islands were no longer safe from direct attack.

The strike was typical of the attacks to follow over the next three months. Hansell's basic plan was to make maximum-effort attacks against high-priority targets in good weather with an available force of at least 60 Superforts. Secondary targets were to be attacked when the weather was not good enough for visual bombing and when the available force was smaller. And every night, a combined weather and strike mission was to go.

*Top right:* 'Throw your oxygen mask away, General LeMay is here to stay!' And that's the General himself, aircraft commander of this B-29 just touching down on a new runway in the Marianas. Wartime secrecy being what it was, not even the island is identified further. / *XXI Bomber Command via Boeing-Wichita*

*Centre right:* With bombs and guns loaded and props aligned, this B-29 waits for her crew on the hardstand at Saipan. / *Mrs Thomas Isley Collection*

*Below:* It's April 1945, and some of the 500th BG's B-29s have been marked with the big Z on the vertical tail while others still retain the smaller Z, the square of the 73rd Wing and the aircraft number as their identification. For the moment, this aircraft is alone on the hardstand, surrounded by jacks, maintenance stands, boxes, and oil drums that help to keep her in the air. / *Mike Janosko Collection*

'My first mission to Tokyo was a very eventful one. I hadn't flown in combat before; I'd been an instructor pilot for three years before I got my chance. I recall vividly flying in a formation some 1,600 miles up to the island of Honshu, and approaching our IP, which was Mount Fuji. Over Fuji we go, head into the bomb run, and we have what is now known as the jet stream. But back then, nobody had heard about jet streams.

'We're at 35,000 feet and we're doing about 500 miles per hour ground speed. Things were really happening fast. We were told that the flak wouldn't reach us at that altitude. It did. We went through, and just about the time we passed out of the flak, the fighters hit us. We had also been told that the fighters couldn't get to 35,000 feet either.

They were there, and they pressed their attacks very aggressively.

'We stayed in formation, nine B-29s of the 873rd Bomb Squadron, and we flew on to the target, released our bombs, and flew off the target together. I looked out to the left, and I looked out to the right, and I saw those gorgeous machines tucked in close and I thought, the Japanese haven't a chance. We're going to whip them. No question about it'. *Jack Catton*.

On 27 November, the 73rd Wing flew a second mission against the Nakajima plant at Musashino. No damage was done to the target, but back at Isley Field, ten to 15 Japanese raiders came in fast and low and destroyed three B-29s while the mission was over the home islands. Earlier that day, two twin-engined Japanese bombers had run in from Iwo Jima and had blown up one Superfortress.

The B-29s flew a night radar-bombing raid against Tokyo on 29 November, and on 3 December went back to Musashino and Target 357 for another try. Six of the Superforts were lost on that mission, and still the Nakajima plant continued to turn out engines for the defending Japanese who were beginning to take the measure of the big bombers both over Japan and back on Saipan.

On 7 December, Japanese planes attacked Isley Field again, and blew up three Superforts and damaged 23. These raids were becoming a serious threat to the B-29 operations and it was said, only half-jokingly, that it was safer to be over Japan in a B-29 than on the ground at Saipan. Before the raids ended, the Japanese attackers had destroyed 11 Superfortresses, had done major damage to eight more, and minor damage to 35. Airplanes could be replaced, at a cost; but the 45 dead airmen left in the wake of the raids could not. Additionally, more than 200 were wounded in the attacks.

To counter them, a major strike was planned against the Japanese airfields on Iwo Jima, co-ordinated with an attack by B-24 bombers from the 7th AF. On 8 December they flew the 600-mile trip; 62 Superforts dropped 620 tons of bombs and 102 B-24s dropped 192 tons. It was a deterrent; the Japanese strikes stopped for a while.

So far, it had been downhill all the way for the B-29s. They were accomplishing little, losing many. But the next attack reversed their fortunes, at least temporarily. It was a daylight raid against the Mitsubishi Heavy Industries Co, Ltd engine plant at Nagoya, a major source of powerplants for defending Japanese fighters. The Superfortresses made 13 December a lucky day. Ninety bombers took off for the attack; 16 of them aborted and three dropped on other targets. But the

It's time to go, and the ground crew begins its treadmill, turning the giant prop blades through a few times by hand before the starter is called into play by the flight engineer.
*/ Ingram T. Hermanson Collection*

*Above:* Led by *Fancy Detail,* Z-Square-50, of the 500th Bomb Group, the long line of Superfortresses trundles along the taxiways towards takeoff and the flight to Japan.
/ *Mike Janosko Collection*

*Centre right:* T-Square-9, *Devil's Darling* (42-24629), from the 498th Bomb Group, lifts off the runway at Saipan on a mission against Japan. On her 23rd mission, she was hit hard by fighters and her airplane commander was killed. With two engines out, she ran out of fuel and ditched 20 miles off Saipan. All the crew, except for the commander, were rescued.
/ *Mrs Thomas Isley Collection*

*Bottom right:* The ground crews watched them go and waited for them to come back. This is Saipan, and the B-29 is from the 500th Bomb Group.
/ *Ingram T. Hermanson Collection*

main force of 71 dropped 500lb general-purpose bombs and incendiary clusters and destroyed almost 18 per cent of the roofed-over plant area, according to post-strike photos. But the pictures failed to reveal the true extent of the damage. It was so severe that machining of parts was halted at Plant 4 in the target array, and engine production from then on depended on the inventory of parts at 13 December, augmented by parts from outside suppliers. Further, the attack initiated a programme of factory dispersal to underground sites, but it was done so poorly that no engine production ever came from the dispersed sites.

It was a short-lived success. The big bombers made two return trips to Nagoya, on 18 December against the Mitsubishi aircraft plant there, and on 22 December against the engine factory again. Neither raid did much damage. The 22 December strike was a daylight incendiary raid, with the bombers carrying only fire bombs. It was in response to pressures from USAAF Headquarters, based on the success of the

18 December raid by **XX** Bomber Command against Hankow, China. It was regarded as a test of the fire raid concept, and it was supposed to be flown with a force of 100 B-29s. But the strike on 22 December dispatched 78 bombers and did very little damage.

On 24 December the Superforts struck Iwo Jima again, hammering the airfields in another tactical diversion from the strategic air offensive. It was Musashino again on 27 December, and once again the attack failed to do any substantial damage to Target 357.

The 3 January mission against Nagoya was more nearly the test fire raid that had been suggested by Arnold's Headquarters. At take-off, 97 Superfortresses left the runway at Saipan, each carrying 4,900lb of incendiary clusters and one 420lb fragmentation bomb. It was another bad run; only 57 bombed the primary target, starting some fires. The test was inconclusive.

Target 357 was hit again — or perhaps missed is the more accurate term — 9 January. One warehouse was destroyed; it

A mixed formation of Superfortresses from the 497th and 498th Bomb Groups soars serenely above cumulus on the way to the home islands of Japan. Left to right: T-Square-44, *Patches* (42-24624); T-Square-51, *Houston Honey* (42-63475); T-Square-50, *Forbidden Fruit* (42-24607); T-Square-?; A-Square-44, *Ponderous Peg* (42-63431); A-Square-?; A-Square-?; A-Square-11; unmarked; A-Square-9. / *AAF Pacific 1233-11 via Boeing-Wichita*

cost six B-29s. On 15 January the bombers flew against Nagoya and Mitsubishi's aircraft factory, dropping four bombs in the target area out of the loads carried by 40 B-29s.

XXI Bomber Command broke its losing streak on 19 January with an assault on the main aircraft and engine plant of Kawasaki Aircraft Engineering Co, Ltd, at Akashi, 12 miles west of Kobe on Japan's Inland Sea. The plant was a major one, producing twin-engined fighters, and engines for single-engined fighters. The raid was a rousing success; 62 B-29s out of the 77 dispatched bombed the factory and knocked it out of the war. The company closed the plant, moved the machine tools to another site, and used what was left for very limited assembly.

It was Hansell's swansong as commander of the XXI Bomber Command. The next day, LeMay was moved from XX Bomber Command to take over Hansell's command, and Hansell was on his way back to the United States to work in the B-29 training programme.

Hansell said later that there were four major problems with the early B-29 operations. First, he had to convince the 73rd Bomb Wing that precision bombing was better than radar night bombing. Second, the bombing accuracy was very poor. Third, the abort rate was much too high, almost one out of every four sorties never getting to the target area. Fourth, losses due to ditching were too high and air-sea rescue operations needed to be improved.

The mission pattern stayed much the same after LeMay's takeover. Strikes against the top-priority targets — aircraft engine plants — dominated the list, and Target 357 was assigned its share. LeMay tried his luck 27 January, sending 76 bombers against Musashino. But the weather protected the area; 56 of the bombers dropped on their secondary targets and six bombed the alternate targets. Nine Superforts were lost, and one almost didn't make it back. It was *Pride of the Yankees*, Z Sq 24, from the 500th Bomb Group, and its commander was Lieutenant Frank A. Carrico. This was his debriefing report:

'When we hit the coastline, we picked up our first fighter, which came up, got our altitude, and followed us in and out of the target. Just before the IP, we picked up a twin-engined Irving (Nakajima J1N1 'Gekko'), nine o'clock level, which stuck out there for a few minutes throwing bursts at us from his turret, then he made an attack on our ship and the boys got him.

'We were jumped good and hard before we got our bomb doors open. All guns were blazing away and just as we let the bombs go, a Tony (Kawasaki Ki-62 "Hien") got a good burst in our number two engine. Lt (Morris M.) Robinson was flying because we were on the left side of the formation, and I told him to stay on the controls and stay in formation.

'I tried to feather the damned prop and naturally it won't feather. It's burning good by this time, and I yell to Lt (Albert E.) Woodward, my engineer, to cut it off and pull the extinguisher. He'd already cut it off and when he pulled the fire extinguisher, the whole installation came out of his panel.

'Just about that time, the prop ran away and blew the fire completely out. Our speed dropped, and we lost the formation. In the meantime we had another attack on the nose which shot out two of the large glass panels and put a bullet through the side, under my instrument panel and between my feet. My bombardier was wounded in the legs, and that left our nose unprotected. After we dropped out of formation, we received nine concentrated attacks on the nose.

'Our astrodome was blown out when we lost pressurisation, and we had a wind blowing through the nose compartment which I thought would surely freeze Lt Robinson and myself; it was 40 below zero Centigrade outside. We had on jackets, gloves and boots, but our legs were freezing, so we gathered flak suits, maps and anything else we could find to wrap around them. One man would fly for a few minutes and then start shivering so much he couldn't stay on the controls. The crew in the meantime had gotten ready to bail out, because I didn't want them to ride the burning plane down from 25,000 feet.

'I told Lt Robinson to fly until the prop came off so I could watch and see where it

*Top left:* Three different Superfortresses carried the T-1 designator from the 498th Bomb Group; two were lost after enemy action, and the crew of one of those was rescued. Here one of them drops a string of 14 500lb bombs from both bomb bays. / Donald L. Miller Collection

*Bottom left:* Danny Mite, T-Square-28 (46-69777), starts dropping a train of 500-pounders by invervalometer. She was lost on Mission 72 on 24 May 1945, after she lost two engines over the target. She was last heard reporting that they were headed toward the ocean. / Donald L. Miller Collection

*Below:* Ponderous Peg, a Marietta-built B-29-16-BA (42-63431) and A-Square-44 in the 497th Bomb Group, is coming home with numbers three and four dead and feathered. Major F. L. Trickey is at the controls, nursing A-44 back to Saipan, one of the first times a B-29 has come home 1,500 miles on two engines. Low cruise power and rpm makes it appear that all four props have stopped. / A. F. Migliaccio Collection

Left: The lead bombardier (in second aircraft from left) has just called 'Bombs away!' and the bombardiers in the other four B-29s from the 497th BG have reacted and triggered their bombs on his drop. Each plane has unloaded five bombs.
/ A. F. Migliaccio Collection

Below: The clouds below the Superfortress duo may be heavier over the target, and make bombing more difficult. Japanese farms lie below and in the distance is Tokyo.
/ Mrs Thomas Isley Collection

Bottom: That's flak and it's too damned close for comfort. It bursts to the left of my plane and misses all three of us. But they've got the altitude setting right...
/ A. F. Migliaccio Collection

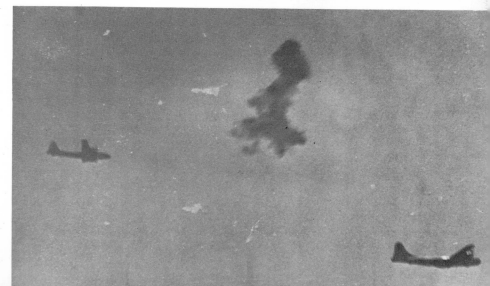

went. By this time, I had all the men in their ditching positions. At 1625hrs, the prop came off, but it hadn't read the SOP (Standing Operating Procedures) on how props were to come off. The metal of the nose section melted on the inboard side and the prop peeled off to the left in flat pitch. It held there an instant and then went hurtling into the number one engine. It broke the two bottom mount braces and bent the upper two; at the same time all four blades on the number one prop bent almost double. The prop would not feather and the vibration was terrific.

'The left wing was vibrating through an arc of about 20 feet, and I had the crew ready to bail out again and was just pressing the mike switch to give the order when the damn prop feathered. Capt (Horace E.) Hatch came up then and asked what our condition was, so we got an accurate position report from him and worked out an ETA (Estimated Time of Arrival) to our base. We didn't have enough gas to make it.

'I asked Capt Hatch to stick close, as all our navigation aids were out and all we had to navigate with was a map and a pencil. We flew until dark and the moon was very bright, so I decided to keep going and make a moonlight ditching. After dark I found my instrument lights were out, and the moon was bright enough to counteract the fluorescent paint glow from my instruments, so Lt Robinson flew until 2100.

'At that time we ran into instrument conditions and it took both of us to hold the ship. We both flew from his panel; he kept the wings level and I held altitude.

'We figured a very accurate ETA to the base and we were ten minutes short of gas. I called Capt Hatch and told him we would fly until 15 minutes remained and then we would ditch under the overcast. I got the crew in ditching positions again, and then my engineer called to say he'd found 75 more gallons of gas in the centre tank. We came on in.

'When we got to the base, we had to make the normal right-hand traffic pattern because I couldn't turn the plane into the dead wing. We held 2,000 feet of altitude, and when I got on base leg, we took out all the trim and let down the wheels. I flew the approach at 1,500 feet until I knew we could get down, power off. We chopped all power and stuck the nose down and still lost too much speed because when we got below 140 miles per hour we lost aileron control.

'But when we levelled off, we picked up our aileron control and she landed good. Our landing was strictly a two-man job also. Everyone was okay with the exception of the bombardier and myself; we both picked up a little flak in our legs.' *Frank A. Carrico*

Carrico's return was one of the first times that a B-29 had been flown back from a mission on two engines. It was a difficult, tiring, and risky condition for a fresh crew; it was doubly difficult, tiring and risky for a crew that had flown to Japan and fought its way to the target. Not many B-29s with two engines out made it back.

One of the nine B-29s that didn't come back carried tail gunner Sergeant Olinto F. Lodovici. He described his experience on that mission against Target 357:

'Our regular crew was changed; we got a new aircraft commander, a new engineer and a new navigator, and we were assigned to a strike against Target 357 on 27 January 1945. That was the tough target and they were waiting for us when we arrived. The first pass by a fighter got our pilot, co-pilot and bombardier. We heard the pilot ask the co-pilot for a hand, because he'd been hit bad in the chest, and the co-pilot told him that he couldn't help much because he'd been hit in the head.

'Our number one and number two engines were burning, and when I realised how bad it was, I tried to call somebody up front and got no answer. So I got out of my seat and looked through the glass toward the aft section of the ship. The aircraft was burning pretty bad inside, so I knew I had to get out of there. And that's a hell of a decision to make because you think maybe they'll make it back and leave you dangling on a chute over Japan. And I couldn't communicate with anybody up there. But I knew it was just a question of time before she blew.

'Besides, I didn't have any more ammunition. It was no sense trying to bluff them out, because I couldn't see out of my window. They'd blown my guns to hell and the window looked like spiderwebs.

'So I released the escape hatch, grabbed my chest pack off the floor, hooked it on one side of the harness — because I knew I couldn't get out of the hatch with the thing all hooked up — and I pushed myself out. I pulled the

That's Sgt James B. Krantz hanging outside the port gunner's blister of A-Square-7, *American Maid*, of the 869th Bomb Squadron, 497th Bomb Group. The Superfortress was at 29,000 feet when his blister let go, and Krantz was sucked outside to dangle over Tokyo on a harness he made himself. The aircraft commander Lt J. D. Bartlett, dove the plane to a much lower altitude to save Krantz and the gunners in the rear, and — after 15 minutes — Krantz was hauled back inside through the combined efforts and muscles of four crewmen. Krantz was severely frostbitten from the extreme cold at altitude, and injured by the buffeting from the slipstream that hammered him against the side of the fuselage. But he lived to tell the tale, one of the most remarkable in a war that was full of remarkable experiences.
/ *Donald L. Miller Collection*

*Above:* There are two out and feathered on the port side, and T-Square-10, 498th Bomb Group, is headed back toward Saipan and down toward the Pacific simultaneously. At least six B-29s bore the T-10 designator with the 498th. One was destroyed on the ground by Japanese bombers in an early hit-and-run raid. A second was missing after a raid on 3 December 1944. A third ditched in the ocean after running out of fuel on 27 January 1945. The fourth was named *Homer's Roamers*, and nothing further is known about her. The fifth was destroyed in an emergency landing, which the crew survived, on 6 April 1945. The sixth was named *Lucky Strikes*, and nothing further is known of her history, either.
*/ Donald L. Miller Collection*

*Top right:* And that's what it looks like from inside, when one of those Wright engines packs up and the engineer shuts down the engine and the pilot feathers the prop and a buddy comes up alongside to stick with you while you're in trouble.
*/ A. F. Migliaccio Collection*

*Bottom right:* Now the long mission is over, and we're set up on final approach over Magicienne Bay, coming in to Isley and rest. The flaps are all the way down, the gear is down and locked, and we're going to squeak down just past the threshold and roll out along the runway with one more mission gone and that much closer to going home. It's a beautiful sky, and a pretty island, and a hell of a long and hard trip out and back.
*/ Donald L. Miller Collection*

chute through after me, and I sat on the little fairing of the left stabiliser. I took my chute and finished hooking it on and checked it, sitting back there, and believe it or not, the slipstream just didn't move me for some reason.

'I sat there for a while, enjoying it, and then I started to push myself away from the aeroplane. But my damn boot — I had them open and forgot to lace them — hung up in the cleat of the hatch. So I'm hanging down alongside the fuselage with one foot hung up on the aeroplane. I just kept pushing and pushing and finally broke loose. As I was free-falling, the airplane blew.

'I delayed opening the chute, because I had my bailout bottle on, and I waited until I could see Mount Fuji sticking up above the clouds, sort of at eye level. Then I popped the chute. Some fighter made three or four passes at me and I was swinging the chute, trying to make myself hard to hit, and I damn near collapsed it. He gave up and I landed just off shore in Tokyo Bay.

'I was captured immediately by civilians and they beat me up pretty bad until two home guards came up and protected me and then turned me over to a Japanese officer who came riding up on a horse. The civilians were still trying to get at me, and this soldier finally took his sword in the scabbard and laid around with it, to convince the people that they should clear out and let me go with him quietly. That's the guy that saved my ass.

'I was worried there; civilians captured some of our guys and just pulled them apart. Well, our people would have done the same thing, I guess. It's a hell of a thing to have bombers over your homeland.' *Olinto F. Lodovici, tail gunner, 870th BS, 497th BG*

Between attacks on the Japanese aircraft industry, LeMay's bombers worked over the islands of Iwo Jima, Moen and Dublon, softening their offensive and defensive capabilities in preparation for the planned invasion of Iwo.

There was another 'test' incendiary raid, this time against Kobe on 4 February. It was the first strike flown by two wings; the 313th, now operational, joined the 73rd in the attack. They dropped 160 tons of incendiaries and 14 tons of fragmentation bombs from high altitudes with substantial effect. They wiped out fabric and synthetic rubber production, halved the capacity of one shipyard, and generally raised a small amount of hell.

But the B-29s stayed with their basic doctrine of precision bombing of single targets, sending a heavy strike on 10 February against Ota and its Nakajima aircraft factory that was producing the Ki-84 (Frank) fighter. Eighty-four B-29s bombed the primary target, damaged some buildings and ruined 74 of the fighters. It cost 12 B-29s, the highest loss so far.

The results of the 4 February fire raid continued to absorb the staff at Arnold's headquarters. On 19 February they issued a new target directive, redefining priorities. The top priority targets continued to be aircraft engine factories, but incendiary attacks on urban areas was the first of two secondary target policies specified, and the second was aircraft assembly plants. That directive marked the change in policy that elevated fire raids to a second level of priority. That day the XXI Bomber

Command went out in force against Target 357 again, dispatching 150 aircraft. But the target was completely closed in by weather, so 119 bombed the secondary target and 12 hit the target of last resort. Six B-29s were lost, and Musashino continued to stand firm.

The conclusive test of fire bombing came on 25 February. It was the biggest strike to date, involving aircraft from three wings then active in the Marianas: the 73rd, 313th and the recently arrived 314th Bombardment Wing (Very Heavy). They flew to the Tokyo urban area, and 172 Superfortresses bombed the primary target. Only 30 hit the alternates. When the smoke had cleared, 28,000 of Tokyo's buildings were in ashes. About one square mile had been levelled.

There was one more attempt to knock out Target 357 by precison bombing. On 4 March, the XXI Bomber Command sent a strong force of Superfortresses to bomb Musashino; weather defeated them again and 159 aircraft had to be content with bombing the secondary target. It was the end of precision high-altitude visual daylight bombing in the Pacific theatre, although nobody said so very loudly at the time.

Eight times the B-29s had flown against Target 357 in a total of 835 bombing sorties. They had destroyed less than four per cent of the factory area. Worse, a single attack on 17 February by Navy carrier-based aircraft had done more damage than any single assault by the powerful B-29 forces. It was high time to examine the whole traditional doctrine of bombing and to find out why it wasn't working in the Pacific.

# All she wore was a great big friendly smile

Nose art! Where would books like this be without at least a half-dozen well-chosen pictures of nearly nude women, painted in provocative poses along the length of the forward fuselage?

Nose art is almost as old as the airplane itself; its definitive history awaits the dedicated researcher. But by the late days of World War 2, the art form had reached a very high level, and it graced at least one of every type the military forces flew.

The long fuselage nose of the B-29 was a natural canvas for the imaginative, or the copying, artist. There were sign painters in the military, some good and some very good, who turned their spare-time talents to the decoration of aircraft. The going price, it is said, was from $60 to $100, depending on size, complexity, and other factors, such as what the traffic might bear. A good artist, with the blank aluminium sides of a squadron's ships beckoning, could make $1,000 or more in a few hours of his spare time. And that was when $1,000 *was* $1,000.

As long as the images were kept reasonably decent, or had minimal clothing, the upper echelons of command went along with nose art, officially not seeing anything at all on those fuselage sides. Official pictures for release back in the States were taken generally from the right side of the airplane, because the nose art was almost invariably confined to the left side.

'In the 314th Bomb Wing, we reserved the starboard side of the fuselage for the formal name. Each aircraft was officially and formally named the *"City of Someplace"*. Ours was the *City of Arcadia;* we figured we might get a crate of oranges out of it. We didn't. Each flight station was labelled with the name of a wife or girl friend. On the port side, we had the customary nose art, or the unofficial name. Ours was *No Balls Atoll.' Charles B. Hawks*

'Our aircraft was T-42, *Sweet Sue.* When the word came down that we could add the names of our wives or girl friends at our positions, we jumped at the chance. I figured that our daughter was born just about the time we were over the target at Ichinomiya, so I painted her name, Ellen Dorothy, just outside the side window of my tail turret.' *Mike Janosko, tail gunner, 875 BS, 498 BG*

The B-29 ladies got a little barer, and the captions got a little bolder, and one day the chaplains had enough. Perhaps we shouldn't blame the chaplains; it may have been a

There were probably a dozen or more B-29s that were named *American Beauty*. Most of them featured a lovely girl; one featured a monstrous caricature. But this one featured a bottle of fine bourbon, an 'American Beauty' indeed. She was assigned to the 444th Bomb Group. / *Ron E. Witt Collection*

morally outraged general officer. Anyway, late in the war, the girls had to go. The voluptuous virgins were erased, and replaced by a simple chaste symbol and a neatly lettered and innocuous name. Just who was being corrupted by these lovely ladies, reminders of home, mother and girl friends, is hard to say. But morality, legislated or commanded, works in strange ways.

That's why you could have seen a 73rd Bomb Wing B-29 with its yellow streamer labelled *Kansas Farmer.* You just know that in an earlier day the plane would have been named *The Farmer's Daughter,* and the decorative theme would have been a young, concupiscent blonde in very short shorts, lots of leg, low-cut blouse only half on . . .

Nose art in the Korean war has been largely undiscovered. Few collections of photos of the lovelies exist. The left side of many B-29s had been pre-empted by Strategic Air Command insignia, and SAC took itself and its insignia very seriously indeed. But the right side of the fuselage was bare, and soon so were the beauties who suddenly appeared on the B-29s once they had been deployed to Japan or Okinawa where few could see and complain.

Some of the titles or names found in the nose art of that war are a bit difficult to understand, unless one remembers contemporary American slang, or can translate Japanese expressions — many of the artists were Japanese employed on or near the base — not normally used between diplomats. *Miss Minooky,* for example, does not memorialise a small town in the state of Minnesota. And *Miss Megook* manages to offend Koreans, women, and Korean women simultaneously.

*Top: Bockscar,* from Salt Lake City, Utah, to Nagasaki, sits alone in the desert after the war. Flown by Major Charles W. Sweeney, she dropped the second atomic bomb on 9 August 1945. / *Boeing P 9710*

*Above:* A close-up of the nose art on *Eddie Allen,* a B-29-40-BW of the 45th BS, 40th BG, after the crew had completed seven flights over the Hump and six bombing missions. / *Boeing 88802*

*Left: Miss Megook,* lovely in her long blonde lines, probably has little in common with the Korean ('gook') woman on the mind of the guy who chose the name. / *Thomas H. Brewer Collection*

In both wars, the themes for nose art were predominantly sexual, with a name or title that was often double entendre: King Size, Cream of the Crop, Over Exposed. There were comic-strip characters, taken from the pages of hometown newspapers: Sad Sac, Lonesome Polecat. There were caricatures of the crew with humorous overtones: The Herd of Bald Goats, The Honeybucket Honshos.

Sometimes there were more involved stories behind the nose art, and here is one example from the Korean war:

'One of the B-29s in the 92nd Wing was named *The Wanderer*, and there's a story there. We had a Lieutenant Colonel named Ralph M. Wanderer, commanding the 325th Bomb Squadron of the 92nd, and he was pushing for full colonel at the time. Nothing wrong with that; we understood. Captain Norman B. Hemingway was the aircraft commander of a new B-29 that needed a name and he chose *The Wanderer*. The nose picture showed a tramp, with a butterfly net, chasing a couple of little — well, they looked like butterflies at first glance. But if you looked real close, you saw that they were little silver eagles, the insignia of a colonel.

'So that B-29 immortalised Lt Col Wanderer's chase for his colonel's eagles, and how Norman B. Hemingway had the guts to do that I'll never know. He got away with it.' *Vern Piotter, navigator, 92 BW, Korea*

Nose art has disappeared again from contemporary aircraft, replaced by super-graphic colour schemes. All that is left now are the pictures of the works of the forgotten great masters of the time. Some of them have been reproduced here as a tribute to the brave crews that, like medieval knights, carried their ladies' favours into battle.

*Top right:* When the nose art came off, the luscious ladies were replaced — at least on the 73rd Bomb Wing aircraft — by this black winged device, the black globe, and the yellow streamer carrying the aircraft name in black letters. This aircraft is *Kansas Farmer*, with the name superimposed on the streamer, in turn superimposed on what has been described as a headless chicken carrying a bowling ball. *Kansas Farmer* was aircraft 47 in the 73rd Wing; she flew 50 combat missions, and her crew downed six Japanese fighters. / *Weber*

*Below:* This B-29 of the 313th BW, based on North Field, Tinian, honoured the Navy's 'Seabees'. / *313th BW*

A Litany of Some B-29 Names in Alphabetical Order

*Adam's Eve and Andy's Dandy,*
*American Beauty, American Maid,*
*Booze Hound, Bock's Car, Bengal Lancer,*
*Battlin' Betty, Bedroom Eyes,*
*City of Pittsburg, Constant Nymph,*
*The Challenger and the Coral Queen,*
*Dragon Lady, The Devil's Delight,*
*Dauntless Dotty and Destiny's Tots,*
*Esso Express and Eddie Allen,*
*Forbidden Fruit, Filthy Fay,*
*Fire Belle, Fever from the South,*
*Gunga Din and Gertrude C.*
*Gravel Gertie, Geisha Gertie,*
*Heavenly Body, Homer's Roamers,*
*Hell on Wings, Honshu Hawk,*
*Inspiration, Island Princess,*
*Jokers Wild and Jumpin' Stud,*
*The Kayo Kid and Kickapoo Lou,*
*Limber Dugan, Lady Be Good,*
*Lethal Lady, Little Jo,*
*Miss Lace, Miss Hap, Miss-Leading Lady,*
*Mary K. and Mustn't Touch!*
*Noah Borshuns, Next Objective,*
*O'Reilly's Daughter, Oregon Express,*
*Pride of the Yankees, Pocahontas,*
*Party Girl, Patches, Ponderous Peg,*
*Ramblin Roscoe, Raidin' Maiden,*
*Rodger the Lodger, Rabbit Punch,*
*Stripped for Action and Supine Sue,*
*Sure Thing, Sweet Thing, Super Wabbit,*
*Tanaka Termite, Terrible Terry,*
*Tokyo Twister and Thunderbird,*
*Uncle Tom's Cabin, The Uninvited,*
*Victory Girl and Vanishing Rae.*
*Wichita Witch and Windy City,*
*Winnie II and Willie Mae.*

*Below left:* On occasion, the lovely ladies on the B-29s had to be covered. The artist here expressed his indignation with the label 'Censored' and the lower label of characters generally indicating profanity in comic strips. This B-29 was operated by the 676th BS, 444th BG, 58th BW, and was named *Lady ————*, just what may never be known. / *Weber*

*Below: Dream Boat*, a B-29 from the 444th BG, carried this shield and motto on her nose. The Latin translates as, 'Through victory to liberty'. / *Weber*

*Above: Constant Nymph*, a Bell-built B-29-21-BA (42-63487), carries markers for seven bombing missions and one photo-reconnaissance flight. / *Weber*

*Left: 'Ho-Hum'* and, in smaller letters, *'Let's Do It Again'* was a B-29-80-BW (44-70123). She carries the green identifying colour of the 676th BS, 444th BG, 58th BW. / *Weber*

*Below left:* The Circle R and red tip of the vertical tail marks this B-29 as one assigned to the 6th BG, 313th BW. Aircraft 1 probably was assigned to the 24th BS of that Group. / *Weber*

*Top right:* Back from battle, a lineup of B-29s stretches along a Wichita runway. In the middle distance is *Fire Belle*, a B-29A-40-BN (44-61653). She was aircraft 22 of the 676th BS, 444th BG, 58th BW, and was flown by a lead crew. / *Weber*

*Centre right:* Landing gear retracting, off the runway lifts aircraft A-46 from the 497th BG, 73rd BW. / *Weber*

*Bottom right: High and Mighty*, aircraft 60 of the 677th BS, stands out in the right foreground of this lineup at Wichita, Kansas. / *Weber*

Above: *Joy-ous Venture*, if the art work is to be believed, looks forward to a peacetime reunion in New York with a girl named Joy, complete with cocktails — note the symbolic cherry in the glass — music, and a view over the river. She was a B-29A-50-BN (44-61821), a sister ship to *Pacific Princess*. She carries the squadron insignia of the 678th Bombardment Squadron, a hooded cobra superimposed on an Ace of Spades and spitting out a bomb. / *Weber*

Centre right: Aircraft 230 of the 444th BG, 58th BW, was *Airborn*, a B-29-28-MO (42-65268). / *Weber*

Bottom right: Only the name *Flyin' Jackass* and the formation number of 39 are known for this B-29. In the background looms the tail of a 444th BG aircraft, a B-29-40-BW (42-24580), still carrying its CBI theatre markings. / *Weber*

*Above:* The Japanese horse-drawn cart that serviced the latrines was the inspiration for the name of *Honeybucket Honshos.* / *William F. Dawson*

*Centre left: Lonesome Polecat* runs along the side of this B-29, a long way from Dogpatch and Al Capp's 'Li'l Abner' comic strip. / *William F. Dawson*

*Bottom left:* The ultimate plunging neckline does little to conceal the fine figure of the young woman on this 98th Bomb Wing B-29. And the French expression lends sort of a classic touch, doesn't it ? / *William F. Dawson*

The following photographs are of B-29s from the 98th Bomb Wing, Yokota Air Base, Japan.

*Above:* The crew of *Rapid Rabbit* bailed out of their B-29 inside their own lines after losing two engines on a combat mission. / William F. Dawson

*Centre right: Lady in Dis-Dress:* pretty girl, pretty awful pun. / William F. Dawson

*Bottom right: Bust'n the Blue* is, if this author remembers, a copy of a photograph of Lilly Christine, the Cat Dancer. Right or wrong, that nose art could have been taken from the pictures of any one of a dozen strippers. / William F. Dawson

90

*Above:* There was always one airplane that seemed to have more mechanical trouble than others, and this one, *Sheer Madness*, was crewed by Abortin' Nortin and his Malfunction Ten.
/ *William F. Dawson*

*Above left: Nip-pon-ese;* well, do we have to explain that name?
/ *William F. Dawson*

*Centre left: Hearts Desire II* implies that there was a 'Hearts Desire I', but she could not have been prettier.
/ *William F. Dawson*

*Bottom left: The Big Gass Bird,* red-rumped and shedding feathers and a bomb, graces the nose of this 98th Bomb Wing B-29 in Japan.
/ *William F. Dawson*

# Twelve Times to Target 357

One-seventh of all the bombing missions flown against Japan by the B-29s in the Marianas were directed at the infamous Target 357, the main engine assembly plant of Nakajima Hikoki KK (Nakajima Aircraft Co, Ltd), in Musashi, a suburb of Tokyo. Twelve times the Superfortresses struck at Target 357, and once the Navy sent a carrier-based force of dive bombers and torpedo planes against it.

Militarily, it was the single most important target on the home islands of Japan. One out of every three engines used in Japanese combat aircraft was built in one of the several plants of Target 357. The Ha-35 Sakae and Ha-45 Homare radial powerplants were the principal production engines at the time of the B-29 raids. During the time period from January 1939 to 10 August 1945, the plant built more than 40,000 engines.

Target 357 was a relatively new plant, having been erected in 1938 as part of the Japanese industrial expansion in support of the war with China. Further expanded in 1941, the factory area covered almost three million square feet and employed a maximum of 45,000 workers. (For comparison, Pratt & Whitney's main plant in East Hartford, Connecticut, was almost as large in area and employment during the war.)

The buildings were a mix of single-storey steel-framed and wooden-roofed structures; a 1941 addition was a multi-storeyed reinforced-concrete building. They stretched over an area of 130 acres.

The first raids on the Musashino plant dropped a mix of demolition and incendiary bombs, using the latter because of the wooden roofs on the main plant area. Later raids used only high-explosive bombs.

Soon after the first raid on 24 November 1944, Nakajima began a dispersal programme and finally stopped all production at Musashi on 30 April 1945, following three heavy strikes on 2, 7 and 12 April.

Yet when all the results of the 13 raids were scored, they showed that less than ten per cent of the total bomb tonnage had hit within the plant area, and that a little more than two per cent of the tonnage actually hit buildings. Casualties were correspondingly small; 220 workers were killed and 266 were injured.

The attacking force of B-29s lost far more in casualties. Two groups alone — the 497th and 498th of the 73rd Wing — lost 40 airplanes in their assaults as part of the strike forces against Target 357. Forty B-29s carried 440 men.

On 7 April 1945, a heavy strike was mounted against Musashino. The mission was to be flown at medium altitude — around 12,000 feet — and the load was demolition bombs. Fighter escort would be provided by P-51s from Iwo Jima.

Capt Charles T. Moreland, of the 500th Bomb Group, was flying his aircraft, Z Sq 42 (*Supine Sue, the International Figure*) on that mission. One extra piece of equipment was on the plane: a wire recorder hooked up to the intercom system. It had been tried before, several times, but those B-29s never returned. 'We thought it was a jinx,' said Sgt Don Hetrick, a gunner aboard Z Sq 42, 'And we were apprehensive, but we figured we could break the jinx. That mission was quite a chore. It was the first one for which we had fighter escort, and the Japanese met it and us with everything they had. The flak was intense and we were the lead crew.'

'We had been hit, and a foot-wide stream of oil was coming over the wing. We needed oil to feather the prop, otherwise we'd have a runaway and generally a runaway prop spun off, ripped right off the engine and often hit the prop next to it. So before the runout, we feathered the engine and flew the rest of the mission on three. The secondary crew took over the lead position.

'We were jumped by an awful lot of fighters, and bombed by some others. They used those damned white phosphorus bombs on us, and when they burst, the effect was spectacular. I think they got at least one of our B-29s that way on this mission. We lost one crew to fighters just off our left wing; they took a direct hit in the cockpit, rolled over and spun in. I never saw any chutes at all. It was one hairy mission.' *Don Hetrick, gunner, 500th BG*

The excitement of that mission survived in the recording. Hetrick kept a copy of the transcription, which has no identification of the speakers. But that is hardly necessary as you read the crisp chatter:

'Fighter coming in low at ten o'clock . . . we're streaming oil . . . I'm feathering number one . . . twin engine outside right . . . one coming in at nine o'clock . . . ten o'clock high . . . four o'clock low . . . two o'clock . . . engineer, you're gonna have to cut number two . . . it's all right, going all right . . . things don't look too bad.

'Nine o'clock high . . . one at about ten o'clock over Z Square 56 . . . one o'clock high . . . one o'clock high coming in level . . . get him! You got him right alongside the engine . . . you got him! Good boy!

'Look at number one engine on 49 . . . who? . . . 49; he's got fire on it, smoke coming out pretty bad . . . fighter coming up at four o'clock low . . . nine o'clock coming up level . . . one at eight-thirty . . . what the hell is that?

'Coming in at two o'clock, fighter coming in . . . one at nine o'clock low . . . can't get him . . . one o'clock . . . number 49 seems to have his fire out, but it's smoking a little bit.

'Got a little hole in our right aileron . . . a *Little* hole?

'That was 47 that went down . . . did 47 get hit? . . . I was busy at the time, I didn't see it, maybe one of the blister gunners saw it . . . Roger . . . who was flying that? . . . Lt King . . . Oh, damn it!

'How you doing, radar? . . . I think he must have fainted . . . fainted, hell, I was so scared I couldn't talk.

'Squadron on our left side . . . get the numbers . . . 48, 40, 54, 43 . . . how many on the right? . . . one that I can see . . . what the hell are *we* doin' here?

'Four o'clock high . . . shut off the gas on number one . . . we still have about 65 gallons of oil on the gauge for number one . . . fighter at twelve o'clock level . . . come on, baby, give me a kiss . . . can you see him? . . . one fighter coming in at about five o'clock . . . fighter at nine o'clock, hit him . . . fighter low . . . look at those P-51s . . . two of them way high; come down and give us a hand!

'That damned phosphorus . . . they hit the tail . . . are you okay, Dietz? . . . anything serious? . . . nothing.

'There's the target . . . have you got the doors open? Roger . . . 31 is dropping . . . Bombs away! . . . Close doors . . . Roger . . . plane coming in, two o'clock . . . got one . . . coming in from the lower left . . . one coming in from two o'clock . . . nine o'clock level . . . low . . . two o'clock level . . . B-29 flaming way below us.

'Nine o'clock coming in high . . . we got him . . . got that son-of-a-bitch . . . ten o'clock low . . . another one at seven-thirty . . . ten o'clock level . . . four o'clock high . . . nine o'clock, ambitious . . . one coming underneath . . . look at those

phosphorus bombs . . . nine o'clock high . . . something's leaking out of number two . . . nine o'clock high . . . it must be moisture.

'Which one is 49 . . . 49 below us, 1,200 yards . . . three ships behind us all together . . . is that 53 behind us also? I believe it is . . . no, I just saw him feather number one . . . 50 is just behind us.

'Did anybody see the bombs hit? . . . I saw some hit, I know about where . . . I just wondered if they hit the target . . . pilot to radio operator . . . putting his headset on, sir . . . this is the radio operator . . . is that dictaphone still on, Agee? . . . yes, sir, I think it is . . . turn the damned thing off, will you?'

The nine B-29s of the 500th Bomb Group, Hetrick's outfit, claimed 13 Japanese fighters shot down, two probables, and 13 others damaged. The 497th Bomb Group, along on the same mission, claimed 37 Japanese fighters destroyed, 14 probably destroyed and 15 damaged. There were 130 fighter attacks noted during the running battle, and 29 of the 497th Group's aircraft were damaged by flak and enemy attack.

When the prop departed the number two nacelle on Z-Square-24, *Pride of the Yankees*, it took a big chunk of the cowling with it, and severely damaged the number one prop and nacelle. But Lt Frank Carrico brought Z-Square-24 back on what he had left, and this is the way that nacelle looked when the maintenance people arrived. / *Mrs Thomas Isley Collection*

# Bombing up the B-29s

While Major Ingram T. Hermanson was Group Ordnance Officer for the 500th BG, he directed a project to document photographically the major steps in the movement, assembly and loading of the bombs for the B-29s. He loaned his original album for this work, and from it, these photos have been chosen. They show four of the several different bomb types carried by the B-29s.

*Above:* Munitionsmen attach the fin assemblies to the 2,000lb HE bombs that will be loaded aboard Z-44, *The Big Stick*, standing in the background.

*Left:* The 500lb incendiary cluster bombs arrived in steel packing cases and were removed by using the bomb winch on an M6 bomb service truck.

*Top left:* Now resting on the M1 bomb lift truck, the 500lb incendiary cluster has its shipping band removed by an ordnance technician.

*Centre left:* The fuses have been installed and the ordnanceman is threading the arming wires through the two tail fuses of the incendiary cluster.

*Below left:* Trundled under the rear bomb bay, the 500lb cluster is ready to be hoisted into place.

*Below:* Working inside the open bomb bay, ordnancemen winch the 500lb incendiary cluster into place on the centre bomb rack.

*Above:* The 100lb M47 all-purpose chemical bombs were filled with gas gel and used as incendiaries. They were loaded in racks of six, and here ordnance and armament personnel are attaching the shackles and the adapter cluster cables to the initial bomb of each cluster.

*Centre right:* The crane on the M27 bomb service truck delivers 2,000lb high-explosive bombs to the hardstand area. Incendiaries on the ground in the background are available if the mission is changed to a fire raid on short notice.

*Bottom right:* There is a final inspection by ordnancemen of the bombs before they are loaded, and then the 2,000lb bombs will be hoisted into the bomb bays.

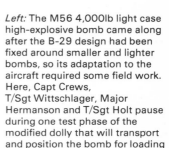

*Left:* The M56 4,000lb light case high-explosive bomb came along after the B-29 design had been fixed around smaller and lighter bombs, so its adaptation to the aircraft required some field work. Here, Capt Crews, T/Sgt Wittschlager, Major Hermanson and T/Sgt Holt pause during one test phase of the modified dolly that will transport and position the bomb for loading into the B-29.

*Below:* Almost ten feet long and almost one yard in diameter, the 4,000lb LCHE bomb is shown before being rolled under the bomb bay on the dolly and tracks.

# Fire in the Islands

*Above:* A 505th Bomb Group B-29, doors open for the drop, skirts the boiling smoke clouds billowing upward over the burning target. Flak is bursting ahead and at ten o'clock. */ 313th BW*

*Right:* The 14 May 1945 raid against Nagoya was the first of the four-wing missions, flown by B-29s from the 58th, 73rd, 313th and 314th Bomb Wings. They put 472 bombers over the target, and here we are in the nose of one of them from the 497th Bomb Group, 73rd Bomb Wing, while the bombardier sights the target, and smoke from the burning city boils up ahead. */ A. F. Migliaccio Collection*

*Left:* Hundreds of incendiary bombs cascade from the bellies of B-29s of the 500th Bomb Group in a daylight raid on Yokohama, 29 May 1945. The lead crew for this raid was commanded by Capt Ferd J. Curtis, flying Z-12, and it was the left gunner, Sgt Howard J. Clos who took this photograph. It was widely reproduced, and was later used as the heading photo for a propaganda leaflet dropped on named Japanese cities to warn them in advance of a fire raid.
*/ Ingram T. Hermanson Collection*

Weather was the worst enemy of daylight, high-altitude precision bombing. It affected the results far more than the best defences the Japanese could mount. And worst of the weather phenomena was the jet stream.

It was — and still is — a shallow, roaring rapids of wind, strongest at the latitudes and altitudes where the B-29s were working, and worst during the winter months above Japan. It howled out of the west on a twisting course, bowling along at speeds that routinely reached above 200mph and occasionally touched 300mph.

It was a new realm; aircraft had not penetrated the jet stream before the raids on Japan. Navigators checked their mathematics and their plots; radar operators recalibrated their sets, twisted the knobs again, changed the scales. The figures showed ground speeds of less than 100mph on headings generally toward the West; when the bombers made their runs on Tokyo from an initial point near Mount Fuji, southwest of the city, the ground speed jumped to 400, 450 and 500mph as the big B-29s were swept along in the raging torrent of the jet stream.

The ballistics data books, compiled so carefully for each of the bomb types carried, were useless. The range of ground speeds just did not extend as high as 500mph or as low as 20 or 30. (Or even zero, as one crew found to its shock. They suddenly were standing stock-still over Japan, hanging there like a balloon in the sky, with the big Wright R-3350 engines roaring and propellers flailing, and the wind blowing them backwards as fast as the airplane was flying forward in the moving air mass.)

Some of the effects of high winds can be cancelled or at least reduced by flying cross-wind. But these winds were too fast to use that strategem; the bomb ballistics and the bomb sight never could have handled the amount of drift.

About the only advantage of a downwind approach was that you got in and out of the target defences very fast. But you left your bombs scattered all over the countryside below. Upwind, you hung there, drifting slowly while every anti-aircraft battery on the ground had time to boresight you and fire a string of bursts.

This problem was certainly a major factor that led to a shift in bombing tactics, away from the concept of the high-altitude precision strike by daylight to the low-altitude sweep by night with incendiaries.

There were other advantages to going in low over the targets. The winds at the lower levels were down to 25 to 35 knots, which could be handled within the normal range of bomb ballistics data and the capabilities of the bomb sights that were used. It would not be necessary to limit the direction of the approach, either; a bombing strike at low level could be mounted from any direction of the compass.

Clouds, the major drawback to visual bombing, were almost ever-present, but they were less numerous and thinner at low altitudes.

The radars, relatively primitive at that stage of their development, were able to 'see' better at low altitudes, and the scope pictures were of better definition.

Flying at lower altitudes was an easier task for the engines, stressing them less and burning less fuel. The fuel saved could be traded for bomb load, and the lessened strain on the engines translated to a simplification of the engine maintenance problem. Improving maintenance meant that a higher number of B-29s would be available for missions at any given time, and that meant in turn that there was a higher number of B-29s over the target with more bombs.

Since precision bombing was not going to be required with the new approach, the attacks could be flown at night. Formation flying, developed to give the maximum defensive firepower massing, would not be necessary at night, nor even desirable, and that meant lower fuel consumption on a mission to the home islands of Japan. Formation flying involved a lot of jockeying of throttles to maintain position, and it burned extra fuel.

If maximum defensive firepower was not a pre-requisite, then the ammunition load for the turrets could be reduced, again trading the weight saving for fuel or bombs or both.

The crews were experienced in night navigation, because they returned home in darkness after many of their long missions to Japan.

And finally, the intelligence assessment was that the Japanese were not believed capable of putting up an effective night-fighter defence, a supposition that was proven in the months to come. Automatic weapons fire was expected to be largely ineffective above 5,000 feet, and the accuracy of the radar-directed heavier flak deterioriated badly below 10,000 feet altitude.

For all of these reasons, the low-altitude fire raids were planned for altitudes between 5,000 and 8,000 feet. The B-29s would be stripped of excess weight, including guns and ammunition. Originally, only the tail gunner had any ammunition on these flights. The bomb load was entirely incendiaries on most of the missions, with an occasional mixed loading of high-explosives and incendiaries to attack specific target complexes.

The bombers were to attack individually, in a bomber stream of the type pioneered by the Royal Air Force in its night-time bombings over Europe. They were to drop on fires set by a small, highly trained and daring pathfinder force, again taking a leaf from the RAF's book.

*Above:* Hang on, because it's gonna get rough! B-29s of the 498th Bomb Group, their vertical tails emblazoned with the large T identifier, fly over turbulent and boiling masses of smoke from the burning Japanese city below. Aircraft at the left carries a black lead crew flash on its fin.
/ *Donald L. Miller Collection*

*Bottom left:* The incendiary clusters fall away and the lightened Superfortresses heave buoyantly into the air. This group, from the 497th BG, are dropping through scattered clouds and a thin undercast of stratus in a fire raid after April 1945.
/ *Mrs Thomas Isley Collection*

The first mission in the experiment was scheduled to leave on 9 March 1945. The time was fixed to get the best weather over the target. The main force, following the pathfinder strikes, was to make radar approaches to the targets, using visual corrections if possible for the actual drop.

The concept, and the decision to carry it through, came from Gen LeMay. It was a daring approach, and a fateful decision. LeMay made it, the B-29s carried it out, and they burned most of Japan's industrial cities to the ground.

'The 881st Squadron started operations on Saipan with only ten of our authorised 20 aircraft, and early losses in combat reduced this number further. I flew only two combat missions in December 1944, and one of them was a weather reconnaissance flight on Christmas Eve.

'Replacement aircraft started arriving in January, and the second one was assigned to my crew and designated Z Sq 12. At the same time, we were designated a lead crew.

'Our bombing accuracy in the early missions left much to be desired. The formation — nine to twelve aircraft — dropped bombs on the lead aircraft signal to insure the planned impact pattern. By designating a lead crew and allowing them special training flights, we improved bombing accuracy.

'Our crew was given scarce B-29 time for four such training flights in January and again in February, and we were assigned to combat missions only as the lead or the deputy lead crew. We continued in that assignment, and flew more training flights on 3, 5 and 7 March. On 8 March a very unusual Wing meeting of all staff personnel, and including all lead crew aircraft commanders, was called. Gen LeMay outlined the concept of the low-level incendiary strike against heavily defended Tokyo. Since this was going to be a maximum effort, my precision-

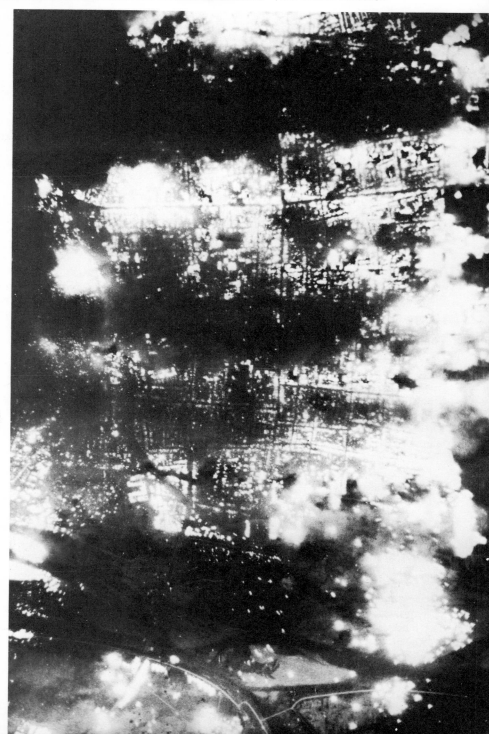

trained lead crew was going to be part of this mass strike.

'My initial impression was of a B-29 traffic jam with the air filled with bombs and machine-gun rounds; it was a frightening thought. But as the details of the strike unfolded, we began to see the safeguards that had been planned to reduce the chance of self-inflicted losses.

'Ammunition was removed from all but the tail guns. Several routes were used to the target area to avoid congestion en route. Indicated airspeeds for cruise and the bomb run itself were assigned, as were staggered altitudes over about a 4,000-foot spread to provide controlled bomb waves over different aiming points.

'The big unknown was what kind of a reception we'd get. I've forgotten what we were told in the intelligence briefing about their defence capabilities, but as we approached our bomb run it looked like all hell was breaking loose ahead of us, and I wasn't sure if that was good or bad.

'As it turned out, it was good for us; Tokyo was burning.' *Ferd J. Curtis*

The B-29s were loaded with about six tons of bombs in each plane. Each lead aircraft carried 180 M47 napalm bombs, and each of the main force aircraft carried 24 of the 500lb M69 incendiary clusters. One by one, they surged down the runways on Guam, Saipan and Tinian, 334 Superforts from the 73rd, 313th and 314th Bomb Wings, headed for Tokyo on the night of 9 March 1945.

'On the long trip to the target, I found it hard to believe that such a serene and tranquil sky could, at any moment, become filled with so much violence and destruction. And in the face of that beauty, the thing that bound us all together in a common bond was that we were scared to death.

'My first fire-bombing mission was also my first night mission. The fire from earlier drops was so bright we could see it from miles away as we approached the target. We were without guns — to save weight for fuel and bombs — and carried only two gunners on the trip as scanners. We went in on the target individually, because it was too dangerous to fly formation at night. I never liked those night raids. It felt too much like you were alone. Just the sight of other planes helped.' *George S. Gray*

It was the first of the great fire raids. The planes went in low, in an area attack on a section of about 12 square miles of Tokyo. They dropped from altitudes between 4,900 and 9,200 feet. The fires were spread by the wind, and blown to other parts of the city. They raced through the wood and bamboo and plaster houses and small factories, leaped roads and fire breaks, blended into an enormous fire storm.

'She was a very tough lady. The low-altitude runs took us close to target fires sometimes. What turbulence! Worse than any Texas thunderstorm I'd ever experienced. The smoke was filled with the litter and the smells of a burning and dying city.

'One one occasion we were tossed upside down in the smoke and survived a 90-degree split-S recovery made on instruments. The 90-degree turn was to miss a mountain ahead. All of us had some injury; I chipped my front teeth on the control column. And the flak suits were going up when we were going down and vice versa, flailing at our faces. From that time on, most of us sat on them.' *Charles B. Hawks*

The target is urban Nagoya, the date is 14 May 1945, and the time is 0955 hours as these clusters of small incendiary bombs drop away from our B-29. The steel bands holding the shells together will separate at lower altitude, and each of these clusters will break into dozens of six-pound bombs of gelled gasoline, and magnesium powder. And that will take care of Nagoya. / *Del Shaffer Collection*

When it was over, it was to stand as the most destructive air attack of the war, over-shadowing even Hiroshima and Nagasaki. One-quarter of all Tokyo's buildings were destroyed; a million people were homeless; almost 84,000 had been killed and 41,000 were injured. Fourteen B-29s were lost.

Ernie Tyler was then a 19-year-old Staff Sergeant and right gunner in a B-29 of the 40th Bomb Squadron, 6th Bomb Group, 313th Bomb Wing on Tinian. He kept a diary and recorded these impressions of his second mission to Tokyo on the night of 9 March 1945, in *Grand Slam*

'Mission No 2
'Night bombing

| | |
|---|---|
| *Primary:* | Tokyo |
| *Results:* | Excellent |
| *Takeoff:* | 1910 |
| *Target:* | 0230 Alt 5,200ft |
| *Landed:* | 1030 |
| *Total time* | 15:20 |

'The night of the 9th and the morning of the 10th we hit Tokyo again. Our second mission — scared the blue blazes out of us. This time we were to carry 32 bombs but we only got 24 loaded before it was time to go. The trip up was very turbulent. We hit the mainland at 0230. All the lights were out. 300 planes going in, in rat-tail fashion and bombing from 5,000 to 6,000 feet. We were at 5,000 feet. We got a little flak and auto fire. Saw fires started by planes ahead of us from about 70 miles away. Over the target the turbulence caused from the heat of the fires was beyond belief. We could smell the smoke and the sky was red from the glow. We dropped our bombs . . . immediately afterward we hit a huge smoke cloud which caused everything loose in the ship to hit the ceiling. Everything was tossed around and we all thought we were going down. Then the pilot said, She's OK, men, take it easy — we'll get out of here in a minute, just as calm as if he was talking to a Sunday School class.

'The whole city seemed to be on fire. The long trip home was okay and then on the final approach all hell broke loose. We started the putt-putt (auxiliary power unit) and it caught fire. The battery blew up. The interphone amp burned up. Both inverters burned. Voltage regulators burned out. The whole electrical system went out next. Number three engine feathered itself and we hit the runway for a beautiful landing, all electrical power gone. Right landing gear collapsed and we eventually came to a stop. No one was hurt, thanks to our pilot, Lt Charles Neal. It sure was good to walk around on the ground again, but I sure hated to see our airplane ruined. There'll never be another one like *Grand Slam*.' *E. L. Tyler, right gunner, 40th BS, 6th BG*

'We were usually met at our hardstand after a combat mission by the crew chief and his crew ready to start on the long task of mending and maintaining the aircraft for the next mission. The morning after the first night incendiary strike on Tokyo we landed, taxied up to the hardstand, and saw bomb loading trailers. The new tactic had proven highly successful, and we were going back for an encore the next night. As it turned out, our aircraft — Z Sq 12 — stayed in commission and we flew all five of the fire raids against Japan during nine days.' *Ferd J. Curtis*

On 11 March, 285 B-29s hit Nagoya. On 13 March 274 Superforts bombed Osaka. On 16 March, they hit Kobe:

'We made an emergency landing on Iwo coming back from one of the fire raids. The fight for the island was still going on, and the Japanese still held the area around one end of the runway. We landed downwind and downhill to avoid them.

'Down at the other end, we were visited by some GIs and Marines, who had fought for that island for days and had gone without sleep or baths or shaves and had worn their uniforms for days. And we were sitting in the B-29 wearing clean T-shirts and cutoff pants for shorts, and eating well.

'So they said to us, hey, you guys been over Japan? And we said, yeah, that's where we were coming from. And one of them said, Jesus, I wouldn't trade jobs with you guys for anything! And he meant it. They were really impressed that we had actually flown over Japan and had been shot at by flak and attacked by fighters.

'Before we took off, we gave them whatever food we had left, including some fresh bread. And when we were getting ready to leave, some Marines wanted to give us hand grenades to chuck at the Japanese when we took off. They were real disappointed that we couldn't use them.' *E. L. Tyler*

On 19 March, the B-29s hit Nagoya again, because the first strike had not been completely effective. And that raid brought an end to the March fire blitz. LeMay's forces had run out of bombs. Four cities had been burned out. B-29 losses were light. Morale was very high, compensating for the long and hard work done by maintenance crews and for the fatigued pilots and airmen.

There was a hiatus in the fire-bombing campaign while the Superfortresses were diverted to support the invasion of Okinawa, and while the bomb dumps were resupplied from off-shore ammunition ships. On 14 May the bombers went out again, this time against Nagoya with the first of the four-wing raids.

The 58th, 73rd, 313th and 314th put 472 B-29s over the northern urban area of Nagoya and burned out major portions of it. A few nights later they were back to burn the southern urban section, with 457 Superforts that dropped for almost three hours over the ill-starred city.

The largest single mission of the B-29's war was sent against Tokyo's urban industrial area on the night of 23 May. A force of 562 aircraft left Saipan, Tinian and Guam for the strike; 510 of them bombed the city. Two days later they went back, with 464 Superforts, dropping incendiaries on the areas they had not hit on previous strikes. It was a costly raid; 26 B-29s fell to the enemy. But Tokyo was finished as a factor in the Japanese war plans.

'Different tactics were evolved as the war progressed, to reduce our losses over specific targets. One of them was the pathfinder mission, pioneered by the Royal Air Force in night bombings of Germany. I don't believe it was widely used against Japan, and our lead crew only flew one such mission. I don't know how we were selected; it was the 500th Bomb Group's turn to furnish the Wing Task Force Commander for the mission, and the Deputy Group Commander, Lt Col Harry S. Brandon, flew with my crew. That may have influenced our selection.

'Some targets weren't very good aiming points for a radar bomb run; their return characteristics were pretty bad or could be confusing. There was one good one in the Tokyo area, a fine radar target, but it had to be approached across the heavy flak defences of that city. It was a command decision to make the pathfinder runs on the target from that approach, and we expected to get heavy flak.

'On the way up we had better winds than forecast, and I decided to hold to the time schedule for the strike, so I killed some time to compensate for the wind. The others didn't

A trio of 504th BG Superfortresses bounce skyward as they drop their loads of fire bombs over a Japanese city. Low haze partially screens the target, and smoke at the left indicates the city is already burning briskly. The dark bursts are flak, and it's close, and — if this picture is any indication — heavy. / 313th BW

wait; they dropped when they got there, and they alerted the defences, who were sitting there waiting for us when we sailed in toward the target. It was my roughest mission. We wound up with flak holes in all four engine cowlings, and more skin damage than on any other mission we'd flown.' *Ferd J. Curtis*

'Pathfinder missions against Tokyo seemed suicidal. Maybe 12 aircraft would draw that mission, with very specific target points they had to hit with incendiaries to mark the area for bombing by the main force.

'We'd fly in, fast and low, always in searchlights with every gun in the city banging at us. Only the rugged speed and manoeuvrability of the B-29 — plus some fancy flying — allowed us to survive.' *Charles B. Hawks*

'We came back from one of those Tokyo nights in *Torchy*. It was 1,500 miles to go, with no electrical controls or instruments for anything in or on the left wing, and the rear spar of that wing was shot through. When we began the letdown, our number one and two propellers were fixed in high pitch at low rpm and at cruise power. We had to shut them down by feathering as soon as we touched down.

'When *Torchy* rolled to a stop, the left wing drooped until it had no dihedral at all.

They counted the machine gun and cannon holes in the plane and quit when they got to 800 holes.' *Donald L. Miller*

'The number two engine on our plane, *Sweet Sue,* always ran hot and the ground crew never could find anything wrong with it. On our last mission to Tokyo, we had a hot number two again, and so we started the usual routine of babying it for the trip back home. When we came off the target, we were supposed to head south, but we saw what looked like a lot of action down there and the pilot decided it might be better to go east for a while. Besides, the smoke from the fires was blowing that way, and it was up at our altitude, and he thought we might be able to get behind it and use it for cover.

'We got hit by flak in the dark, and the airplane was running rough, so we decided to land at Iwo. But Iwo was socked in by weather, and we flew around for a while hoping it would clear. After three hours, the pilot called in for a decision, and the crew decided that we'd rather bail out than ditch anytime.

'So the ground gave us a heading for Mt Suribachi, where we were supposed to bail out. I was back in the aft pressurised compartment by then, because I always left my tail gun position empty until 100 miles before landfall and then left it 100 miles after

Sakai was burned early in the morning of 10 July 1945, and this is what the strike looked like from one of the B-29s in that raid.
*/ Mrs Thomas Isley Collection*

we left the coast. We bailed out of the main hatch, and I counted to five real fast, then a slower five and pulled the rip cord. Prettiest sight I ever saw. I drifted down and landed on a soft field being graded by a Seabee running a bulldozer.

'Everybody else got out all right, and we stayed on Iwo for two days. We heard small arms fire every night; the Japanese weren't really through defending the island.

'Anyway, when we got back, the other crews that had flown in that airplane came around on the quiet and thanked us for losing the plane.

'It was an expensive way to fix a hot engine.' *Mike Janosko*

Yokohama went on 29 May, victim of 454 B-29s. Osaka was hit 1 June by 458 aircraft; Kobe on 5 June by 473. It was Osaka's turn again on 7 June, when 409 B-29s attacked with fire bombs and left the city in ruins. More than 55,000 buildings were destroyed. It was hit once again on 15 June by 444 aircraft, and that strike concluded a month of concentrated and devastating fire raids. The first phase of the planned destruction of Japanese urban areas had been completed. The top six industrial centres — Tokyo, Nagoya, Kobe, Osaka, Yokohama and Kawasaki — had been levelled.

There had been a total of 17 attacks, with 6,960 sorties dispatched, or an average of more than 400 Superforts on each strike. They had dropped 41,592 tons of bombs and had lost 136 of their number to the Japanese defences.

With the major industrial cities off the target lists, the XXI Bomber Command planners looked to the smaller cities. These held many industrial plants and transportation centres, so they were legitimate strategic targets. They also were congested, and typically Japanese cities, so they would burn well.

Beginning on 17 June 1945, these cities were systematically fire-bombed in night attacks, with radar bombing techniques.

The first four to be hit were assigned, one each, to the four combat wings of Superfortresses in action. The 58th struck Omuta; the 73rd flew against Hamamatsu; the 313th attacked Yokkaichi, and the 314th hit Kagoshima. More than 450 B-29s headed out on the strike, and the results were highly successful. The pattern of the attack was to become standard for the rest of the war.

Whenever there was a B-29 force ready to go, and whenever the weather conditions indicated that radar bombing was the technique of choice, they were dispatched against the cities on the target list. Usually four cities were chosen, one for each wing. Once in a while, one target would seem to require the attention of two wings, so that only three targets would be assigned for that raid.

Sixteen of these raids left Saipan, Guam and Tinian, on an average of about twice each week until the end of the war. They met increasingly less opposition; the defence systems around these smaller cities had been neglected by the Japanese in favour of concentration of effort at the major cities.

LeMay took another chance in late July. It seemed like a bold gesture, and it was; but it also was a very shrewd appraisal of the Japanese psyche at the time. LeMay had a leaflet printed in Japanese, warning that some of the 11 cities listed would be hit the following night in a bombing raid, and urging the residents to leave those cities for their own safety. Six B-29s roared over the eleven cities on the night of 27 July and dropped 660,000 leaflets. The following night, the first six cities on the list were hit hard. Fighter opposition, even with the advance warning of 24 hours, was weak. LeMay's psychological gamble had worked, and he used it again on 1 and 4 August. Those leaflets convinced thousands of Japanese civilians that the war was lost, and that their government had been lying to them for months about the strength of the defences of the home islands and the power of their military forces.

The fire raids against the smaller cities were generally as successful as those against the six major cities. These secondary raids hit 57 cities, three of them twice. They burned out an average of forty-three per cent of their areas, with the most destruction being wrought at Toyama, which was 99.5 per cent destroyed.

The momentum built in those last terrible days of the war, as city after city crumbled into ashes. The strength of each attack increased as LeMay's forces grew in number and ability. A force of 300, 400, 500, even 600 B-29s was not unreachable.

On 1 August 627 Superfortresses hit four cities with incendiaries; it was one part of the day's effort — its largest — by XXI Bomber Command. In addition to the fire raid, 120 B-29s went after an oil depot at Kawasaki, and late that afternoon 37 B-29s were sent to mine the Shimonoseki Strait and six other sites. A total of 836 Superforts was dispatched from the island bases; 784 bombed their primary targets.

It was a massive effort, recalling the day-and-night, 1,000-plane raids over Europe a few months earlier. But even these powerful assaults were to be erased from memory by the effects, short- and long-term, of two strikes yet to come.

# One Damned Mission after Another

And it seemed that way. Load up, make the long flight to the target, drop your bombs, fight your way home, debrief, hit the sack. Then get up and do it again.

That was the other guy's mission. Yours was always different, remember? You came back on three engines, or you ditched and got rescued by a submarine, sent your way by a circling Superdumbo. It was your B-29 that a Japanese fighter rammed and took off a chunk of the tail; you got back, but that sure as hell wasn't a routine mission. Remember getting turned over when you hit that cloud of smoke in a fire raid? How about the time you watched in horror as your bombs neatly spaced themselves to miss the wing and tail of another B-29 that had slipped beneath you at that moment?

But underneath all the exceptions, there was the routine, the established Army way, the SOP of a combat strike.

'We completed our crew training at MacDill Field, Tampa, Florida, and it was time to head out to the Pacific and a combat assignment. Our shiny-new B-29 was waiting for us at the staging area in Kearney, Nebraska.

'She was elegant. She had all the brand-new smells of upholstery, fibreglass, miles of rubber-insulated wiring, dozens of little and big motors throughout her frame, new aluminium, hydraulic fluid, and that exclusive smell of high-octane aviation gasoline that no longer exists. It's a shame that these long-gone smells couldn't have been recorded, like a Glenn Miller tune, to be played back later for reminiscing. She even had good-luck messages pencilled on her framework by an anonymous Rosie the Riveter at Marietta.

'The more we checked this new bird out, the more we liked her and the prouder we became of her, especially because the Wright engines didn't even once catch fire when we took off on check flights, unlike some of the ships in which we had trained. How could we lose with such a fine piece of machinery?

'When everything checked out OK, we took off for Mather Field, Sacramento, California, found a place in Air Transport Command's pipeline that cleared us out over the wide Pacific, and headed for Guam via Honolulu and Kwajalein. We saw our first enemy flak when we flew too close to Japanese-held Motji on the approach to Kwajalein. But we really remember

The bombs are loaded on Z-51 of the 500th Bomb Group. She carries 34 mission markers and three Japanese flags on her starboard nose; at 35, her crew goes home.
/ Dr Lyman C. Perkins

Kwajalein because that's where somebody stole our case of Scotch.

'We landed at Guam, unloaded a bomb-bay full of mail and spare parts, and picked up orders assigning us to the 6th Bomb Group, 313th Wing, on Tinian. That station was about 25 minutes' flying time north of Guam, and on the way up we saw our very first enemy fighter. It was a dead-duck Zero, sitting broken in the middle of the knocked-out Japanese airstrip on the island of Rota, bypassed in the campaigns to take the Marianas.

'We landed at Tinian, and taxied in past more B-29s than I had ever seen, a crew-of-the-week from MacDill, red hot and hot to trot. After the "Follow Me" jeep had parked us on a coral hardstand, we loaded a 6 × 6 truck that took us several miles away to a Quonset hut marked, "Headquarters, 39th Squadron, 6th Bomb Group (VH)". Our pilot, who was a major and a veteran of 100 missions over Europe in B-24s, went inside to report that the crew that would win the war had arrived.

'In fifteen minutes he came back out, mad as hell, to report that our crew had been broken up for replacements and that our shiny new B-29 had been taken away and assigned to another bomb group. What kind of a war was this? How could we ever beat the Japanese this way?

'As luck would have it, I was the first one to be reassigned to another crew. The crew of Capt Catts was short a top CFC gunner; he had been severely wounded and two other

crewmen had been killed by a direct flak hit on a mission over Osaka. They had just returned from R&R (Rest and Recuperation) in Hawaii, and I am sure they were delighted to get a new, green top gunner. As it turned out, they were a great team and never showed me anything but help and friendship.' *J. R. Pritchard, Jr, CFC gunner, 39th BS, 6th BG*

'Aircraft availability was the key to crew selection for a strike mission. Almost all of the major strikes through March 1945 called for a maximum effort, that is, every combat-ready airplane was assigned to the mission. That pretty much selected the crews automatically; the crew or alternate crew primarily assigned to each aircraft was selected.

'The final target was chosen — by Wing prior to 25 February 1945, and then by XXI Bomber Command — after the strike was ordered, based on target priorities and weather forecasts.

'The responsibility for crew selection at squadron level for heavily defended targets was eliminated by this procedure, even though it had not been developed for that purpose.

'Every effort was made to keep a crew together for their entire combat tour. The concept of flying a crew only in their own aircraft on any major strike was really beneficial to the abort rate. The big psychological factor was the pride and confidence you had in your own aircraft. If your own was not available, you might be assigned to another if it was going to be a relatively "easy" mission.' *Ferd J. Curtis*

The men walk into the hot Quonset hut, make their way through the crowded benches and sit, facing an elevated stage and a podium. A large sign above the stage tells them, 'Stand up when you talk. Hand up if you can't hear.' At the edge of the stage is another sign, propped against the panels. It reads, 'Do not walk or stand on benches.'

Captain Marmion begins the briefing. Behind him are huge charts with the plan of attack, the course from Saipan to the target, the call signs and radio frequencies.

A blackboard at the left of the stage lists the altitudes for the mission. It assigns the 73rd Wing to route altitudes between 3,000 and 3,500 feet, and attack altitudes between 7,000 and 7,800 feet. The 313th Wing will fly between 4,000 and 4,500 feet to the target, and attack from altitudes between 6,000 and 6,800 feet. The 314th will be the low wing, cruising between 3,000 and 3,300 feet, and attacking from 5,000 to 5,800 feet.

In large letters the blackboard shows the name of the force commander: Col Dougherty. Below his name, the timetable: Stations at 1730K time, start engines 1825K, takeoff 1840K. Radio silence requires a timed operation.

The room is filled. Captain Marmion continues to describe the mission, and the men take notes, quietly. An occasional question, a request to repeat a number comes from a crewman. To many, it's a familiar

*Above:* Boarding ladder in place, this B-29 waits quietly for the action to begin. */ Dr Lyman C. Perkins*

*Top left: Censored,* aircraft 11 of the 39th Bomb Group, 314th Bomb Wing, taxies out of the hardstand area at North Field, Guam. It's late afternoon; the shadows have begun to lengthen and the clouds have built up. */ via Boeing*

*Bottom left:* This well-known picture of a B-29 of the 504th BG over Osaka is shown once again to correct the impression earlier users had that the number three engine was losing oil. That was not unusual for the B-29 engines, but in this case, the dark area behind the number three engine is the shadow of the B-29 fuselage from which this picture is being taken, and the shadow of the upper aircraft's number two engine nacelle can be seen on the upper fuselage of the plane in the picture. Regardless of details, Osaka is burning, and the moated palace on the right has been untouched by bombs. */ 313th BW*

*Above:* Four little friends — P-51 Mustangs from the fighter base on Iwo Jima — fly escort to B-29s of the 498th Bomb Group. The fighters were escorted, in turn, by the big bombers because most of the P-51s were very poorly equipped for long-range navigation. So it's up on the ladder and clean off the T and the Square and the number, and paint the big T of the 498th Bomb Group on the rudder. One B-29 generally shepherded the fighters to and from Iwo on long strikes.
*/ Mrs Thomas Isley Collection*

*Top right:* Shiny, late-model B-29s of the 29th Bomb Group, 314th Bomb Wing, fly a tight combat formation on the approach to the target.
*/ Charles B. Hawks Collection*

*Bottom right:* It's April 1945, and the powers that be have decreed that the old identifiers be removed and gigantic single letters replace them for group identification. So it's up on the ladder and clean off the T and the Square and the number, and paint the big T of the 498th Bomb Group on the rudder.
*/ Mrs Thomas Isley Collection*

run; they've been to that target before, hit it a number of times. But the factories continue to produce engine parts for the Japanese fighters. This time, they think, we'll get 'em.

Other briefers take the stage, describe the weather, the target, the air-sea rescue services, alternate fields. And then the general briefing is over, and the crews file out, breaking into smaller groups headed for specialist briefings: Navigators over here, radar operators there, bombardiers in that building, gunners down by your aircraft.

The machinery of the mission has begun to turn. It will build momentum and maintain it for the next 24 hours or so, until each of the strike aircraft has returned or is accounted for.

'My first mission ever was a night incendiary raid on a fuel storage and refinery area in Nagoaka, across Honshu island northwest of Tokyo on the Sea of Japan. It was a mere 1,800 miles from Tinian, a 3,600-mile round trip.

'We were briefed for an afternoon takeoff which would put us over the target around midnight. The ground crews did ninety-nine per cent of the work preparing each plane for its mission, but our crew went down to the flight line anyway to pre-flight the B-29. The gunners helped the armourers load the .50-calibre ammunition into the turret cans. We did all this in the afternoon before takeoff.

'Our crew had lost its aircraft to the junkpile on Iwo Jima after staggering in there on the proverbial "wing and a prayer" following their sad and terrible experience over Osaka. So we were assigned a combat veteran B-29 named *Irish Lullaby* that had belonged to a crew of the 24th Squadron who had completed their missions and had gone home.

'She was resplendent with the "Pirate" insignia of the 6th Bomb Group on the nose, yellow Pirate, blue triangle, white, red-edged "wing" painted back toward the leading edge. *Irish Lullaby* was painted in black script, shaded in green. And of course, she had the red cowl panels and rudder top common to all aircraft of the 6th Bomb Group.

'With all its twelve turreted .50-calibre machine guns loaded and pointed up or down for safety, its ten tons of thermite incendiary bombs that could burn through two inches of steel plate, and some 12,000 gallons of gasoline on board, she was a formidable war machine. But parked just a few hundred yards across the field was another B-29 named *Enola Gay*, and within a few more days, our tough *Irish Lullaby* would look like a pussycat by comparison.' *J. R. Pritchard, Jr*

The B-29 stands fuelled, bombed and loaded with ammunition, on the coral floor of the hardstand. Its guns are stowed off the horizontal, a sure sign they are loaded and

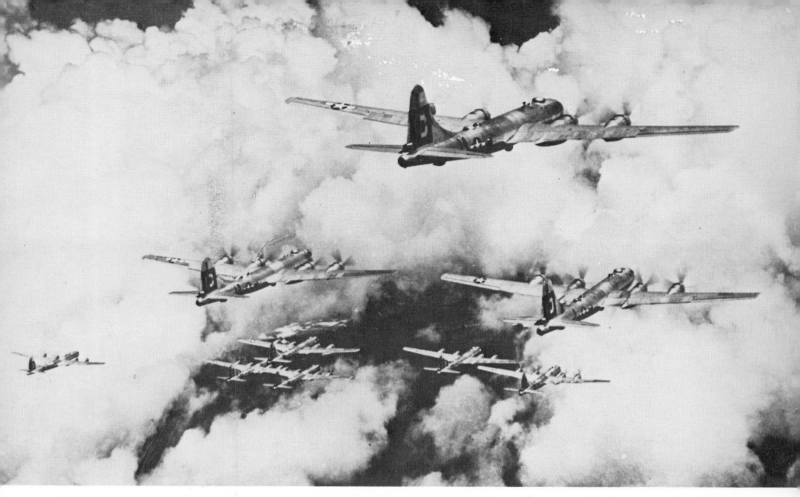

hot. The crew chief, some mechanics and armourers, a radio technician stand and wait, their tasks done for the moment.

'I used to ride around to the hardstands just before mission time, just to hang around and talk a bit with the crews, maybe ease their tensions. One night, coming toward Z Sq 42, Capt Moreland's plane, I heard a lot of fuss and saw a couple of guys sliding down the props. Now we had a notice on the bulletin boards that they were not to slide down the props; it was hard enough keeping those things working without having guys knocking them out of line or whatever by using them as a quick way down from the wing.

'Anyway, somebody spotted me and there was the usual type of covering talk, the kind that anybody who's ever been in the service knows is just trying to divert attention. So I said, okay, men, what's the problem? Well, there was some fidgeting and then one sergeant said, "Sir, we have a mouse on board Captain Moreland's plane and we check before every mission to make sure he's there and ready to go, too."

'They took me into the bomb shelter, where they kept a running score of missions for the crew and probably some other stuff, and there was a board with the crew's names and at the bottom was the twelfth crew

113

member, Mister Mouse, credited with five missions.

'That mouse had been along in the B-29 for five rides over Japan and — the last I knew — he had completed 14 missions and was expected to stay on the crew for the rest of its tour.' *James J. Garrity, adjutant, 883rd BS, 500th BG*

The truck brakes to a stop by the hardstand, and the crew jump off. They unload their personal gear, chutes and manuals, flak suits and dinghies and life vests. The pilot and flight engineer start a walkaround inspection; the rest of the crew tosses equipment aboard the B-29, stows the food, jokes with the ground crew. The pilot gives the order to board, and the crew enters.

Soon, the auxiliary power unit starts, its rhythmic stutter the reason for its nickname of putt-putt. The tail gunner, whose job was to start the putt-putt, moves to his station. 'Interphone check', says the pilot, and the crew calls back, co-pilot, bombardier, navigator, flight engineer, top gunner, left gunner, right gunner, radar operator, and tail gunner. In similar rotation, the crew makes a check of the control surfaces, reporting on their condition, and a station check of equipment ready to go.

Outside the airplane, the armourers have pulled the safety wires on the bombs in the bomb bays and are standing clear of the ship. The pilot acknowledges their task.

'We bombed our own hardstand once, and that was a thrill. I was CFC gunner in the crew of *Dragon Lady* on a night mission to Nagoya, with the Group Commander aboard. We were loaded with 500lb demolition bombs, and we got in the airplane as usual. The procedure was that after everybody got in, and when we were ready to start the engines, the right gunner turned out the light in the bomb bay.

'What he didn't know, and what the ground crew had neglected to tell us, was that they had just completed a modification changing the position of two switches. One was the bomb bay dome light; the other was the emergency bomb salvo switch. You can guess the rest.

'The right gunner felt around where he thought the dome light switch was, and found it safetied. So he got his pliers, cut the safety wire, and flipped the switch. And the sickening rumble of those bombs dropping out on to the hardstand I will remember forever. From my perch I could look through a plexiglass window into the bomb bay and I could watch those bombs go. We left the plane hurriedly.

'The Colonel was cool; he asked for an explanation and got it, then called for the

armourers to reload and we went off on the mission.' *Robert B. Hill, CFC gunner, 871st BS, 497th BG*

Inside, the flight engineer gets his orders to start the engines, and he energises the starter switch on number three engine. The blades swing through their huge arcs to the whine of the starter motor. Six, seven blades go through the vertical and 'Eight!' yells the fireguard watching number three. The engineer flips the ignition switch. The Wright R-3350 wheezes, coughs, chugs a few times, spews clouds of exhaust, and the prop changes from individual blades to a blur. The engine roars its power. It is time to roll.

All four engines are noisily idling; the throttles are advanced, the big bomber begins to bounce, to lighten on her gear; then she is free of friction's grasp and starts to roll away from the revetment.

The gunners call in that the landing gear and tyres look okay. The flaps whine down all the way, then retract to 25 degrees for takeoff, monitored by the side gunners.

The B-29 reaches the end of the runway. The pilot calls for one more crew check and they respond, in the same order again, ending with, 'Tail gunner, sir'. The engines go to full power, howling their strength into the afternoon quiet.

Ponderously, the Superfortress starts its takeoff roll. It accelerates smoothly, wheels rumbling over the hard-packed runway surface. Pilot, co-pilot and engineer work easily, their persuasive movements easing on power, feeling for control reactions,

'Hey, Lieutenant, I got this great idea for a publicity shot! We'll get a crew down by the airplane — I think they're B-29s or something like that — and we'll have them loading bombs and bullets and they'll be painting things like "Screw you, Tojo" on the bombs and . . .' That's what seems to have happened to this unwitting B-29 from the 500th Bomb Group, as ground crews swarm over her with 'busy' work for the camera. Painting insults on bombs, yes. Sitting on the prop, sure. But did any of the armourers out there ever, ever load the top fifties that way ? / *XXI Bomber Command via Boeing-Wichita*

watching the runway ahead, sensing the great surging power of the engines. Their practised actions conceal the tension below the surface, the knowledge that every second of this takeoff run is critical, that if anything happens they have a split second to react and to make the correct judgment and take the correct action. Miss the fleeting opportunity, and they are all dead.

The wing seizes the air, deflects it downward and begins to lift the weight off the landing gear. The shock absorbers stretch, showing more of their chrome-plated struts. Back pressure on the controls, now. The nose wheel lifts off the runway; the nose rises. And then the main wheels also rise, slowly. The landing gear starts to ease into the wheel wells.

Watching, you see the great bird hurtle down the runway, hell-bent on a suicidal jump off the cliff at the end. She begins to rotate before the edge, she eases into the air at the very end of the runway, and almost immediately drops from view as the pilot lets her down to the level of the waves pounding against the base of the cliff. She accelerates slowly in this heat and with that load, and he uses gravity to help him gain a few extra feet per second of flight speed.

You watch, while a second and a third B-29 move down the same runway, make the same jump off the edge, disappear below the lip. And then you see the first one, coming into your line of sight miles offshore, climbing slowly toward Japan.

The island shakes to the sound and the echoes of the engines, full-throated howling

in quartettes, three airplanes on the runway at once, one holding, one rolling, one lifting, twelve engines screaming out their full power.

'The early B-29s, operating from Saipan, had cooling problems. Saipan was hot, which didn't help. We just couldn't make an engine run-up and an ignition check at any reasonable power on the ground, standing still. So we did those tasks during takeoff. There was a marker along the runway at a critical distance; if you reached it and everything was running smoothly, you continued. If things were troubled, you cut the engines at that point and refused takeoff.' *Haywood S. Hansell, Jr*

'We had a two-mile runway at Guam, downhill the first half and uphill the second, with a 500-foot drop off a cliff at the end. I learned to get her out of the starting gate fast. If you lost anything during the second mile of the run, you'd had it. The way we were loaded, it did no good at all to try to raise the nosewheel off the runway at anything less than 210mph.

'We aborted takeoffs twice, and the first time was a beauty. We lost an engine just at the halfway point. We made all the drag we could: dropped the flaps, opened the bomb bay doors — and a couple of bombs shook loose, just to add to the fun — and we burned out our brakes. We drove off the runway and over the rough coral shoulder separating the strip from the jungle. We bent the props and blew a tyre. Then, we had just

The nose of a B-29 frames a trio of sister ships from the 505th Bomb Group. Two have been marked with the Circle W of that group; the third is probably a replacement aircraft, fresh from a delivery flight and not yet marked. / *313th BW*

enough speed to get back on the runway, so we taxied down and across traffic to get on to the nearest taxiway. It was all in a midnight blackout, and with other aircraft taking off at thirty-second intervals from the same runway, we didn't have much time to clear the strip.

'Within minutes I reported, by request, to General LeMay who was in the tower during this takeoff. Actually, he did all the talking, and I agreed with everything he said!' *Charles B. Hawks*

'We did a night takeoff I'll remember. In our ship, the bombardier — that was me — called off the airspeed for the pilot and co-pilot. They liked it that way.

'Anyway, we were rolling and I had just called off our decision speed where we had to keep flying or abort, and a waist gunner called that there was fire in number four engine. The flight engineer called that number four was losing oil pressure. Our load was a gasoline tank in one bomb bay and bombs in the other, and we sure wanted to fly rather than ditch off the end of the runway.

'We went off the end, over the cliff and headed for the water to pick up speed. The pilot feathered the engine and asked me to jettison the load. I figured we were too low and told him so, and he came back and *ordered* me to jettison the load. So I dumped both bays.

'The airplane was so close to the water that the gas tank couldn't drop clear. It hit the rear bulkhead of the bomb bay and bent the doors. I swear I could have stuck my foot out and dragged it in the water. And after that,

we had to fly until the rest of the strike force was launched before we could go back in there and land.

'The worst part was when there would be somebody burning on the water underneath you as you took off.' *Del Shaffer, bombardier, 874th BS, 498th BG*

'The photo lab reported that there were salt deposits on the films they got from our camera. The camera installation was just aft of the exit door, and we used it to take pictures of the target after we dropped. It was a convenient hatch, and the first thought was that the guys in the back were using it as a urinal.

'That wasn't it at all. The real problem was that we got pretty close to the water right after takeoff, trying to pick up some extra speed. And what we were doing was kicking up spray off the ocean with our props. It was seeping into the camera hatch and depositing on the film, the camera and the whole installation.' *Robert B. Hill*

'T Square 5, *Jolting' Josie*, was Major Catton's plane, but she was being flown by another crew when she crashed on takeoff. I had been at the living quarters and got a call to the flight line to service some of the aircraft. I got a lift from a GI driving a weapons carrier, and as we came around the northeast end of the runway, he stopped to watch a couple of the takeoffs, and he stopped right at the end of the runway.

'There was a wind blowing, maybe 20 or 25 miles per hour, and the B-29s were taking off as usual. *Joltin' Josie* had just reached the

end of the runway by the cliff where they usually started to fly, and the wind just stopped. Dead. Flat calm. And T Square 5 just kept on going down to the water and hit. Nobody got out.' *H. W. Douglas*

And then the noise fades. The last of the Superforts has disappeared over the lip of the cliff. You watch, see it rise once again, and climb to join the rest of the formation, now only distant specks on the horizon.

The island is suddenly quiet. It will stay that way for more than twelve hours, while the planes go to Japan and come back. You walk back, in twos and threes, already starting to sweat out your ship.

'To keep the statistical people happy, we had to increase our bomb tonnage dropped. This meant lighter fuel loads, and the only way we could do this was to stay at low altitude for the flight to the target. We did it on the deck, skimming the sea at maximum cruise power, dodging small tea-growing islands in the moonlight.

'We flew through or below the usual two weather fronts on our trip north, and over and through the same fronts on our return. Those trips almost always included a sunrise and a sunset. The variations in light and colour in the Pacific were fantastically beautiful. They softened our own strain and anxieties over the war'. *Charles B. Hawks*

'Basically, we navigated by dead reckoning and by shooting the stars at night. The astrodome was in the tunnel between the two pressurised compartments and I had to crawl

*Above: Jumbo II*, aircraft A-50 of the 497th Bomb Group, carries 53 tiny bomb mission markers plus three that can't be identified in this photo. She also has 13 Japanese flags stencilled on her nose above the numerals 50. A tough airplane, and it seems as if she had a fighting crew as well. / *James J. Garrity Collection*

*Top left: Ponderous Peg*, sure of her identity, carries both the large A identifiers of post-April 1945, and the earlier A-Square-44, which can be seen under the large A on the tail. / *Mike Janosko Collection*

*Centre left:* Neatly lined up in Isley Field revetments, these 500th Bomb Group Superfortresses sun themselves in the mid-day brightness of the tropics. / *Mrs Thomas Isley Collection*

*Bottom left:* It did indeed rain on Saipan, and these B-29s of the 497th Bomb Group are reflected in the shallow puddles under the leaden skies. / *James J. Garrity Collection*

Aircraft 62 of the 444th Bomb Group coasts in for a landing on West Field, Tinian, as another B-29, engines idling and flaps partially down for takeoff, waits to take over one of the two 8,500 foot parallel runways. / *Ron E. Witt Collection*

into the tunnel with my sextant, climb up in the astrodome and shoot the stars.

'Later, we got some Loran stations on Iwo, and in the Marcus and Philippine Islands, so that we could get a good set of Loran lines for navigation between Saipan and Japan.

'Then toward the end of the war, the crew complement began to change. We got commissioned, rated navigators as radar operators, replacing the sergeants we'd had earlier. The sergeants were okay, but they hadn't been trained well. About all they could do was to turn the set on and off, and trouble-shoot it a little. That was important, but it didn't help navigating that much.

'The APQ-13 got to be reliable after some initial problems. It had a full 360-degree presentation, so it was good for navigation and only secondarily a bombing radar. The APQ-7, on the other hand, was designed to scan a 45-degree segment directly in front of the airplane, so it wasn't too great for navigation. But it was some bombing radar. We bombed from 25,000 feet in training using that system, and we often dropped within 100 feet or so of the target from that altitude.' *Vern Piotter*

'Before we got to the islands, we put on our flak suits. They were some protection, but they were heavy and cumbersome. This was long before nylon armour, and the suits were made with small metal plates sewed individually into pockets. We were supposed to wear them, but most of us sat on them to protect the family jewels.

'The B-29 had some internal armour plating to protect various crew stations. It was weight that we thought we could use to better purpose, and so our crew voted to remove all of it except for one piece. That

was the piece that was forward of the tail gunner. We wanted to feel that we wouldn't shoot off our own tail, or kill the gunner by accident, or by a round that cooked off in a gun.' *Robert B. Hill*

'The APQ-13 was called a bomb-nav radar, but most everybody used it primarily as a navigation aid. It was, by today's standards, very primitive and it worked part of the time most of the time. We used it a lot to define landfall, because it did a good job of defining a coastline and separating land from water, so you knew when you were coming over the coast. We didn't bomb with radar that much unless we really couldn't see the target.

'The way we bombed was standard procedure. When we got to the IP, the bombardier directed the turn on to the target heading, based on his maps and the pre-flight briefings. The pilot actually made the turn, and then levelled the plane to align it on course for the target.

'If we were bombing by radar, which the navigator operated for the bomb run, he would give me corrections during the run, based on what he saw on the scope.

'Then the bombardier took over for the bomb run, synchronised the bomb sight, and held the airplane heading while the pilots controlled and held airspeed and altitude. We had to have all three steady and constant during the run. It made for better bombing, but it also simplified the computations for enemy anti-aircraft.' *Del Shaffer*

'Our bombing got better as the war went on. You have to remember that we were really doing on-the-job training, because back in the States we had been hampered by not having enough B-29s to train in and even fly.

*Right:* Three P-51 Mustangs from Iwo Jima stick close to a B-29 during a flight over cloud cover. The escort fighters are carrying long-range auxiliary fuel tanks, and they are outbound to Japan.
*/ Donald L. Miller Collection*

*Below:* Dead centre in the picture, a Nakajima J1N 'Gekko' ('Irving' in Pacific name codes) is photographed by the strike camera on one of the 500th BG B-29s. Target is unidentified, but it is a heavily settled urban area with a major railroad line running through the centre and feeding a large complex of factory buildings or warehouses at the lower right of the picture.
*/ Elmer Huhta Collection*

So it was natural that we started out with some pretty poor bombing accuracies.

'Our best effort came on a daylight mission to Osaka, with Hitachi as a secondary target. The wing put up 12 squadrons. We took off from the parallel runways at North Field (Saipan) with a launch every 25 seconds. Normally, each ship flew toward the rendezvous area alone, or maybe in a very loose formation with one or two others. We usually set a rendezvous point about 150 miles off Japan. The pilot of the lead ship would lower the nose gear to identify himself as lead, and the rest of us would form on him. He'd circle for 20 minutes or so until the rest of the squadron joined in and established the formation. This was at maybe 1,500 feet to 3,000 feet altitude.

'Then we'd start the climb to bombing altitude as a formation. I've forgotten if that was our exact procedure on this particular mission, but it was typical. Our primary target was cloud-covered, so the Hitachi Engineering Works became the target. The sky was clear as we flew our bomb run at 19,000 feet. We had a good run, and all the planes dropped on the signals from their lead bombardiers, and all dropped within 20 minutes as successive formations came over the target.

'The post-strike photos showed that we had gotten 98.5 per cent of our bombs within the predicted CEP (Circular Error Probable), and I believe it was the most accurate of all bombing raids in all theatres during the war.'
*Bernard J. Mulloy, aircraft commander, 869th BS, 497th BG*

'There's total darkness everyplace, you can't see anything — anything — around you, and all of a sudden, right underneath you or right

*Above:* A combat formation of Superfortresses from the 29th Bomb Group, headed for Japan and another combat mission.
/ *Charles B. Hawks Collection*

*Left:* Three B-29s from the 444th Bomb Group fly past Mount Fujiyama, Japan's most prominent landmark and IP (initial point) for many a bomb run on Tokyo and its environs.
/ *Ron E. Witt Collection*

*Above:* B-29s of the 444th Bomb Group fly over their home base of West Field, Tinian. / *Ron E. Witt Collection*

*Top right:* Z-41, of the 500th Bomb Group, at bombs away. Aircraft at upper right still carries the old identifier of Z-Square-number, and so this picture must have been taken early in April 1945, the month the markings change took effect. / *Don C. Hetrick Collection*

*Bottom right:* Bombs dropping from this 6th BG Superfortress form a figure-eight in midair. / *313th BW*

over you, there goes a B-29. And the searchlights are continually, frantically searching for you. You see an airplane in front and the lights have caught him and they follow him for miles. Once they catch him, they'll keep the light on him all the way. Sometimes the beam would flash past your window and the light would be so bright that you just couldn't see anything for a while after that. If you were ever caught, and followed a while, they'd get you, almost certainly.' *Del Shaffer*

Through the searchlights on the bomb run, holding a steady course while flak blazed underneath, or fighters bored in from ahead, then the relief of 'Bombs away!' and almost immediately, 'Let's get the hell out of here!', and the B-29 turning, diving maybe, working its way through the smoke or the lights and the flak. Head for the coast, navigator. The run over enemy territory, sometimes free, sometimes chased by determined fighter pilots pushing their light aircraft to the limit. Cross the coast, take up a heading for Saipan. The fighters stay for a while, throwing a last defiant burst, and then break away. You're safe, so far, and now all you have to worry about is getting the airplane back in one piece.

'We used to take one can of beer per crewman — we were rationed to three cans per week on Saipan — along on a mission. We wrapped them in rags and paper to keep them from freezing, and stowed them in the unpressurised tail compartment between the aft pressurised compartment and the tail gunner's position. After we were clear of the target area and the defences, the tail gunner

would bring the cold beer forward, and we'd open it and wash down our cold Spam sandwiches with a very cold beer.' *Robert B. Hill*

'There was always an informal competition to get home first, and there was a practical reason, too. It was a lot less congested in the traffic pattern if you got there first and early. We seldom flew in formation after leaving the target, and it was every man for himself after leaving the Japanese mainland.

'We had problems with the jet stream going up and over the target, and one day it hit me that maybe we could use the jet stream to get back home faster. So I worked the natigational problem, and learned to take advantage of the pattern of the jet stream going home. We'd head out from the target as if we were going to cross the Pacific, and we'd drift with the changing direction of the jet stream. The object was to fly a constant heading from "coast out" to home base.

'Once I gave the pilot a heading on leaving the Japanese coast, which he held constant all the way home. We arrived over Isley and split the field on course. Boy, was I proud of that navigational job! We were actually pioneering the practical use of "pressure pattern" navigation which in later years became a SAC training requirement.

'We were especially in keen competition with the crew commanded by Capt Thomas P. Hanley. They were a replacement crew and flew a brand-new, late-model, Renton-built ship. It gave us a special satisfaction to arrive home in our old, war-weary *Coral Queen* (A Sq 17) ahead of Hanley's new model.' *Vern Piotter*

'It was a long trip back, because our mission times varied from nine to as much as 25 hours in the air. I'm almost certain that some B-29s just fell into the sea with everybody aboard asleep.

'Just short of Guam once, we tried to rouse one; we watched him peel off course in a descending turn and dive straight into the sea. Even bennies (benzedrine) and coffee had their limits.

'The total mission time — from briefing through de-briefing — must have averaged about 24 hours during the time I was flying.

'My first experience sleeping was also the last time I ever shut my eyes in a B-29. I had dozed off, and when I woke, I found the entire crew asleep and the ship ghosting along on autopilot. So I took to mixing a little pure oxygen with the "Voice of America" and Tokyo Rose, and managed to stay awake on the rest of the missions.

'A six- to eight-hour return flight over the peace and quiet of the Pacific gave us time to settle our nerves, and even the big lady seemed pleased to have her load lightened. Her props turned over slow and easy, flying a gradual descent from maybe 20,000 feet to touchdown over 1,500 miles of water.'
*Charles B. Hawks*

'As bad as the weather was, it didn't produce icing conditions very often. In fact, icing was so rare that we took the de-icing boots off the airplanes for combat. We figured we could use the drag saving, because every little bit helped.

'So naturally we did pick up ice on one mission, and it was bad. We knew we

couldn't make it back to Saipan, so we headed for Iwo and landed there. Believe me, if Iwo hadn't been there, the wing would have been wiped out. There must have been 100 B-29s on the ground at Iwo that day.'
*Bernard J. Mulloy*

'We must have set some kind of a record for most forced landings per hour of flying time in the B-29. On our very first mission over Japan, we ran out of fuel and were lucky to make a safe landing on another strip just five miles short of home. It would have saved a lot of sweat if Iwo Jima had been available for that one.

'Once we were coming back from Japan on two and one-half engines, and we had to go into Iwo before they were really ready to handle us. The battle for the island was still going on, and the Marines wanted to keep the small Japanese fighter strip clear, after they'd gone to so much trouble to take it. They were going to push our B-29 into the sea to clear the strip, but my crew would have none of that. They argued down the Marines, took five days to repair the ship, and flew one rescued airplane and crew back to Guam.

'One night, during a violent tropical storm, we had to choose between ditching or trying to get into Iwo. We elected for the landing, on a small, muddy strip with an unperfected GCA system. We made it, but we never saw the ground until the next day after spending the night stuck in the mud.

'Twice we ran out of fuel on final after a long mission, and landed dead stick on auxiliary strips a stone's throw from home base on Guam. In the approach attitude, small amounts of gas were trapped in the wing cells and were unusable, even though they read as fuel on the gauges. So you'd come in, thinking you had just enough to make it, and trim her for final approach. Suddenly, you have a very quiet airplane as the engines quit.' *Charles B. Hawks*

If you had fuel, and if you had no trouble with the airplane as a result of combat, and if it was a nice day and you felt like it, you could have some fun on the way back with the B-29, strictly unofficially, of course. The Air Force and Navy pilots in the area maintained the usual inter-service rivalry. Navy fighters would bounce the B-29s on test flights; Air Force pilots would pit their Mustangs against the Grumman Hellcats the Navy flew. And the B-29s waited for a chance to strike back with a gesture of their own.

'One of our B-29 pilots was returning from a mission with a light airplane, feeling pretty good, and he spotted a Navy carrier miles ahead. He feathered one engine, and set up the B-29 on a long glide toward the carrier. He entered the pattern on the downwind leg, turned on to base, lowered the flaps and landing gear and set up a final approach just as if he were going to land on the damned carrier.

'You should have seen the waving from the signal officer. They had deck crews out there waving their arms, their jackets, their hats, anything. And the old B-29 kept coming down the groove. At the last minute, the pilot cleaned up the airplane, poured on the coal, and roared down the length of the carrier, turning away as he did so.

'In all the fuss, nobody bothered to get his tail number or identification, which was just as well. The next day the Navy issued a notice that unidentified aircraft in the landing pattern would be fired upon, and that ended the buzzing of carriers. We figured the Navy was not being a very good sport about it all.'
*H. W. Douglas*

'Once we were committed on final approach, and we did not have enough fuel to make a go-around. That's when the landing gear chose not to extend and lock. There are two-man hand cranks for this particular emergency, and they are fine when you have plenty of time, because they take about 400 turns to extend the gear and lock it. The manual says it takes twelve minutes to do that.

'The navigator checked the manual and told me that the gear did have to be fully extended to support the weight of the B-29. My co-pilot told the tower that we were probably going to crash.

'We touched down while the gunners were still turning the cranks, and rolled to a stop. No crash. I firmly believe that the tough gunners I had in the crew just held that gear down with the hand cranks and muscle-power.' *Charles B. Hawks*

Now, climb out of the seat, stretching the legs that were riding the rudder pedals until a couple of minutes ago. Down through the hatch by the nose wheel, away from the B-29 after signing the form and turning the ship over to the crew chief.

Sorry, Sergeant, we got some holes in her. That's okay, sir, we'll fix 'em.

Climb in the truck, head for the debriefing, tell the intelligence officer about the new fighter squadron we saw on the way in. Diagonal yellow strip around the fuselage back of the cockpit. Aggressive; they jumped is in pairs, and they came in much too close. We got hit, but our gunners got three, they think, and a couple of probables.

I'm tired; Christ, am I tired!

Back to quarters, stumble into the hut, fall on the bed, kick the boots off . . . sleep . . .

# Special Missions, Special Planes

Just in case the atomic bombs didn't work, there were a few alternate ideas that were evaluated and tested. One was to increase the size of the bombs carried by the B-29s by slinging them on underwing external racks, thus avoiding the limiting dimensions of the bomb bay structure. A Wichita-built B-29-75-BW, serial number 44-70060, was converted to a test bed for these wing-rack experiments. Each of the underwing racks could carry one 22,000lb British 'Grand Slam' bomb, or one 12,000lb British 'Tall Boy' bomb, or a pair of M56 4,000lb light case demolition bombs. These latter bombs were carried inside the B-29s in combat; but it was a tight, tricky installation and required special loading equipment. The biggest bombs were to be turned against Yokohama. That city is sited on a coastal shelf with a well-defined fault line behind it. In theory, 'Grand Slam' bombs — they were also nicknamed 'earthquake' bombs — could be dropped so as to trigger the failure of the shelf along the fault line and dump Yokohama into the ocean. In this picture, the test B-29 is loaded with a pair of sand-filled dummy 'Grand Slam' bombs, checking the flying qualities of the aircraft on a flight out of Wichita on 29 June 1945./ Boeing

As the war progressed, the Superfortresses were assigned to changing missions. They had started with the expectation of doing the traditional job of precision daylight bombing from high altitudes. Weather, primarily, forced a change from that tactic, and the B-29s went on to score their greatest successes in area night raids, dropping fire bombs from low or medium altitude. They shifted then to a mix of high-altitude precision strikes when weather permitted, and low-level fire raids when the weather did not permit. Since the latter case was the predominant one for Japan, more fire raids were flown than precision strikes.

The Navy never gave up its fight to get the B-29s assigned to the mining of Japanese home waters. They, and the Army Air Forces, knew it was a job that had to be done, that it would pay off strategically, and that only the B-29s had the range and load capabilities to do it properly.

Finally and grudgingly, the USAAF gave in. LeMay designated the 313th Bombardment Wing (VH), based at North Field, Tinian, to do the job. The decision was made late in January 1945, and the wing began training for the special assignment the following month. They flew four to eight practice flights per crew, with five radar approaches to a target on each flight.

The basic tactics were to be night attacks by individual aircraft, dropping on radar scope presentations. To get maximum load and best performance, the crews assigned to those missions lightened their aircraft by removing all the .50-calibre ammunition and by leaving two crewmen home. Further stripping of the Superforts would have hampered their speedy transition to other missions flown alternately with the night mining efforts.

The problem had simplified itself by early 1945. Japanese shipping lanes had been lost, one after another, to Allied forces that controlled the area. Only a few remained, and the most important of these was a single eastern approach to the Inland Sea, a nearly landlocked body of water that lies south of Honshu Island. There are two southern approaches to the sea, but they were so open to enemy attack that the Japanese had stopped using them by 1945. Most of Japan's shipping cleared the Shimonoseki Strait at the eastern end of the Inland Sea.

It was a narrow approach, ideal for mining, and on 27 March 1945, 92 B-29s from the 313th Wing dropped a mix of 1,000 and 2,000lb acoustic and magnetic mines in the strait. Three nights later, 85 aircraft finished the job, closing the strait and all approaches to it. The Japanese, caught by the suprise attack, could only recover with hasty and often suicidal minesweeping operations.

The demand for B-29 support of the Okinawa invasion halted mining activities for a while as all available aircraft turned to tactical support of the campaign, but the results were still coming in after only two strikes against the strait. No large warships were able to get out of the strait after 27 March. Some destroyers tried it during the Okinawa battle; they were desperately needed by the Japanese forces defending the island. But at least four of them were sunk by mines. And by 27 April, 18 Japanese ships lay on the bottom, or had been permanently disabled in the Shimonoseki Strait.

LeMay knew better than to argue with success, and ordered the 313th to keep one group assigned to the mining task whenever it wasn't called to the top-priority mission of hammering the home islands of Japan. The 505th Bombardment Group (VH) was the chosen unit, and they started with a flurry of 14 missions between 7 June and 3 July 1945. They put up 404 B-29 sorties, dropped 3,542 mines in ten major shipping lanes in the Inland Sea and the Sea of Japan.

The mining mission produced some of the longest flights of the war and one in particular, to the Korean port of Rashin, set a record. On 11 July 1945, one of the 6th Bomb Group's B-29s flew from its base on Tinian to Rashin, 2,362 miles away, dropped its mines, and returned non-stop logging a total of 4,724 miles on the journey. It was in the air for 19 hours and 40 minutes.

Most of the aircraft flying this route, or going to the other Korean ports they mined, did stop at Iwo Jima for fuel either on the way out or the way back. Bombardiers started their runs at the initial point 60 miles south of Vladivostok, Siberia, after spending three hours flying across Japan. After the drop, they turned and crossed Japan again on the way home.

It was a superb effort, and it effectively bottled up what was left of the Japanese merchant fleet, the Empire's lifeline. The last missions of the 313th were leaflet drops, propaganda messages urging the Japanese to surrender as the only alternative to starvation. It was a very real possibility, because the mining, coupled with the destruction of stored rice in the devastating fire raids, had reduced the Japanese diets to a near-starvation level.

In the short time that the B-29s had been mining Japanese waters, their efforts accounted for more than ten per cent of all the merchant shipping lost to Japan. They dropped more than 12,000 mines and, as a contemporary note, many of those mines remained unswept for years after the war. As recently as 1975, the Japanese began construction of new minesweepers which, when completed, were to be assigned to

locating and destroying the mines remaining from those raids of the 313th Wing in 1945.

### Supporting an Invasion

Okinawa is an island in the Ryukyu group, about 300 miles from the nearest Japanese home island, Kyushu. In the island-hopping strategy of the Pacific theatre, the importance of Okinawa loomed large. It was intended to be a base for 20 additional B-29 groups, which would be used to pound Japan in preparation for the planned invasion by ground forces.

The Japanese defended Okinawa vigorously; they knew its value and the effect its loss would have on the outcome of the war. In that defence, they unleashed a relatively new weapon: the kamikaze aircraft. First used against naval forces in the Battle of Leyte Gulf, the suicide sortie became almost co-equal with conventional air attacks by the Japanese.

The invasion campaign got off to a conventional start, with a pair of supporting strikes by the B-29s against Japanese airfields on Kyushu island. But a few days after the invasion, the Japanese counter-attacked by air, mixing kamikaze and conventional strikes to send two destroyers, two ammunition ships, a minesweeper and a landing ship to the bottom. About 700 combat sorties were made by the Japanese from Kyushu, about half kamikaze, half conventional.

The Superfortresses went back to the home airfields on Kyushu and hit them, or secondary targets, in two strikes during April

1945. The Japanese struck back even harder, and began a series of ten major assaults that included almost 2,000 kamikaze sorties. During this time, they sank 25 ships and damaged scores of others.

The seriousness of the situation called for a major shift in B-29 bombing activities. Beginning in mid-April, the Superfortresses struck against the Japanese airfields on Kyushu, or against secondary targets nearby, with the aim of denying use of the airfields to the Japanese fighter and kamikaze units, and keeping at home those that did get off the ground.

About three-quarters of the B-29 combat sorties during the period between 17 April and 11 May were flown to support the Okinawa campaign by diverting the attacking Japanese aircraft. The big bombers flew more than 2,100 sorties against airfields, hitting some of them several times. The Japanese defenders kept their fields in action a large part of the time by rapid repair of the cratered runways, and there is recorded evidence that most of the Japanese fighter attacks were flown on the same day that their bases had been hit by B-29s.

The B-29 was not a tactical bomber, even though it was flown well in the hands of pilots who made bomb runs at low altitudes and walked their bombs neatly across runways. That was asking the B-29s to fly interdiction missions like fighter-bombers did, and the crews responded.

Nobody can identify the plane or the crew involved in one specific incident, and there's

127

*Left: Regina Coeli* — Queen of the Skies, for you non-Latin speaking people — was a B-29 assigned to the 315th Bomb Wing and its special missions of blasting oil refineries and storage areas. The B-29B versions were stripped by removing the upper and lower gun turrets, leaving only the tail gunner for defence. They used the AN/APQ-7 'Eagle' bombing radar for night precision strikes against well-defined targets, generally located at the edge of a body of water. / *Murray Singer*

*Right:* The Diamond Y identifies a B-29B of the 501st Bomb Group, 315th Bomb Wing, based on Guam at Northwest Field. Note the absence of the upper and lower gun turrets and the black-painted belly to minimise searchlight reflections. / *Murray Singer*

a chance that it is an apocryphal story anyway, but it's in character with the B-29's capabilities and the proclivities of some of her pilots.

One of the aircraft commanders in the strike force against a kamikaze base in Kyushu had never gotten over the idea that he had been born to be a fighter pilot. He took his B-29 right down to the ground after his bomb run, swung it around in a long pattern and went roaring down the main runway of the Japanese field, belly close to the ground and all guns blazing. The gunners went wild, and shot up the parked aircraft as if they had been sitting ducks.

Several B-29 pilots mentioned this story, and there are guarded references to it in official histories. It's a good story and probably happened. But wouldn't a photograph of that run be great?

By 11 May 1945, the island of Okinawa had its own defence force, US fighters operating from airfields at Kadena and Yontan, and from an auxiliary strip on the island of Ie Shima. The B-29s were released to go back to their primary tasks.

### Blasting the Oil Supplies

Near the end of the war, specialised precision bombing attacks were assigned to the newly arrived 315th Bombardment Wing (VH), which had reached Northwest Field, Guam, in May and June of 1945. The 315th had done its unit training as a night radar-bombing outfit, at the expense of learning about visual bombing and daylight formation flying.

Their aircraft were B-29B models built by Bell at Marietta. They were equipped with

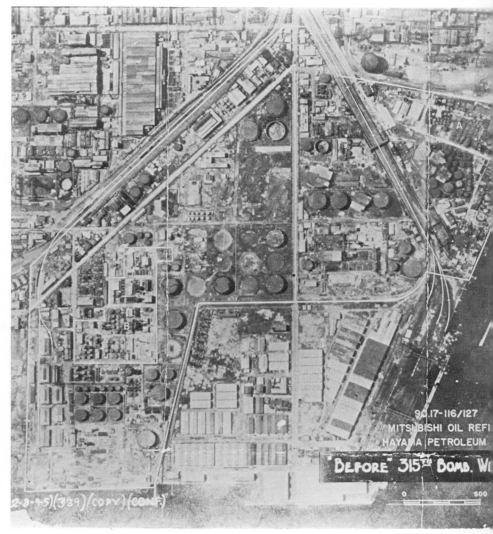

9C.17-116/127
MITSUBISHI OIL REFI
HAYAMA PETROLEUM

BEFORE 315TH BOMB. WI

*Left:* The Mitsubishi Oil Refinery and the Hayama Oil Refinery were located on a peninsula of reclaimed land, roughly rectangular in shape and clearly defined by the APQ-7 radar capabilities. Before the 315th Bomb Wing struck it, this was its appearance from the air. */ 315th BW via Murray Singer*

*Right:* On the night of 1-2 August, the 315th BW raided the two petroleum refineries, levelling a major portion of the target area. */ 315th BW via Murray Singer*

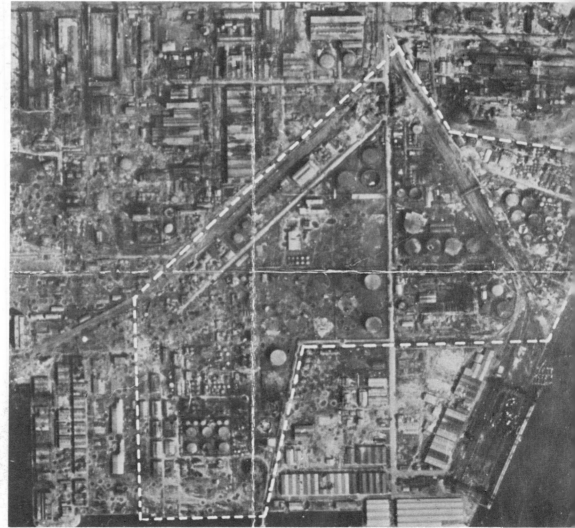

129

the new AN/APQ-7 Eagle radar housed in a small wing slung below the fuselage on two struts. The 315th B-29s lacked any turrets except for the tail gun position, and their bellies were painted glossy black as a protection against searchlight detection.

One characteristic of early radar was its relatively good performance against ground patterns that were clearly defined, such as a coastal area where water and land met. Logically then, the best targets for the 315th would have to be fairly large and located on the Japanese coast. Oil refineries and storage depots filled that requirement, and accordingly the 315th was sent out to strike Japan's oil industry.

Their first attack was mounted against the Utsube Oil Refinery at Yokkaichi on the night of 26 June. Between that first strike and the end of the war, the 315th flew 15 missions against ten targets. The Superfortresses dropped 9,084 tons of bombs — the 500lb general purpose type — in 1,095 sorties. Because of the lack of armament, extra weight was available for bomb load, and the B-29s of the 315th started by carrying an average of 15,000lb per airplane. On their last mission, the planes were lifting close to 21,000lb each, and might have gone to even higher bomb loads had the war lasted.

They lost four aircraft to enemy action, and 66 of the B-29s were damaged by flak. It was a very low price to pay for the work done.

Typically, a 315th mission would begin in the late afternoon with takeoffs at 45-second intervals from Guam. The first group of bombers would climb to 8,000 feet and the second to 10,000 feet for the cruise to the target. As they neared the coast of Japan, they would climb to the bombing altitudes of 15,000 feet.

At the initial point, the groups established three converging tracks to the target, separated horizontally by about ten miles at the IP. Bombing was done by individual aircraft, rather than by the formation, flying in a stream with a 200-foot altitude separation of the converging streams.

Ideal bombing weather for the 315th was solid cloud cover, with a minimum of turbulence. When cloud cover was not available at the target area, the B-29s faced the ever-present radar-controlled searchlights of the Japanese forces. Aluminium foil 'rope' was used to decoy the radars; as soon as a searchlight locked on a bomber, the countermeasures operators ejected some 'rope'. Generally the resulting target strength caused the Japanese radar to lock on to the aluminium foil cloud and leave the B-29. If the response was slow, other searchlights

TARGET 90.32 - 1841
UBE COAL LIQUEFACTION CO
BEFORE 315TH BOMB. WING STRIKE
5-6 AUG 1945

would join the first to catch the B-29 in its beam. In that case, the B-29 pilot would try to evade the flak that would surely follow by going to full power and top speed.

The use of the APQ-7 radar modified the usual bomb run procedure. The radar was synchronised electrically with the optical bombsight in the nose of the B-29. The radar bombardier and his scope were further aft, in the navigator's compartment. He tracked the target, aligning it with a reticle on the radar scope. This information was fed to the optical bombsight and resulted in a display of the track to fly, presented on an indicator in the cockpit. The radar data also gave ground speed and time for release for the optical bombsight.

The pilot set the plane on automatic pilot, turned to the track displayed on the PDI (Pilot's Direction Indicator), and held that course to the target. He also stabilised the airplane speed and altitude, so that the pilot himself was controlling all three parameters of the bomb run. In the usual approach to optical bombing, the pilots only controlled speed and altitude; the bombardier held the course.

The Ube Coal Liquefaction plant was another well-placed target for radar bombing, with its characteristic geometry set off by surrounding water. It was targeted for the 315th Bomb Wing late in the war.
/ 315th BW via Murray Singer

TARGET # 90.32 - 1841
UBE COAL LIQUEFACTION CO.
"DESTROYED AND SUNK" BY
315TH BOMB. WING 5-6 AUG 45

N

(315PL)(286X 8-5-45Xc.P7X CONF)

'Down in the nose the bombsight indicators come together, my red light comes on, bomb doors have snapped open. Bombs away! The aircraft lifts as the forty 500-pounders leave us in a minimum train stick. I break away right and down since we're the lowest aircraft in the stack. My co-pilot, Major Greg Hathaway, is on the inside of the turn and has the best view of the tremendous explosions which even light up the clouds above us. We've hit pay dirt! We were all decorated for that mission; the target (Maruzen Oil Refinery) was ninety-five per cent destroyed.' *Boyd Hubbard, Jr, commander, 501st BG*

But strategically, the 315th missions — however well executed — had only small significance. By then, the blockade and the losses of Japanese shipping had dried up most of the country's oil resources. Domestic production had never been very important; the bulk of Japanese crude oil came in from overseas, which was the overriding reason behind their early drive south to take the Netherlands East Indies, source of tremendous crude oil reserves.

In another setting, the record of the 315th against the Japanese oil industry would have been hailed as outstanding. But in the context of Japan's last days, it has to be judged as of limited strategic value.

*Ravens and Porcupines*

At night, the heavy Japanese defence around the major industrial cities relied on radar to direct searchlights and anti-aircraft artillery. The Japanese radar, unlike the German types in the European theatre, operated at a relatively low frequency. 'Chaff', or 'window' as the Royal Air Force called it, worked well in the European air war decoying German radars. But the narrow, short strips of aluminium foil were almost useless in the Pacific theatre.

'Rope' was developed instead. It also was aluminium foil, but the pieces were one inch wide and were from 100 to 400 feet long. By the end of the war, B-29s were carrying a load of 600lb of 'Rope' on night missions against Japan.

Gun-laying radar was a different problem. Some of the Japanese equipment had been developed from British units that had been

*Yokohama Yo-Yo* was an F-13A-40-BW (42-24621) converted from a standard B-29 to the reconnaissance role and assigned to the 73rd Bomb Wing on detachment. Here she shows 11 photo mission markers.
*/ Donald L. Miller Collection*

captured in the fall of Singapore, and their characteristics were available to US radar experts for the development of counter-measures. They developed a jamming system and verified it in 'ferret' flights.

Special equipment, operated by trained officers called 'Ravens', was installed in the B-29s to meet the threat. It could intercept and analyse Japanese radar signals so that appropriate jamming signals could be sent out.

Initially, there was a severe shortage of the 'Raven' operators. On the early raids against the home islands, only a few planes in each major formation carried the operators. Late in the war, they were carried on many more aircraft, often on all the planes in the formation.

Night raids were a different and more difficult problem for solution, because of the bomber stream tactics, with individual aircraft making separated runs over the target. Each airplane would be the focus of a number of Japanese radar sets, operating at a number of different frequencies, and it was too much for one or two 'Ravens' aboard to handle.

One solution was to modify a batch of B-29s for radar countermeasures (RCM) work. These planes carried as many as 18 sets of intercept, analysis and jamming equipment.

'We had a "porcupine" mission one night; they were named for the aircraft, which had many antennas protruding in all directions from the fuselage. It was intended as a super radar-jamming platform, and we interfered

with their searchlights, their flak, their radios, everything.

'The "porcupine" had to arrive at the target first and leave last. About an hour of circling and dodging the searchlights and flak was fun, with the crew dropping rope, playing jamming records, and the like, and me in the lightweight B-29 making like a fighter pilot. Sometimes we carried intelligence people along to plot flak positions and to observe the bombing results. They had a grandstand seat for what was then the greatest show on earth!

'Our waist gunners were identical twins, and they carried letters from General Arnold advising that they never were to be separated in combat assignments. They saw their 21st birthday in on a "porcupine" mission over Tokyo.' *Charles B. Hawks*

These early RCM aircraft were very effective, given the state of the radar art of their day, and they were the basis for further development that continued after the war. Between World War 2 and the Korean conflict, special RB-29s based on the 'porcupine' aircraft of the Pacific campaigns flew dangerous and unpublicised missions around the edges of the Soviet Union and other countries. Operating as weather reconnaissance squadrons in Alaska, or as detachments from a weather squadron, these RB-29s monitored Russian radar developments and deployments until a later generation of RCM aircraft and equipment replaced them on station.

## Photographic Reconnaissance

The availability of the Superfortress with its very long range changed the reconnaissance situation in the Pacific. When the B-29s first went into action, there was no reconnaissance aircraft that could make the post-strike photos of the target that are so necessary to the analysis of bomb damage. With reasonable haste, some B-29s were field - modified to be used for the task.

Normally, all B-29s carried a single camera on their missions and used it to record the initial bomb drop — the lead plane in the formation held his bomb run for 45 seconds after the drop to get photos — and possibly to catch the early hits of other planes in the formation. Once the target began to burn or crumble, there was little chance to see it until the smoke and dust cleared away, some hours or days later.

The modified B-29s were so successful at their new mission that Air Forces reconnaissance specialists at Wright Field initiated a special modification programme to produce the F-13, a photo-reconnaissance version of the basic B-29.

The F-13A aircraft that saw service from the Marianas held a number of K-18 and K-22 camera installations for both vertical and oblique coverage. Its bomb bays held long-range fuel tanks.

A small number of F-13As made up the 3rd Photo Reconnaissance Squadron, detached for duty on Saipan. One of them, *Tokyo Rose,* flown by Capt Ralph D. Steakley, was the first American aircraft to fly over Tokyo after the Doolittle raids of 1942. Steakley's crew photographed the urban areas around Tokyo on 1 November 1944, from 32,000 feet, and brought back pictures of Japanese targets that had not been photographed before then. The single mission produced more than 7,000 photos of the area, a reconnaissance bonanza.

F-13 crews from then on flew over the home islands of the Japanese Empire on a frequent basis. Flying singly, they would make the run at high altitude to escape fighter interception. The Japanese tried; on a number of occasions they scrambled large numbers of fighters, vectored to intercept the F-13s. But the fighters did not have the performance to get to altitude and stay there while closing and manoeuvring for firing.

It was a very different situation for the RB-29s (redesignated from F-13) in the Korean war. Russian-built MiGs made the skies very inhospitable for all reconnaissance aircraft, and particularly the RB-29s. They were slow, outmoded, and belonged to another war, another age. Yet their crews made the maximum effort. After one disastrous engagement, the RB-29s were ordered not to go to the Yalu River again.

Yet in spite of this setback, the RB-29s continued to fly reconnaissance missions. The 91st Strategic Reconnaissance Squadron moved to Yokota, Japan, in November 1950, five months after the war began, and started flying routine missions against target areas. The first MiG-15 to fall to the guns of any B-29, bomber or recon version, was shot down by one of the gunners from the 91st SRS.

*Les's Best,* an F-13A operating out of Saipan on photo-reconnaissance missions, has 20 mission markers emblazoned on her nose. The officer in the cockpit is Capt James Garrity, adjutant of the 883rd Bomb Squadron, 500th Bomb Group. / *James J. Garrity Collection*

133

470119

From where I sit, I can see one dead engine, and that's bad. But I can also see a Superdumbo, and that's good. This Superdumbo — more properly, an SB-29 — was converted from a Wichita-built B-29-80-BW, serial 44-70119. More radio, better radar, more observers, and much more rescue equipment, including a lifeboat slung under the belly, outside what was the bomb-bay area, made the SB-29 a very useful and versatile search and rescue aircraft. Still it was, at best, a stop-gap measure and was replaced by later and better aircraft. This photo is a late wartime — possible post-war — shot, and the B-29 with the dead engine is a late model with Curtiss reversible-pitch props and cooling cuffs at the roots.
/ Boeing 148125

## Rescued by a Big Elephant

There are many miles of open water between the home islands of Japan and the Marianas. A pilot of a B-29 in trouble had only one place to set down on route before Iwo Jima was captured: the Pacific Ocean. And it was a wild ocean, with violent storms, rain squalls, whitecaps, and heavy waves.

Ditching a B-29 — landing it on the open sea — was not an enjoyable prospect or experience. Procedures had been worked out in model tests by the National Advisory Committee for Aeronautics at its Langley Memorial Laboratory, and in one full-scale test ditching in calm and sheltered waters.

But even under ideal conditions, the B-29 was an inconsistent performer in a ditching. A few, skilfully or luckily landed, did float; one B-29 ditched in the Bay of Bengal floated for more than 24 hours and drifted ashore. But most of them broke in two and sank fairly rapidly. Getting out, getting life rafts deployed and emergency equipment from its storage places required more time than often was available. And if the crew did get out, the prospects for rescue depended on an earnest, but disorganised, search and rescue effort involving Navy submarines and patrol planes, joined later by Army amphibians of a special rescue squadron.

The best answer lay in the B-29 itself, converted to a search and rescue aircraft, the SB-29A 'Superdumbo'. For some reason, rescue aircraft had been dubbed 'Dumbo', after the Disney flying elephant, and the B-29, being super-everything, became the 'Superdumbo'.

It carried extra crewmen, extra emergency gear and provisions, and a lifeboat slung below its belly. Working as part of a developing search and rescue team, the Superdumbo was able to stay on station for as long as 14 hours, scanning thousands of square miles of ocean in search missions. They retained their armament as well, and were able to fight off enemy aircraft or ships that attempted to interfere with the rescue operations.

Mission time in the 'Superdumbo' counted as combat time, because the search and rescue patrol was dangerous. Often the planes orbited just out of fighter range off the coast of Japan, but if needed, they closed to the coastal waters. They coordinated pickups in the Inland Sea, a land-locked body of water heavily defended and surrounded by Japan.

The capability for search and rescue increased as the war went on, and on the very last B-29 mission from the Marianas, the strike force was supported by an air-sea rescue team that included 14 Navy submarines, 21 Navy seaplanes, nine SB-29A 'Superdumbo' aircraft, and five surface ships. More surface ships were stationed on the waters off the ends of active runways, and Navy patrol planes circled those areas. More rescue aircraft were on standby at the bomber bases. For every three B-29 crewmen on that mission, there was one man on the surface ready to help rescue downed crews.

When the final statistics were in, they showed that an airman had about a fifty per cent chance of surviving if he were forced down at sea. Ditching was to be preferred to crashing or bailing out, obviously, but all of them offered far better chances of survival than being captured did.

# Bail Out!

If you bail out over Japan, pray that you are picked up by soldiers. The civilians will beat you to death.

That advice, often an unofficial part of a pre-mission briefing, only hinted at the real truth. The B-29 crewmen had few illusions about the treatment they could expect if they were captured. Tokyo Rose, American-born, English-speaking radio voice and propagandist for Japan, frequently reminded them they would be treated as war criminals, tried, and executed. Death in combat is a standard risk of war; but death at the hands of irate civilians, or in a prison camp, was not anywhere in the fine print. And there was, of course, a Geneva Convention that laid down the rules and practices for humane treatment of prisoners.

Some survived the treatment. One of them was 1st Lieutenant Victor Morris, a flight engineer with Captain Zweifel's crew of the 874th Bomb Sqdn., 498th Bomb Grp. Morris wrote to the squadron adjutant, Capt Bernard M. Kearns, after he had been repatriated by a Navy team:

'Dear Bernie and all members of the 874th Bomb Sqdn:

'I am sure this letter will come to you as a surprise, but I am alive and in good health aboard the Navy's newest hospital ship. Am suffering from malnutrition and loss of weight. I and practically all flying personnel have lost thirty-five (35) to seventy (70) pounds weight.

'Very few men from the 874th are aboard this ship. While in prison camp I came across Sgts Evans, Reynolds, Sam Soucci, all from Lt Smith's crew. John Houghton was badly burned and injured so they decided to give him medical attention, only after spending

This stricken Superfort from the 29th Bomb Group is in deep trouble. The number four engine has been feathered, and that trail of white smoke is probably an induction system fire that has ignited either some magnesium or some aluminium parts, or both.
/ Charles B. Hawks Collection

two weeks lying in terrific pain and agony. Believe me, we have all gone through hell . . .

'We were shot down by heavy flak concentration. Our wing was blown off. The ship certainly was a blazing inferno as were the buildings below us. I just missed bailing out into a burning building . . . I really had the "hell" beaten out of me by civilian women and children. The army saved my life, as the civilians were doing a good job of clubbing me to death. Have quite a few scars on my head and legs.

'We were given the third degree at interrogation and kept under constant fear of being killed. They kept telling us that we were under trial for murdering innocent civilians. You can't imagine how they hated B-29 and P-51 men. We were classified as "Special Prisoners", never permitted to talk, see the sun, or breathe fresh air. Food was deplorable, three (3) small rice balls and a glass of water per day . . .'

One of the six B-29s that was lost on 3 December 1944, in a strike against Target 357, was flown by Major Robert Goldsworthy. He had been operations officer of the 881st Bomb Squadron, 500th Bomb Group, and had not been in that slot too long. 'One of our aircraft commanders was having

ear trouble and couldn't fly, and we needed every plane and crew we could get. So I traded jobs with him; I took his crew and plane, and he became squadron operations officer.

'On 3 December 1944, we headed to Tokyo to bomb an aircraft engine plant. We were in a 12-plane formation and my plane was the lead ship. I was a Major and flight leader, and my co-pilot was Col Richard T. King, Jr, group commander of the 500th, flying as flight commander. We also had Col Byron Brugge, intelligence officer from Wing Hq, with us as an observer.

'Just after the bomb drop, we were hit by fighters. They punctured the inboard left wing and the gasoline sprayed out all over the airplane. Naturally it caught fire, and our intercom was out and the nose wheel had dropped. We lost altitude, I rang the bailout bell and we started to go out of the airplane in order. Col King said later that he counted eight, possibly nine chutes as he was floating down.

'We were picked up by civilians, who bound us with the shroud lines from our own chutes, and turned us over to Japanese soldiers. They blindfolded us, loaded us in a truck and drove into Tokyo.

'After rough interrogations, we were put in solitary confinement at military police headquarters. Food was mixed rice and barley, sometimes a little fish, and not very often we'd have thin soup for breakfast.

'In March we were moved to Omori prison camp, and we were listed as special prisoners. There were thirty-six of us, and all but four were B-29 crewmen. "Pappy" Boyington was in another section at Omori, with another group of special prisoners.

'They kept us there until 15 August, separated from the rest of the prison camp. On the 15th, they started giving us more food and medication, and we were allowed to mix through the camp. We were finally liberated on 27 August, by a Navy team under Commander Harold E. Stassen — right, that Stassen — and taken to a Navy hospital ship for treatment. Dick King, who had been an All-American football selection and an end on the West Point team, weighed 126lb instead of his usual 195. We were all skin and bones, but we were alive. A lot of men never lived through the experience. Colonel Brugge was in the cell next to mine in MP headquarters, and he was systematically beaten to death because he wouldn't answer their questions in interrogation. It was terrible, the treatment they gave him.' *Robert F. Goldsworthy, operations officer, 881st BS, 500th BG*

# Rescued by Mao's Guerrillas

Rescuers and rescued pose for a picture in the winter sunlight of a Chinese village. Seated, left to right, are Commissar Deng, 4th Div, New Fourth Army; 1st Lt W. G. Warburton, flight engineer; Major F. B. Morgan, observer; General Chang, 4th Div Commander, New Fourth Army. In the rear row, same order: Unknown; Leo Young, New Fourth Army interpreter; S/Sgt Dwight E. Collins, radio operator; 1st Lt Felix O. Sinicrope, navigator; Sgt George R. Schuchardt, tail gunner; Major Wu, New Fourth Army, Commander of Cavalry. / Francis B. Morgan Collection

From the Miami (Florida) *Daily News,* 11 November 1944 (Saturday):
'WASHINGTON, 11 Nov. — (AP) — B-29's Saturday hit three vitally important targets — Nanking and Shanghai in Japanese-occupied China and Omura on the Japanese home island of Kyushu.

On the basis of preliminary reports, one of the B-29's is missing, the 20th Air Force said in a communique.'

One man aboard that missing B-29 was not a regular member of its combat crew. As a group communications officer, his assignment normally kept him on the ground. But the circumstances for this trip were different, and the result was an adventure that few B-29 crewmen had. Francis B. Morgan, then a Major in the Signal Corps and 40th Bomb Group Communications Officer, tells his story:
'We were having troubles in mission communications. The radio operators didn't

have much to do, because they kept radio silence on the way to the target and through the bomb drop. When they crossed the Yellow River on the way back, they sent a single code word, repeated three times, to indicate they had completed the drop and were on the way home.

'They were supposed to monitor the radio, through, for the entire mission. But twelve hours is a long time to wear a headset. I wanted to find out if we could do anything to ease the situation and so I arranged to fly on a mission as an observer.

'On 11 November 1944, I boarded *Sir Trofrepus* (42-6237) — the name is Superfortress backward and slightly changed — and we took off from A-1 at Hsinching to bomb Omura. Just after liftoff, a scanner noted we were siphoning gas out of one wing and the pilot decided to abort the mission. When he turned to go back, the siphoning stopped, and so he decided to go on to the rendezvous. We usually flew east to a

請敬 逢遊菲治潔時 四午下日八月二 於定蒞
光臨

太行軍區 □□魯豫 邊區政府 謹訂

We cordially request the pleasure of inviting the company of Major Francis B. Morgan to dinner on February 18th at 4 P.M. at our Tai En.

Chin-Ki-Lu yu Border Region Government.

*Above:* This formal invitation requests the company of Major Morgan at dinner on 18 February at 4pm. The invitation came from the Chin-Ki-Luyu Border Region Government, and was one of many examples of the hospitality shown to the rescued B-29 crewmen by their Chinese hosts and rescuers.
*/ Francis B. Morgan Collection*

*Left:* Major F. B. Morgan (front centre) and seven other American fliers pose with General Chang, commanding the 4th Division, New Fourth Army, on their way out of China to American bases in India.
*/ Francis B. Morgan Collection*

139

rendezvous over a lake about 800 miles away, formed the group and headed to the target. The problem with the siphoning delayed us about ten minutes or so, just long enough to arrive late at the rendezvous. The group had formed and gone on ahead, so we continued in their wake. Over the Yellow Sea, our radio operator received a mission abort signal because Omura was solidly covered with cloud. Our secondary target was Shanghai.

'We were circling alone, over the Yellow Sea, and by the time we got the message decoded, the formation had changed its course and backtracked toward Shanghai and passed us below and about 15 miles away. We swung in behind them, still way behind, and the formation bombed Shanghai. For some reason, our pilot — 1st Lt Richard Vickery — decided to bomb Nanking, and we went in alone over that target.

'The flak briefing had indicated weak to moderate intensity, inaccurate to fairly accurate, with a maximum ceiling of 20,000 feet. We flew at 22,000 feet and due south at bombing speed. We were carrying bombs in the rear bay only, and gas in the front bay. The doors cranked open for the bomb run and just at "Bombs away!" we felt a thump. We thought it was a bomb hung up in the bay, and we saw the bombs hit our target of warehouses on the river.

140

*Left:* Sandlot baseball, Chinese style, involved the efforts of American fliers and Chinese troops. It was one of the ways to pass the time during the long march homeward.
*/ Francis B. Morgan Collection*

*Below left:* The American and Chinese flags fly above a banner reading, 'The Nations of America and China Unite !' This kind of banner always greeted the arrival of the American airmen in any new town or village, unless — as Morgan said — there were Japanese or Chinese puppet governments around.
*/ Francis B. Morgan Collection*

*Below:* A welcoming crowd of Chinese has gathered under banners reading, 'American People & Chinese People Will Always Be Friends !' and 'Welcome Our Brave American Aviators !' This also was a typical occurrence on the trip out of China.
*/ Francis B. Morgan Collection*

'But the thump had been a near-miss flak burst. It set the number four engine on fire and also ignited the fuel transfer system in the rear bomb bay. The rear bomb bay was in flames. The flight engineer called the CFC gunner and asked him if he could put out the fire. "Shit, no!" said the CFC gunner. "We gotta get out!"

'Vickery decided to stay with the airplane as long as possible, because we wanted to get as far from Japanese-occupied Nanking as we could. After all, Tokyo Rose had said that captured B-29 crews would be executed.

'We believe the gunners in the waist jumped then and didn't wait, because Vickery gave the bail-out order about ten or fifteen minutes after we were hit and got no response from the waist. The tail gunner acknowledged the order. Our nose wheel was down so we could bail out the wheel well. The radio operator and I tied down the key so that base could get a DF fix on us, and got ready to destroy our code books and other crypto material. The navigator bailed out first, then the flight engineer, and the tail gunner had gone as soon as he heard the order. The aircraft rolled to the right suddenly and I was flung into the flight engineer's compartment. I was standing on the window, trying to reach the wheel well and that's the last I remember until I came to, free-falling through the air. I could see people

on the ground, and I must have fallen 19 or 20,000 feet.

'I pulled the D-ring but nothing happened because my right hand was lacerated and I couldn't pull hard enough. So I pushed on the ring with my left hand, the chute popped, I swung two or three times and hit in a rice paddy, the only one with water in it for miles around. I tried to push the chute under water to hide it, not too successfully. I looked up and saw pieces of the airplane still falling, one wing with an engine attached still several thousand feet in the air. I saw three chutes and walked about a quarter of a mile to meet them. It was the tail gunner, the flight engineer and the radio operator.

'We had been briefed about Chinese guerrillas in the area, and we talked about it after we landed. Warburton (1st Lt William G. Warburton, flight engineer) had a first-aid kit in the leg of his flying suit, and he bandaged my hand. Warburton and (Sgt George R.) Schuchardt, our tail gunner, had bailed out in the usual way. (S/Sgt Dwight E.) Collins, the radio operator, and I were blown out of the B-29 when it exploded. The four of us were standing there deciding what to do when we were fired upon by unknown Chinese in peasant dress. We hit the dirt, heard more shooting, and then five Chinese came running up, gestured to us to run with them, and with them leading and covering us, we headed for the hills. They were from Mao's New Fourth Army (N4A), there to harass the Japanese and help the US forces. We moved five or six miles real fast.

'We had been shot down around nine or ten in the morning; it was dark when we reached a place to rest more than 15 miles away. Later that night we moved another 20 miles or so on donkeys with pack saddles. The next day, we rested in a small village part of the day, and walked to another one where we rested and ate. That night we travelled another 20 miles on donkeys to another tiny village where we met Sinicrope (1st Lt Felix O. Sinicrope, navigator). Up to that point, we had been escorted by two men and two women guerrillas. In the village we were taken over by Lee Kong, from the N4A.

'Next day we were told we were waiting for Comrade Yu, who was coming in from N4A headquarters with horses. They arrived on 14 November, and the following morning we mounted up at 0730 and rode until 1300 with one stop for lunch. We arrived at a small house near a village, and it had begun to rain so hard that we couldn't travel, so we rested there overnight. In the morning we set out again at 0800 and arrived at the N4A headquarters at 1500 to be greeted by officials there. We radioed the American delegation at Yenan, told them our names and serial

141

*Above and right:* On 7 February 1945, another B-29 crew led by Captain Varoff (initials unknown) was picked up by an American B-25 at Li-Cheng and flown out to India. Morgan's Chinese hosts gave him these pictures of that event, which would be duplicated later when a B-25 arrived for Morgan's party.
*/ Francis B. Morgan Collection*

numbers, said we were alive and well, and requested transportation out of the area.

'For the next few days we loafed, bathed, shaved, were visited by doctors, were given clean clothes, read some books — all Upton Sinclair novels — made a checker board, sent another message to Yenan, celebrated Thanksgiving, and generally enjoyed the care and hospitality of our hosts. They got together a special Thanksgiving dinner for our benefit; they were wonderful people.

'Finally on 3 December we got word back from Yenan that our delegation would make arrangements with the Central Government in Chungking and would notify us of the results. On the 12th, a month and a day after we were shot down, we got the message from XX Bomber Command making four points. First, Col Savoie (an earlier escapee) had arrived back at the Command and had given talks about escape and evasion at all the bases. Second, he had been returned to the US. Third, the Central Government (under Chiang Kai-Shek) refused to accept any more rescued fliers from the N4A. Fourth, could we go to Yenan? Apparently, Savoie had been too laudatory in his remarks about the Red Army units that had rescued and returned him, and the Central Government was displeased.

'It had begun to freeze at night, and we were getting snow, and so the N4A officials recommended that we wait until March to try to get to Yenan. We really didn't want to, and they understood, so they worked out a coordinated plan with the Eighth Route Army (8RA) to leave the day after Christmas.

'On 24 December we were invited to General Chen's place for dinner. We had cold meats, year-old eggs and wine; then fish, chicken, duck, and "lion's head" (steamed chopped meat). Then vegetables with more wine, and little meat balls inside pastry. Then sweets — lily seeds in syrup — then mutton soup and then mushroom soup, more wine and finally coffee. The most I've ever eaten in my life! We then adjourned to a hall of sorts which had two Christmas trees, a painted Santa Claus and other decorations. There we had plates of peanut brittle, sesame seed brittle, peanuts, pears and candies. While we tried to nibble, Liu Young, who was our assigned interpreter, introduced dancers, singers and musicians. Bill sang a solo and when General Chen had sung one at my request, he demanded that I sing in return. Later we all sang carols together, got Christmas cards from others and a bottle of wine and a can of honey from Loh Tsei.

'It was our turn the next day, and we entertained the officers from Headquarters and the doctors at Christmas dinner, with their food, of course. The next morning

Commissar Yao, Dr Wei, General Chen, General Chiang, General Lai, and Doctors Chiang and Gung came over for breakfast and brought more maps to add to the ones we had received earlier from them. Then our pictures were taken and we started off on horseback.

'The weather held us up unpleasantly, and hospitality delayed us pleasantly. We were handed along from unit to unit, greeted, wined and dined all along the route, picked up a fifth rescued airman, a P-51 pilot named Walter Krywy, heard and saw B-29s overhead on a number of missions, picked up three more airmen: Lt Al Fisher, Sgt Pat Patterson, and Sgt Pete Kouzes, pilot, flight engineer and radio operator of a C-46 that got hit. We inspected troops, described our basic training methods, our manual of arms and bayonet drill, received presents of Japanese swords, aluminium chopsticks, souvenirs, new tailor-made uniforms, winter clothing, and padded shoes.

'The Chinese were very considerate, very thoughtful. We were fed when others either did without or got less, and this was in some areas where there was so little food that the people ate leaves off the trees.

'On 15 February we sent a message to Yenan asking that a plane be sent out to a rendezvous point to pick us up. On the 25th we got an affirmative answer and headed for the strip to wait. On 3 March, at 1445, the prettiest B-25 I ever saw came in with a pair of fighters for an escort, and took us off. We got back to A-1 at 1745, were debriefed, fed and placed under a heavy armed guard. The reason was that the Central Government's secret police, the Dai Li, were expected to make an attempt to kill us because of the unkind things they thought we were going to say about the Central Government.

'We left the next morning from Kharagpur, and I stopped off on the way to leave some intelligence information the N4A and 8RA people had given me. They thought it would be helpful in what was expected to be an invasion landing on the Chinese coast. That evening I was back in India, and within a few days I was on my way home to the US.

'It was quite a trip. We covered 850 miles in 30 travel days, much of it through Japanese-controlled areas. I'm glad I knew how to handle and ride horses. We rode typical cavalry style; we'd trot one-third of the time, walk the horses one-third of the time, and then dismount and lead the horses for the remaining third of the time.

'And I can't say enough about the Chinese who rescued us and cared for us. They all went out of their way to do things for us, and to make us feel comfortable in what they knew were unfamiliar and strained conditions for us.'

# One B-29, One Bomb

What the Japanese radio announcer was saying was perfectly credible, given the usual nature of information about B-29 raids released to his intended audience. But it was perfectly incredible, given what had happened.

A small number of B-29s, he said, penetrated into Hiroshima city just after eight o'clock yesterday morning and dropped a small number of bombs. As a result, he added, a considerable number of homes were reduced to ashes and fires broke out in various parts of the city.

It was 7 August 1945, and the morning before, a single B-29 had dropped the first complete model of an atomic bomb, and it had worked. In a millisecond, Hiroshima was nearly obliterated.

In one mission, one B-29 and one bomb had changed the course of warfare forever.

The B-29 had been singled out for the job more than two years earlier. In June 1943, the only feasible atomic bomb seemed to be one based on a plutonium gun design. It was a long device, literally a gun, in which two subcritical masses of plutonium were driven together in a long barrel by explosive charges, and thereupon immediately went critical and exploded. The gun was something like 17 feet long, and it could be carried only in a specially modified B-29 whose two bomb bays would have to be joined into a single long bay for the weapon.

Underwing installations had been considered and rejected. The outstanding British heavy bomber, the Avro Lancaster, had been studied as a possible carrier, but also was rejected on the grounds that it could not be fitted into the existing logistics and maintenance pipelines.

So a test B-29, which was very hard to get even for such a high-priority project as the atomic bomb development, was modified and used for drop tests of the long gun weapon mockup, by then called the 'Thin Man', and for the implosion plutonium bomb of a different design and shape, by then called 'Fat Man'. Test drops of both weapon mockups had been made at the Muroc Dry Lake Bombing Range beginning in March 1944, and the last of a series damaged the carrier B-29, laying it up for repairs and delaying the tests. By June, when the bomber was ready to

fly again, the gun design had been shortened considerably, the bomb was renamed 'Little Boy', and it could fit in one bomb bay of a standard B-29.

By September 1944, the external bomb shapes — which had been changing as the designs were revised — were frozen, as were the aircraft requirements. By the next month, the first of a special lot of 15 B-29s was beginning to be used in drop tests of mock-up bomb shapes over the Wendover Bombing Range, 125 miles west out of Salt Lake City, Utah.

These were B-29s that had been modified for the atomic bomb delivery, not by combining the bomb bays as first planned, but by installing stronger bomb racks — each atomic weapon was going to weigh about five tons — and mounting the new fuel-injection R-3350 engines, with reversible-pitch electrically controlled Curtiss propellers with root cuffs to aid the cooling of the ever-hot Wright engines. Only the tail guns had been installed; all other armament was removed. The bomb bay doors used pneumatic actuators, a feature that was introduced late in the production of the B-29s, to snap the doors open and closed in a fraction of a second.

The operating organisation was a unique one. It was designated the 509th Composite Group, and it included most of everything it would need to be a completely self-contained outfit. It would be equipped with 15 B-29 bombers, assigned to the 393rd Bombardment Squadron, and five Douglas C-54 transports, assigned to the 320th Troop Carrier Squadron, and nicknamed the 'Green Hornet Line'. It would also include the 390th Air Service Group, the 1395th Military Police Company (Aviation), and the 1st Ordnance Squadron, Special (Aviation). The total authorised strength of the 509th was 225 officers and 1,542 enlisted men.

The unit was constituted on 9 December 1944, and activated on 17 December 1944, the 41st anniversary of the Wright brothers' first flight. The 509th was first based at Wendover Field, Utah, where they practised strange flight profiles with single bombs carried to and dropped from great heights.

Parallel to the training of the 509th, several series of test drops were made for

144

NAGASAKI STRIKE PHOTO

development of the atomic weapons. The fuses were to be set for air bursts, and there was some problem getting a reliable proximity fuse that would do the trick. Then somebody noted that the Radio Corporation of America was developing a tail-warning radar, the AN/APS-13, whose characteristic ability was detecting an object at a fixed, preset distance, and then triggering a relay to actuate a warning aboard the aircraft. The APS-13 was adapted for the atomic bomb fusing, and tested in a number of drops made over the Salton Sea, a range facility that offered an overwater approach and a drop to an altitude just about at sea level, something not available at either the Wendover or the Muroc bombing ranges.

California Institute of Technology's Camel Project was charged with the responsibility of solving the problems of the bomb assembly mechanism, and of the combat delivery of the weapons. They produced a number of 'pumpkin' bombs, for tests, built within the casings of the 'Fat Man' implosion bomb, but without the nuclear materials installed. These were dropped at the Navy's Inyokern rocket range, and later by the 509th at Wendover and over Japan, where the 'pumpkin' cores contained high explosives.

By the spring of 1945, the first batch of B-29s assigned to the 509th had revealed a lot of weaknesses, so a second batch of new airplanes was acquired. And about the same time, the 509th started its move to Tinian. The official date of departure from Wendover was 26 April 1945; the advance air echelon had arrived at Tinian's North Field on 18 May. The ground echelons began to arrive on 29 May, and the combat crews flew their aircraft in beginning 11 June.

By 30 June, the 509th was ready to start its combat flight training. They began with a half-dozen practice missions, which typically included a navigational flight to Iwo Jima

146

Above: Hiroshima, minutes after.
/ *James J. Garrity Collection*

Top left: *Enola Gay*, a B-29-45-MO built by Martin at Omaha (serial 44-86292), lifts off the runway at Wendover Field on a training flight. / *Boeing 109360*

Centre left: Bearing the markings of the 6th Bomb Group, 313rd Bomb Wing, for deception, *Enola Gay* comes in for a landing at Tinian after dropping the first atomic bomb. / *Boeing 151200*

Bottom left: At rest, the *Enola Gay* shows her cleaned-up and developed airframe. No turrets break the upper or lower fuselage lines; only the APQ-13 radome protrudes from the belly. Curtiss reversible-pitch props, with blade root cuffs for extra cooling of the engine, were installed on the planes of the 509th Composite Group. The arrow in the circle is the official Group designator. The aircraft number — 82 — was on the nose and fuselage behind the US insignia at the latter site. / *Boeing 2B1855*

with a bomb drop on Rota, the bypassed and beaten island, on the way back; perhaps another pair of short bombing missions to Rota, and a long run to Truk for a drop on that punchboard island. These missions were flown by two to nine aircraft.

It still wasn't certain that an atomic bomb would work. The 509th had gotten this far on the strength of calculations and some very limited experiments. But on 16 July, the Trinity test explosion lit up the pre-dawn sky around Alamogordo, New Mexico, and the scientists knew that their calculations had been verified.

On 20 July, the 509th began flying combat missions against carefully selected targets in Japan, cities that had been hit earlier, or that were near ones that had been bombed, and which additionally were in the general area of those cities on the short list for later atomic attacks. There were 12 of these strikes, flown on 20, 24, 26 and 29 July, involving formations of two to six aircraft, each dropping a single 'pumpkin' bomb. It was hoped that the Japanese wouldn't be disturbed by the strange sight of small formations, after seeing some of them over the islands, dropping single 'blockbuster' bombs.

The first atomic bomb, 'Little Boy', was ready on 31 July, seventeen days after the first — and only — test of a nuclear weapon.

The War Department, Office of the Chief of Staff, sent a special secret order on the afternoon of 24 July, direct to Gen Carl Spaatz, the Commanding General of the United States Strategic Air Forces. It told him that the 509th Composite Group would deliver its first special bomb, as soon as weather would permit visual bombing after about 3 August, on any one of four targets: Hiroshima, Kokura, Niigata, or Nagasaki.

On 5 August the forecast predicted good visual bombing weather over the target areas

for the following day. Gen LeMay confirmed 6 August mission date, and the typewriters began to pound out the words of the orders for Special Bombing Mission No 13. The primary target was to be the urban industrial area of Hiroshima. The secondary was the arsenal and city at Kokura. The third alternate was the urban area of Nagasaki. Only visual bombing would be permitted; the target had to be observed personally by both pilot and bombardier, and they had to agree that what they saw was indeed the target city. The mission was to bomb from an altitude of 28,000 to 30,000 feet at a speed of 200mph.

And so at midnight the crews went to their briefing. At 0137, Tinian time, three B-29s roared down three parallel runways on North Field, headed for Japan and three separate weather reconnaissance flights over the three target cities. Major Claude R. Eatherly's *Straight Flush* headed for Hiroshima. Major Ralph R. Taylor, in *Full House* set course for Nagasaki, and Major John A. Wilson steered *Jabbit III* toward Kokura.

At 0245, Lt Col Paul W. Tibbets released the brakes of the *Enola Gay*; as she began her take-off run, two more B-29s carrying instruments and observers rolled into position for take-off. Major Charles W. Sweeney was at the controls of *The Great Artiste*, and Capt George W. Marquardt was commander of an unnamed B-29 marked only with the fuselage number 91. One after the other, the three aircraft lifted off the runways at Tinian, hauled up their landing gear, and headed into history.

At 0605 they crossed over Iwo Jima, and turned toward the target area. 'Little Boy' was armed, by hand, by Navy Commander Frederick L. Ashworth, working in the cramped and crowded bomb bay. Tibbets started the climb to bombing altitude at 0741, levelled off at 32,700 feet at 0838. The target was spotted at 0909, they made the bomb run and dropped 'Little Boy' at 0915:17 Tinian time.

Forty-three seconds later, Hiroshima ceased to exist as a city.

The second strike, planned against Kokura, was plagued by problems, large and small. Maj Sweeney traded planes with Capt Frederick C. Bock; Sweeney flew *Bock's Car* and Bock flew *The Great Artiste*. They hit bad weather, lost contact with one of the two observing aircraft, made three bomb runs without seeing the target. They decided to bomb their secondary target, found it covered by cloud, and were running dangerously low on fuel. A hole opened in the clouds, the bomb was dropped visually, and it destroyed Nagasaki two minutes before noon on 9 August 1945.

# The Last Days

What can be added to the simple eloquence of the chalked message? The war is, indeed, over, and the long, arduous and hellish journey that began for the world in September 1939 has ended in August 1945. The Superfortresses had been in action for 14 months out of the 72 that the conflict raged. Now the dignitaries were to sign the armistice in Tokyo Bay, and there would be time for a few sightseeing flights, a show of force over the Bay, and then the island hopping eastward over the Pacific, back to the Golden Gate and San Antonio and Oconomowoc and Burlington and the Bronx. The war is over.
/ *George S. Gray Collection*

While the Japanese agonised over whether or not to surrender and under what terms, the XXI Bomber Command stayed with its mission of convincing them beyond all doubt. The day after the Hiroshima atomic attack, 124 B-29s struck the naval arsenal at Toyokawa, and 29 Superforts mined the waters of the Inland Sea. On 8 August, Yawata was fired by 221 B-29s; about 60 others bombed an aircraft plant and an arsenal in Tokyo, and 91 dropped incendiaries on Fukuyama. Nagasaki was hit by the second atomic bomb on 9 August; on the same day, 95 B-29s hammered Amagasaki's Nippon Oil refinery. On 10 August, the Superforts went back to Tokyo and pounded the arsenal with a force of 70 aircraft. That night 31 B-29s mined the Shimonoseki Strait and shipping lanes in the Inland Sea.

The last raids of the war were heavy. With a fighter escort, a force of 302 Superfortresses bombed a naval arsenal at Hikari and an army arsenal at Osaka; another unit of B-29s hammered the railroad yards at Marifu, with

108 bombing the primary target. During the night, more than 160 bombers showered Kumagaya and Isezaki with incendiaries.

The longest nonstop combat strike of the war occurred that night also, when 132 Superforts took off on a planned 3,650-mile round trip to bomb a refinery of the Nippon Oil Company. Still another group of B-29s — 39 of them — mined the Shimonoseki Strait and the Inland Sea.

'...as we taxied out, the *"Fleet Admiral Nimitz"* showed a 200-rpm magneto drop on one of two mags on one engine. When we reached the runway, a jeep drove up in front and an officer signalled "Cut engines". He climbed in and said, "Admiral Nimitz says the war is over." He had departed and I had just finished chiding my crew chief for the only time the *Nimitz* was short of perfection when another jeep arrived with, "Get going! LeMay hasn't received word that the war is over." We cranked up and took the runway knowing that if we didn't get a good power

*Above:* But the war was not over for prisoners in Japanese hands. Often their captors refused to believe the facts of surrender, refused to open the gates, refused to increase rations or add medical attention. The last great missions of the B-29s were errands of mercy, dropping food and medical supplies and clothing to prisoners of war in camps in China and Korea and Japan. Hundreds of B-29s lined up on the fields, nose to tail, to load for these flights. On Isley Field alone, this picture shows more than 117 B-29s lined up on one of Isley's two runways, waiting to be despatched to a drop at a prison camp site.
/ *Prescott Martin Collection*

*Left:* B-29s of the 58th Bomb Wing lined up to load for prisoner-of-war drops. Each airplane carried large letters under each wing, reading P. W. SUPPLIES.
/ *Ron E. Witt Collection*

check and runway speed and had to chop throttles and abort, most probably all aircraft would follow us back to the ramp, thinking that the mission was scrubbed. Thankfully, the *Nimitz* performed and we lifted off greatly relieved.

'President Truman announced the surrender during our return to Guam after dropping a full bomb load on the oil refinery at Akita on northwest Honshu the night of 14-15 August. This was the longest combat strike, 3,740 miles. We met over 300 B-29s and passed through them as they departed Tokyo leaving an inferno. All aircraft had landing lights on and (were) flying at assigned altitudes, but even so it was a bit unnerving.' *Boyd Hubbard, Jr*

The war was over, but the B-29s still had some more missions to fly. This time they dropped supplies — food, medicine, clothing — to prisoners of war in camps in China, Japan and Korea. First of the drops was made on a camp near Peking, China, on 27 August, and about 900 sorties followed during a one-month period. Long lines of B-29s, their wings marked on the undersides with large letters reading, P. W. SUPPLIES, parked on the runways for loading of palletised crates of supplies.

One of the B-29s, Z-28 from the 882nd Bomb Sqdn, 500th Bomb Grp, was on a mission to a POW camp near Konan, Korea, but the crew couldn't locate the camp after arriving in the general area. They were circling and looking when Russian Yak fighters came up and flew formation with them.

The Russian pilots appeared to be waving greetings, so the American crew waved back and continued orbiting. One of the Russian pilots pointed toward the ground and the co-pilot, Lt Robert S. Rainey, thought they had located the camp and were pointing it out. But the Russians had led the B-29 to a very small airfield, and the crew concluded that the Russians wanted them to land there. The field was too small, and there were no orders covering what to do, so they turned away and continued their search for the camp.

'At this point,' said Lt Rainey in his post-mission statement, 'The Russian fighter pilots were becoming very angry and were making all sorts of gestures with their hands, also they were raising and lowering their landing gear.'

The pilot turned the B-29 and headed for the ocean and home, and one of the fighters fired a burst ahead of the B-29's nose. The airplane commander kept his course, figuring that the Russians would leave them when they realised the B-29 was heading home. Instead, the fighter off the left wing angled in, and fired a burst into the number one

engine, starting a fire in the accessory section and the oil tank.

The airplane commander turned back toward land and ordered the crew to bail out. Six of them went, and then one of the gunners reported that the fire seemed to be dying out. The crew were ordered to stop bailing out, and to take their positions for a crash landing. The pilots set the B-29 down on the small airfield the Russians had led them to earlier.

After three days of minor difficulties and some tense moments, the crew and the airplane were released by the Russians. They later supplied a statement, written by the senior officers at Konan, dated 6 September 1945. The translation of that report identified the two as Commander of the 14th Fighter-Bomber Regiment Major Savchenko, and Assistant Commander of Operations Department of the 88th Infantry Corps Senior Lieutenant Churvin. They wrote:

'On 28 August 1945 at about 1430 Korean time, there appeared in the vicinity of the Red Army Airfield at Konan an unrecognised B-29 without signalling to the Russian aerodrome. Commanding Officer and Staff of the Red Army did not know in advance about the appearance of this B-29 in the Konan area and the fighting with the Japanese had not ceased. Due to the fact that during the war with Germany there had been American-type planes flown by German pilots that still had American markings on them, the Russians were not sure who was flying the B-29. In accordance with the above, the Commander of the 14th Fighter-Bomber Regiment ordered all measures be taken to land the B-29. Four fighters were sent aloft to land the B-29. The fighters signalled to the B-29 and pointed out the airport. The B-29 did not land, so the Russian fighters opened fire and as a result the B-29 returned to the airport at Konan and landed. All 13 men of the B-29 crew are now being quartered with a company of English soldiers at Konan. All supplies in the B-29 were received by this company of English soldiers.'

There were 154 camps known to Air Force intelligence, confining more than 63,000 prisoners. The supply effort was a necessary one, not just a gesture; the prisoners had been neglected by their captors, and only after the Japanese finally came to personal terms with the surrender did the prisoners begin to get the minimum food ration and the medical attention they so desperately needed.

And that was it. The war was over, the long process of going home began, and the B-29s began to leave the islands, one by one, heading for home, the scrapyard, the desert storage areas, or later service with a new

*Right:* An hour or so before the estimated time of arrival of the B-29s with supplies, these leaflets were dropped over the Japanese prison camps by other B-29s. They detailed the supplies to come, with items and quantities specified for packages for 50 and 500 men. And the caution: Do not overeat or overmedicate.
*/ Elmer Huhta Collection*

150

# レンゴウグンホリョヘ
# ALLIED PRISONERS

The JAPANESE Government has surrendered. You will be evacuated by ALLIED NATIONS forces as soon as possible.

Until that time your present supplies will be augmented by air-drop of U.S. food, clothing and medicines. The first drop of these items will arrive within one (1) or two (2) hours.

Clothing will be dropped in standard packs for units of 50 or 500 men. Bundle markings, contents and allowances per man are as follows:

| BUNDLE MARKINGS | | | | BUNDLE MARKINGS | | | |
|---|---|---|---|---|---|---|---|
| 50 MAN PACK | 500 MAN PACK | CONTENTS | ALLOWANCES PER MAN | 50 MAN PACK | 500 MAN PACK | CONTENTS | ALLOWANCES PER MAN |
| A | 3 | Drawers | 2 | B | 10 | Laces, shoe | 1 |
| A | 1-2 | Undershirt | 2 | A | 11 | Kit, sewing | 1 |
| B | 22 | Socks (pr) | 2 | C | 31 | Soap, toilet | 1 |
| A | 4-6 | Shirt | 1 | C | 4-6 | Razor | 1 |
| A | 7-9 | Trousers | 1 | C | 4-6 | Blades, razor | 10 |
| C | 23-30 | Jacket, field | 1 | C | 10 | Brush, tooth | 1 |
| A | 10 | Belt, web, waist | 1 | C | 31 | Paste, tooth | 1 |
| A | 11 | Capt, H.B.T. | 1 | C | 10 | Comb | 1 |
| B | 12-21 | Shoes (pr) | 1 | B | 32 | Shaving cream | 1 |
| A | 1-2 | Handkerchiefs | 3 | C | 12-21 | Powder(insecticide) | 1 |
| C | 32-34 | Towel | 1 | | | | |

There will be instructions with the food and medicine for their use and distribution.

C A U T I O N

DO NOT OVEREAT OR OVERMEDICATE                 FOLLOW DIRECTIONS

INSTRUCTIONS FOR FEEDING 100 MEN

To feed 100 men for the first three (3) days, the following blocks (individual bundles dropped) will be assembled:

**3 Blocks No. 1**
(Each Contains)

2 Cases, Soup, Can
1 Cases Fruit Juice
1 Case Accessory Pack

**1 Block No. 5**
(Each Contains)

1 Case Soup, Dehd
1 Case Veg Puree
1 Case Bouillon
1 Case Hosp Supplies
1 Case Vitamin Tablets

**1 Block No. 3**
(Each Contains)

1 Case Candy
1 Case Gum
1 Case Cigarettes
1 Case Matches

**3 Blocks No. 2**
(Each Contains)

3 Cases "C" Rations
1 Case Hosp Supplies
2 Cases Fruit

**1 Block No. 7**
(Each Contains)

1 Case Nescafe
1 Sack Sugar
1 Case Milk
1 Case Cocoa

**1 Block No. 10**
(Each Contains)

3 Cases Fruit
2 Cases Juice

This reconnaissance photo is typical of many that were taken to provide some target identification for the B-29s dropping supplies. These photos were part of the briefing folder and went with the crews aboard the planes. Marked by intelligence officers to show the camp locations, these photos became the target identifiers for drops. / *Del Shaffer Collection*

force structure then being built: Strategic Air Command.

When the war ended, 40 B-29 groups were in being and 21 of them were on station in the Pacific. Japan had surrendered, unconditionally, with about two million men still under arms, countless citizens prepared to defend suicidally every inch of their homeland, and several thousands of kamikaze airplanes held for a final strike.

Two atomic bombs, coming on top of months of fire raids and precision bombing attacks by endless streams of B-29s, had done the job. Whether or not Japan would have surrendered if the two nuclear weapons had not been dropped is an argument that will continue as long as military strategy and history are subjects for discussions and dissertations.

The fact is there. The war was over, and its end was hastened, certainly, and brought about, probably, by the bombing offensive conducted by the B-29s of the 20th Air Force.

That offensive must have seemed a long way off to the men of the 58th Bomb Wing who pioneered the introduction of a new airplane, new engines and a new armament system in combat. The experience was eloquently summarised in the 444th unit history by an anonymous writer:

'. . . only those who readied this plane and flew it can fully know the harsh pains of its birth and dangerously rapid development . . . of explosive decompression at altitude, of engine temperatures soaring above 300C, of props that refused to feather, of remote controlled turrets "cooking off" and spraying wildly, of multiplied stresses from unprecendented loads . . .

'To the men who flew these early planes they were, at the least, serious (troubles) and often fatally dangerous. They meant engine fires, perhaps consuming a wing before men could bail out, gunners "cannon-balled" from the cabin when their blister blew, planes shuddering and mushing off the runway and hugging the ground until they disappeared in the distance in their pitiful attempt to gain speed and engine cooling, ships in formation riddling each other or themselves with .50-calibre bullets . . .

'. . . at that time, the solution of these difficulties was of life and death concern to the pilots and crews who flew these planes with soaring cylinder temperatures, runaway props on takeoff, flaming and disintegrating engines with props that refused to feather in flight. During the first few months the record time before change was 100 hours, average takeoff cylinder temperatures were 290C, and four forced landings because of fire were accomplished on one day. At the end of four months in India, the ironic boast was that now it was a proven fact that a B-29 could be raised from the ground twice in one week without the aid of jacks.' *444th Bomb Group unit history*

Operating from its bases in India and advance bases in China, and in the face of formidable logistics and operational problems, the 58th Bomb Wing struck targets in Manchuria, Korea and the home islands of Japan itself. They dropped about 800 tons of bombs on Japan, a small amount in the light of the weight of the later offensive, but a substantial accomplishment considering the circumstances. As it turned out, these bombings did not seriously disrupt the Japanese war economy. But they served notice that more was to come, and they made some Japanese realise that the war was going to be lost.

The bulk of the bomber offensive started late in November 1944, with Mission San Antonio I against the Musashino plant of the Nakajima Aircraft Co. The first phase of the offensive continued through early March, and was built around the traditional concept of daylight, high-altitude precision bombing, using visual approaches, and targeted against the Japanese aircraft industry, particularly engine plants. The results were moderately successful. As one direct effect, the Japanese began a programme of plant dispersal, but never carried it out as well as they might have done., From November 1944 on, Japanese fighter production began to decrease, and the production curves skidded downward at an ever-increasing rate.

The low-level fire raids began on 9 March 1945, and in ten days destroyed four of Japan's largest cities. The B-29s flew 1,595 sorties, dropped 9,373 tons of bombs, most of them incendiaries, and destroyed — the word applies well — 31 square miles of industrial and urban area.

They shifted to a tactical support role during April and early May, 1945, to support the invasion and the subsequent fighting to capture Okinawa. Their job was to bomb tactical military objectives, often under control of Army ground forces, and including the fighter fields on Kyushu Island that were sending defending aircraft and devastating kamikaze strikes against the invasion forces.

In May the Superfortresses went back to their task of pounding Japan, flying both low-altitude fire raids and higher-altitude precision attacks, depending on the chosen targets. During May and June, they finished off the six largest cities and began going through the list of secondary targets. By 9 August, 66 urban centres had been struck, and 178 square miles of industry and urban area lay desolated.

Parallel to the last few months of these strikes against larger areas were campaigns of attacks on point targets such as oil refineries, and mine-laying in the waters and shipping lanes that served Japan. More than 12,000 mines were dropped in the Inland Sea and in well-travelled shipping lanes, and they sank almost ten per cent of all the merchant shipping tonnage lost to Japan. It was a truly remarkable accomplishment done in a very short time.

When the totals were added, the B-29s had dropped more than ninety-one per cent of all the bombs delivered against targets in the home islands of Japan: 147,000 tons out of the total of 160,800 tons dropped by all Army and Navy aircraft.

The damage done to Japan was about the same as that done to Germany, in terms of its effect on the ability of the country to continue the war. But because of the differences between Japanese and German city and factory construction, layout, protection and defences, it required only about one-ninth of the bomb tonnage dropped on Germany to do equivalent damage.

The B-29 losses were light, militarily speaking, and amounted to 1.38 per cent of all combat sorties. The B-29s flew a total of about 33,000 sorties, so that meant that more than 450 aircraft were lost, with all or part of their crews.

Japanese fighter attacks, although pressed home with determination, were light compared to the strength of the German fighter assaults by day and night against USAAF and RAF bombers over Europe. Only 11,026 fighter attacks were reported over Japan, or one for about every three sorties. Averages, of course, don't convey the real picture. Japanese fighter defences were heavy against the early raids and tapered off later in the war, so that some raids went in and out of the target area completely unopposed except by some sporadic flak.

B-29 gunners claimed 714 Japanese fighters destroyed, 456 probably destroyed, and 770 damaged. These numbers are considerably lower than the claims made in the European theatre and reflect the lighter Japanese defences.

At the end, the Japanese said it beat them. Prince Konoye, of the Japanese Royal Family, said, 'Fundamentally, the thing that brought about the determination to make peace was the prolonged bombing by the B-29s.' And Premier Suzuki said, 'I myself, on the basis of the B-29 raids, felt that the cause was hopeless.'

It was.

# Sunday Surprise

Another Sunday, another surprise attack. At dawn, 25 June 1950, the North Koreans struck across the 38th parallel. Ground forces resisted the brunt of the attack, held briefly and broke before the North Korean momentum. The call went out for immediate help, and among those that answered were the 22 Boeing B-29 Superfortresses in the Far East. They had been sitting in revetments at Anderson AFB, Guam, leftovers from World War 2, nearing the end of their service lives. Now reclassified as 'medium' bombers, they made up the strategic force within Far East Air Forces (FEAF).

'Korea was the swan song for the B-29s, and they were really too old for that war. Our worst enemy was the engine, and after that those old World War 2 airplanes. We lost more in training than we did in combat.

'We lost them in collisions. The problem was that a lot of our aircraft commanders were wartime co-pilots who had been recalled. All of a sudden, this kid finds himself flying a four-engined aircraft, and he has trouble hacking it. Weather flying was rough on them; they hadn't had much experience, and they'd lose control in turbulence.

'The problems of maintenance were also tougher. The airplanes were older, the flight crews didn't baby them, and the ground crews had to work on them in open docks, out in the heat and rain and all the extremes of Okinawan weather. The ground crews lived in tents, and so they didn't have much opportunity for relief from the weather during their off-duty hours.

'The maintenance crews were great, though, and they did one hell of a great job.'
*Robert F. Goldsworthy, deputy commander, 307th Bomb Wing, 2nd Air Force*

There was one other B-29 unit in the theatre, the 31st Photo Reconnaissance Squadron (Very Long Range), equipped with six RB-29s and based at Kadena Air Base, Okinawa. There were 24 weather reconnaissance WB-29s in FEAF, and four 'Superdumbo' search and rescue SB-29 aircraft.

The 19th Bomb Group moved from Guam to Kadena, ordered by 20th Air Force Headquarters to strike against targets of opportunity such as assemblies of tanks, artillery, or troops. On 28 June, four B-29s flew their first combat mission of the Korean war. Two searched the parallel rail and road lines between Seoul and Kapyong, and the other two scanned the line between Seoul and Uijongbu. They dropped bombs on anything that seemed to be a worthwhile target.

The next day nine Superforts bombed Kimpo airfield, dropping 260lb fragmentation bombs from altitudes as low as

'Somewhere over Korea' says the official caption in the usual vague identification of wartime photos. She's an RB-29A-45-BN, serial 44-61727, operating with what was then the 31st Strategic Reconnaissance Squadron, later redesignated the 91st SRS, of the 15th Air Force. She carries at least 45 photo mission markers on her nose. / USAF 82168 A.C.

GREASE RACK
LUBE JOBS BY APPOINTMENT ONLY
FLATS FIXED-OIL CHANGED-BATTERIES
CHECKED WHEEL ALIGNING-BRAKE SERV
-ICE-IGNITION+ELECTRICAL-FLAK HOLES
PATCHED-BROKEN AIR PLANES FIXED
ALL WORK GUARANTEED TO END OF
RUNWAY        HAVE FAITH

SUPER SERVICE - 8 BLOCKS
DUE EAST   GAS, OIL AND MINOR
                    REPAIRS

*Left:* The maintenance hangars at Yokota were enlivened by pin-up calendars, the nose art of aircraft in the docks, and by signs such as this one. / *William F. Dawson*

*Below:* OK, so 'damn' is spelled wrong; the sentiment is what counts. The crew chiefs erected this sign over the entrance to their lounge. / *William F. Dawson*

*Bottom:* Distorted by the plastic sighting blister, this photo shows the main runway at Yokota and the hardstand areas for the B-29s. At least 34 B-29s are visible. / *William F. Dawson*

3,000 feet. They were jumped by three Red fighters; the B-29 gunners shot down one, damaged another. Two other B-29s bombed the main railroad station at Seoul.

Fifteen bombers hit enemy troops and landing craft on the north bank of the Han River on 30 June. Ten B-29s struck Yonpo airfield on 2 July, after reports of a heavy concentration of aircraft at that enemy-held base had been received. Loaded with fragmentation bombs, the Superforts roared over Yonpo, counted 16 airplanes, dropped, and destroyed none at all.

The next day, Gen Hoyt S. Vandenberg, USAF Chief of Staff, moved the 22nd and 92nd Bomb Wings (Medium) from Strategic Air Command to temporary duty with FEAF. And on 8 July, FEAF organised its own Bomber Command (Provisional), headed by Maj Gen Emmett O'Donnell, Jr, a long-time bomber commander and leader of the 73rd Bomb Wing in the Marianas during World War 2. 'Rosey' got his orders: work in the area north of the Han River, and destroy North Korean industry. It was the standard strategic bombing mission and one that O'Donnell and the B-29s were best able to handle.

But the ground forces were in desperate straits, and the B-29s were first thrown into the battle to support them. They dropped on targets of opportunity around the battlefield area and behind the lines, doing what fighter-bombers would probably do better. They stood it for about nine days, and on 18 July, Lt Gen George C. Stratemeyer, who was Gen Douglas MacArthur's top air commander in the Far East, told MacArthur that it was not the way to run a strategic bombing effort, and no way to use the B-29s.

MacArthur agreed, and issued orders for the B-29s to concentrate in the area between the bombline and the 38th parallel, with the idea of isolating the battlefield. The target list they were given was terrible; some of the targets

THROUGH THESE DOORS PASS THE BEST DAM
AIRMEN    IN THE AIR FORCE

CREW CHIEFs LOUNGE

didn't exist, and others were misnamed or mislocated. It was World War 2 and Japan all over again, complained one bomber commander.

MacArthur had, in effect, only changed the task of the B-29s from one of close support to one of interdiction. FEAF wanted to get on with the campaign of strategic bombing. The exigencies of the Korean War demanded that both be done simultaneously.

So Gen Vandenberg offered to send two more B-29s groups to the war, if they would be used solely against strategic targets. MacArthur agreed, and the 98th and 307th Bomb Groups were ordered to make the move.

There was only a handful of strategic targets in North Korea. Five major industrial areas were identified, with a few others of secondary importance. One was ruled off-limits for political reasons; it was too near the Manchurian border, and dropping on the wrong side might kick off a war.

By 27 September the strategic campaign was completed. Any target worth hitting had been pounded into ruins. It had taken just over a month, and 'Rosey' O'Donnell could report to FEAF that Bomber Command had run out of targets to destroy.

The Superfortresses had flown 3,159 sorties against the strategic Korean targets. The 18 available specific targets had been hammered into ruins. One Superfortress had been lost during the campaign.

'Our first mission to Korea was disastrous. At the assembly point over the Sea of Japan, our flight commander got a call that one of the aircraft had lost an engine. The commander told him to leave the formation and head back, and to jettison his bombs after leaving the formation.

'The pilot acknowledged, and said he was dropping them in train. In a few seconds he reported that some of the bombs had hung up, and they were going to try again for release using the intervalometer (for automatic timed release in succession). They were still hung up after he tried that, and so he called again to say that he would hit the salvo switch. (Salvo means to drop the entire load of bombs simultaneously.)

'As the bombs left the bay, two of them hit together, detonated, and blew up the airplane.

'We were still using bombs left over from World War 2, and the RDX explosive was unstable after five years. Nobody bothered to tell us, and we lost a fine crew that way.'
*Vern Piotter, navigator, 92nd Bomb Wing*

But the interdiction campaign never stopped. One of its major features was bridge-busting, certainly a tough mission to fly successfully. Bridges are long, narrow targets and are hard to hit. The North Koreans repaired them within hours after they were hit, or built another one upstream or down, or ran a ferry across instead.

Many of the Korean bridges had been built to modern standards from steel and concrete by the Japanese during their long occupation of the country. They had built them with solid footings and abutments that resisted near misses.

The B-29s evolved a simple tactical approach. They formed a bomber stream at about 10,000 feet, and flew toward the bridge at a 40-degree angle to its span. Each B-29 triggered off four bombs on a single run. There was little or no opposition; they had all the time in the world to get stabilised on the bomb run. No fighters hassled them during this early stage of the war.

Later statistics showed that it took more than 13 runs to destroy each bridge, using 500lb bombs that were the accepted standard for the job. Heavier bombs should have been used, but the bombing problem was complicated by the fact that the crews had to

Aircraft 9894, carrying the Circle H and the insignia of the 98th Bomb Wing, and the insignia of the 343rd Bomb Squadron, stands in its parking area at Yokota Air Base, Japan. / *William F. Dawson*

A trio of B-29s from the 98th Bomb Wing, photographed from the gunner's blister of a fourth, fly formation into North Korea on a combat strike. / William F. Dawson

load their own bombs and never knew quite what missions they would be flying in time to plan a load. Further, not all the B-29s had bomb racks for the heavier bombs. Only the 19th Bomb Group was equipped to load and carry the 2,000lb bombs that would have made an impression on any bridge.

Even so, by the end of the first interdiction campaign, O'Donnell reported that the B-29s had destroyed 37 of the 44 bridges they had been assigned as targets only a month earlier. The remaining seven were useless for carrying heavy traffic.

'Itazuki, Japan, has the best hot baths in the world. There's an auxiliary strip there and if you got into trouble in Korea, you would declare an emergency and go into Itazuki.

'One time I was coming back from a bridge-busting mission at Sinan-ju and I had an engine fire. Well, I thought of that old saying, "In 30 seconds, either it goes out or I do!" But we were over North Korea, and I had been a prisoner of war once in Japan and I didn't really want to do that again. So I stayed with it, encouraged because I could see the battle lines ahead.

'That fire in number four kept burning, and I couldn't feather the prop and I'd already pulled the fire extinguisher to no effect, and we were still over enemy territory. So I sweated that one out and — believe me — just as we crossed the battle line into our own area the fire went out, all by itself. The prop was windmilling, and so I called Itazuki, declared an emergency and we made the strip on three engines.

'And we all needed those hot baths that night!' *Robert F. Goldsworthy*

'Those of us who were based on Okinawa envied the 98th Bomb Wing. They were stationed at Itazuki, Japan, and that was the lap of luxury. They had fresh milk, fresh eggs, fresh women. So when we were coming back from a mission, we'd think of any excuse we could to put in at Itazuki — engine trouble, radio trouble, whatever — just to get some decent food like fresh eggs and bacon.

'Old Tex would get on the intercom and say, "Engineer! We're thirty minutes out of Itazuki; time to feather number four!" So I'd feather an engine, and he'd call Itazuki to report engine trouble. We'd go in, land, have a great breakfast, and then fly back to Okinawa, where the food was lousy'. *E. L. Davis*

The 19th Bomb Group, with its capability to carry 2,000lb bombs, was assigned a steel railway bridge on the line at Seoul. For almost one month, the 19th mounted strike after strike against the bridge, using 1,000- and 2,000lb bombs, and even in desperation some 4,000lb bombs. The decking was blown to bits time and time again, but the bridge still stood.

The Japanese firm that built the bridge furnished its original drawings to try to help solve the problem. The 19th changed fuse settings, hoping to damage the superstructure if they couldn't knock out the footings. Still the bridge stood.

Gen MacArthur said he'd commend any air crew that knocked it out, and Gen Stratemeyer quietly promised a case of Scotch to the crew that did the job.

On 19 August, the 'elastic bridge' finally met its doom. The 19th sent in nine of its bombers, carrying six tons each of 1,000lb bombs. They dropped them from their trail formation, and reported hits. 'We'll finish it off tomorrow', they promised. Soon after,

B-361, a B-29 from the
98th Bomb Wing.
/ *William F. Dawson*

Navy pilots from Task Force 77 came in on the bridge with a mix of 37 Vought Corsairs and Douglas Skyraiders. They dive-bombed the bridge, scoring eight times. After the attack, one Navy plane peeled off, and roared along the bridge to check it for damage. He reported that it was still standing, but useless for some time to come.

On 20 August the 19th Bomb Group returned to the target, thinking to finish it off. They were surprised to see that two spans of the bridge were in the water, evidently having fallen during the night. But they bombed the bridge anyway, and had the satisfaction of seeing a third span drop into the river.

The 19th Bomb Group and the Navy's Air Group 11 both received a trophy from Gen MacArthur, and Gen Stratemeyer bought two cases of Scotch instead of one.

By September, the fortunes of the United Nations forces in Korea had changed for the better. They were driving the North Koreans north faster than the Reds had advanced south. Some of the crack NK units were at the edge of panic in their headlong retreat.

There were no more strategic targets; there was little point in maintaining the total strength of Bomber Command. Near the end of October 1950, the 22nd and 92nd Bomb Groups were sent home. On the 27th of the month, FEAF disbanded Bomber Command.

And for three days, things were quiet. Then it was like 25 June all over again as the Chinese volunteers boiled up out of their airfields on 1 November, flying their MiGs out of the privileged areas on their side of the Yalu, and following these strikes with a major ground assault on the night of 2 November.

The mood changed abruptly at Bomber Command. It was a new contest, and the old

rules were no longer in use. The political restrictions that had banned the use of incendiary bombs in earlier strikes at strategic targets were rescinded. Bomber Command's B-29s were loaded with fire bombs, just as they had been six years earlier, and they headed north. They flew almost continuously for two weeks, burning the heart out of North Korean cities. MacArthur told them to start at the Yalu and work south, and to bomb anything that even resembled a strategic objective. They obeyed the orders.

'Mission day was a big day at Kadena. It was like the day of the big game when I was playing high-school football; there was excitement in the air, and it never changed the whole time I was there. It was hard to eat breakfast.

'Our wing — the 307th — flew every third day, in a mission rotation with the other wings out there. We had three squadrons, and we'd put up a total of 15 to 20 aircraft from all three squadrons. We flew mostly night missions, leaving Okinawa to arrive over the target at moonrise or moonset for visual bombing. It was sometimes a six-hour ride, sometimes a ten-hour haul. We never flew straight to the target, always went on a diversionary approach.

'With a late evening take-off, the day started early in the morning for the ground crews. They had to load the fuel, bombs and ammo, check the systems, and all that. Assuming we had an 1800 take-off, I'd get to the airplane about 1500. The bombs were loaded by then, and there were only radio people and probably ordnance people around.

'We were parked on hardstands in revetments, and I'd go to the airplane with the crew chief, crank up the external power

159

unit, and plug it in. Then we'd do a walkround. It was a standing gag that the B-29 was the only airplane in the Air Force with externally lubricated engines, and the only thing we worried about on the walkround was that we wanted to make sure the oil wasn't pouring out on the ground. Anything less was acceptable.

'Then I'd get into the airplane, with a mechanic or somebody to help run the checks. The inside smelled like a locker room; it was hot on Okinawa and humid besides, and the planes were closed up between missions. They got kind of gamy after a while. So I'd get into the flight engineer's seat and get out the check lists. The mechanic would sit in the pilot's seat and hold pressure on the wheel brakes.

'He'd keep an eye outside and yell, "Clear three!" and I'd engage the starter switch. We turned the engine over with the starter, and the guys standing fire guard on the ground would count the blades as they went through. When the count got to eight, I'd hit the ignition switch, shove the mixture control up over the hump, and open the throttle. The engine would catch as the throttle came up to idle.

'Then I'd wait for the oil pressure and cylinder head temperatures to come up and stabilise, and when we'd gotten all four engines started and idling in a stable condition, we'd do a prop check on all four props, running them into low blade angle. That had to be done by the guy in the pilot's seat, because I had no prop controls at my position. We checked the rpm drop with the blade angle change, reported the prop check at 2,100rpm, checked the feathering, again from the cockpit rather than from my position. After a mag check at 2,750rpm, I'd run all four engines up to full power, and the old B-29 would be sitting there jumping,

with the nose gear bouncing, just wanting to go.

'After the briefings, we'd all go down to the aircraft, lay our flight gear on a canvas mat and stand an inspection by the aircraft commander. Both the pilot and I would follow that with a final walkaround of the airplane, and then we'd climb aboard. The armourers would come out to the plane, pull all the arming wires on the bombs, and we'd close the bomb bay doors, ready to go. The pilot would make an interphone check of all the crew positions, and we'd start the engines.

'We got individual taxi clearances from the tower, and we'd lumber out toward the runway, holding nose-to-tail while we were waiting for take-off. We were cleared for take-off at 30-second intervals, and we'd have three aircraft on the runway at once, one flying, one rolling, one holding.

'We'd have a final crew check at the end of the runway, and run her up to full power. The B-29 was just roaring and stomping and grunting and groaning, and the pilot would release the brakes and we'd go charging off into the sunset. I don't remember the length of the runway at Okinawa, but I do remember that I never thought it was long enough.

'There was just one runway at Kadena; one end ran straight into some mountains and the other was straight into the ocean. Every combat mission took off toward the ocean, because a loaded B-29 never stood a chance of making it the other direction. Our normal combat load was forty 500lb bombs, full fuel, all the gun turrets loaded with ammo, and nine or ten crew members loaded with flak vests, flak helmets, and as many flak curtains as we could scrounge.

'We taxied out one evening bound for North Korea with a brand-new 1st Lieutenant co-pilot. It was a hot night, and

*Above:* Engine start on a B-29 of the 370th Bomb Squadron, 307th Bomb Wing. / *E. L. Davis Collection*

*Above right:* 'With all four engines running up to power, the old B-29 would just bounce and buck and shake, like she had to move'. This B-29 of the 370th BS, 307th BW, is getting a power check well before the scheduled departure of a mission. Her bomb load has been stacked at the edge of the hardstand. / *E. L. Davis Collection*

*Right:* Salvoing both bomb bay loads at once, this B-29 of the 98th Bomb Wing drops demolition bombs on a North Korean target during a mission on 13 July 1951. / *USAF 80340 A.C.*

we were going to use every inch of runway and more getting off. The co-pilot's job on take-off consisted of handling the radios, holding the control column forward, and calling out airspeeds. With the turbosuperchargers on, and the old R-3350 throttles to the firewall, we might — if we were lucky — be able to pull 60 inches manifold pressure on the roll.

'When the brakes released on the old bird, it was like pulling your foot out of a gluepot. The running joke was, "Everybody stand up; it'll make it lighter!" Down the runway we go with the airspeed indicator moving like the hour hand on a Mickey Mouse watch. When we got to the point where we had better think pretty seriously about flying, our co-pilot comes on the interphone with, "The manifold pressure on number three is dropping! Abort! Abort!"

'Not another word was said. I had the throttles locked forward to the firewall with my feet. Well, we managed to get off, as I knew we would, because nobody was looking forward to a swim in the China Sea. After we got the gear up and the climb established, the pilot, ol' Tex, tossed his headset back to me and said, "Engineer! Get me another headset, will you? I can't hear a damned thing out of that one!"

'At climb power it took more than an hour to get to cruise altitude, depending on the load, and so we were off to North Korea and the flak and the MiGs. If we had loaded 2,000lb bombs, we knew that it was going to be a rough, sweaty mission because we were after something big.

'I was scared to death, but I relished it, thought about it, enjoyed it, because I thought we were accomplishing something. I felt pride, fellowship; it made me feel good to do it. But I was scared.' *E. L. Davis, flight engineer, 307th Bomb Wing*

This January 1951 mission photo is one of the classic pictures of the Korean conflict. Three B-29s of the 98th Bomb Wing have triggered their loads almost simultaneously, and the demolition bombs drop in a seemingly endless stream toward the target below.
/ USAF 80327 A.C.

Air superiority in the north was held by the Chinese MiGs and they proved the point time and time again. The B-29 missions were flown with fighter escort. When the big and little friends missed connections, disaster resulted. The 98th Bomb Group arrived late one day for a rendezvous, and their 18 B-29s had to make the run unescorted. Nine MiGs bounced them, damaging ten of the 18 bombers severely, three so badly that they had to make emergency landings at Taegu, in Korea, instead of making the trip back to base.

On 12 April, 1951, 39 B-29s struck the bridges at Sinui-ju on the Yalu, under an escort of high cover and screening fighters. No matter; the MiGs boiled through the formation, fought through the screen, shot down two of the B-29s and hammered six badly. That did it. Those losses were prohibitive, and the B-29 strikes in that area were called off.

'Day raids were discouraging in Korea. The MiGs got eight out of nine B-29s from the 307th Wing on what was to be their last daytime raid. After that, it was night time work, and — other than worrying about intense flak — you just hoped the airplane kept on running. That was your biggest danger.

'We went in on the target in a bomber stream, with the planes about two minutes apart. After a couple of these, the North Koreans started vectoring MiGs up towards us, and they'd get in trail with us and sit there. We could see them more easily than they could see us, because their jet exhaust was a lot brighter than the piston-engine exhaust on the B-29s.

'Anyway, gunners would call in and say, "I've got one right in my sights! Can I fire?", and we'd have to say that they couldn't. The worst thing we could have done was to fire

on a MiG at night, because that would reveal our position as well as if we'd turned on the lights. With a pair of them out there, they were hoping that one would draw our fire and the other could then shoot us down. So we had a lot of frustrated gunners who never shot at anything.

'The jet stream was the big problem in Japan during World War 2, but it wasn't a problem in Korea because we were bombing between 18,000 and 25,000 feet, well below the jet stream effective altitudes. What we did have to contend with was the contrail problem. The North Koreans — or whoever it was fighting with them — would pick up our contrails at night with their searchlights. It was easy; all they did was aim the lights generally upwards and they were bound to pick up some contrails. They then traced them back to the airplane, and vectored fighters in using the contrails as telltales.

'The command level dictated the bombing altitudes to try to avoid contrails, based on forecasts from Tokyo weather central. We also got some information from weather soundings in Russia'. *Robert F. Goldsworthy*

'Those missions were long. We were doing maybe 12-hour missions in Korea. We used a lot of benzedrine, taking it just after take-off which was generally just before dark. Then we'd fly all night, come back in the morning, get our mission whisky, and take a sleeping pill. That was it, alternating benzedrine and benadryl. Sometimes I'd sleep all day and into the night, and right through the night into the next day. Luckily, we didn't fly every day.' *Vern Piotter*

Change was constant in the Korean war, and the USAF F-86 Sabres began to shoulder the fighter load. They swept into combat and seized control of the sky from the MiGs. The B-29s came out of their revetments and

headed north again, and in April pounded all the North Korean airfields, denying their use to enemy MiGs for forward operations.

Bridge-busting continued to get tougher as the war dragged on. Red flak and fighters combined to limit the bombers to a single run at altitudes above 20,000 feet. Bomber Command changed its tactics, and struck the bridges from a formation of four B-29s, coming in at an angle less than the 40-degree standard set earlier in the war. Both the 98th and 307th Bomb Group's B-29s were retrofitted with the racks that could handle 2,000lb bombs.

But their real hope was the radio-controlled bomb. The 19th Bomb Group had experimented with Razon bomb (Range and AZimuth ONly) in the summer of 1950. It was a weapon left over from the closing days of World War 2. Controlled by a direct radio link, the bomb could be corrected in range and azimuth by the bombardier.

The 19th Bomb Group knocked out about 15 bridges that way, but they really wanted the newer and bigger — and supposedly better — Tarzon bombs.

'We had three B-29s that had been modified and equipped to drop Tarzon bombs. They were 12,000lb bombs that had a special fin assembly with control surfaces that could be actuated from the drop plane. The bombardier was supposed to be able to track the bomb after the drop by a burning flare in the tail section, and to steer it in azimuth and range to correct for any ballistic problems.

'The modified B-29s had the bomb bays cut away partially, and they carried the bomb so that two-thirds of it was housed in the airplane, and about one-third stuck outside. The bomb reduced the ground clearance considerably, and so the planes were loaded in a special revetment that had a pit to increase the clearance for convenience in loading and adjusting.

'The whole effort was classified Top Secret, we were told. There was a special weapons loading team that was the only crew allowed to approach the airplane during the loading phase, and it seemed like they took days to get the airplane ready for a drop. They went through a long ritual of levelling the aircraft before they slung the bomb in place. They used special bomb dollies, and they raised the bomb into position, rather than hoisting it in as was done with the smaller conventional bombs.

'A lot of the details have faded, and so have some of the names. But I can't forget the name of Payne Jennings, Colonel, United States Air Force, Strategic Air Command. He was, in many ways, a very likeable guy, but he was also very gung-ho, and gave the impression that he was out to win the war single-handed.

'One of his pet projects was the Tarzon bomb, and he flew several missions with crews on Tarzon drops. We had an aircraft commander in my squadron who was very professional, and very good, and Payne Jennings elected to ride with him on a Tarzon mission.

'They took off and were well along toward Korea when they radioed back that they were having some trouble with an engine. Now the rule was that if an engine gave you trouble with Tarzon aboard, you jettisoned the bomb and came back home. If you didn't, you wouldn't get home. You were carrying a 12,000lb bomb, and that was not a job for three engines.

'Well, they lost the engine, but they radioed that Colonel Jennings had ordered that they press on to the target and that's what they were doing. A short time later they lost a second engine, probably because they had to increase power to stay in the air

B-29s from the 92nd Bomb Wing drop on targets in Korea. The Circle W was the wing identification for the 505th BW in World War 2. That Group was de-activated in June 1946, and its letter became available for use with the 92nd at a later date and in another war.
/ USAF via Boeing

on three, and the second engine couldn't take the stress. But they said they were continuing to Korea, and that's the last word we ever heard from the crew.

'Everybody was convinced that they finally had to ditch — they just ran out of altitude — and that the plane and crew were lost in the ditching. But even at that, some of us believed that Colonel Payne Jennings was somewhere out in the China Sea, astride that Tarzon bomb, paddling like mad for Korea.'
*W. B. Leake, armament chief, 93rd Bomb Sqdn, 19th Bomb Group*

A similar accident that was observed later, again involving a heavily loaded B-29 with a Tarzon bomb, showed that the bomb could not be jettisoned 'safe'. The tail assembly ripped off on impact with the water, and simultaneously armed and detonated the bomb.

The loss of Col Jennings and the crew was attributed to an attempt to jettison the Tarzon bomb in the last few seconds before ditching, rather than as soon as the trouble developed. The bomb probably blew up on hitting the water, destroying the B-29 and killing the crew.

Tarzon bombing was one attempt to advance the art — or science, for the bombardiers among the readers — of free-fall ballistic bombing. Two other techniques were used in Korea.

One was ground-directed drops, using pre-surveyed radar stations on the ground. These accurately sited points located, tracked and directed the bombers on their bomb runs. It resulted in precision bombing at night, something that the bombing radars of the day could not guarantee. Many of these missions were flown in support of ground troops, because the B-29s were able to saturate a small area with the drop. They used 500lb fragmentation bombs with the fuses set for air bursts, and each bomb covered an area about 150 yards in diameter when it blew. On occasion, the B-29s dropped as close as 400 yards to the UN front lines.

The other technique was the Shoran drop. Shoran — for short-range navigation — had been developed during World War 2, along with Loran — long-range navigation — but both were orginally only navigation techniques. These systems transmitted an electronic grid in the sky, in effect, and equipment on board the B-29s could read the transmissions and compute a position very accurately. The same system could be used to drop bombs, and by mid-1951 the Shoran-guided drop was routine in Korea.

The enemy was hurting, and mid-1951 saw their first attempt to arrange truce talks. By the time the truce talks broke down, in August 1951, the Reds had licked their wounds, devised some new tactics and were ready to sally forth to battle. Their sudden and strong assault gave them control of the air again, and FEAF stopped all fighter-bomber strikes against the Yalu area as too risky.

The Reds took advantage of the truce break to start rehabilitation of their airfields, looking towards their use as forward bases for the MiGs. The B-29s went into action against those bases, getting away cleanly on their first strike on 18 October 1951. But the MiGs were there to meet them the next time, and on the third mission. In one week, Bomber Command lost five B-29s, as many as they had lost in the entire war to date.

Further daylight missions were scrapped as Bomber Command began night raids again. The NK countered with radar-directed searchlights, night fighters and an airborne battle commander, who orbited above the bomber stream and co-ordinated the MiG attacks. Glossy black lacquer was applied to the B-29 bellies to cut down their visibility in the searchlight beams, a trick learned in World War 2 and forgotten or filed. Countermeasures — the 'porcupine' missions of World War 2 — were revived to confuse enemy radars.

On 30 September, a combined force of B-29s and Douglas B-26s struck the Namsan-ni Chemical Plant on the Yalu River. First, three B-29s went in on a flak-suppression strike, bombing known positions with air-burst bombs. Equipped with electronic

countermeasures gear, that trio then continued to fly above the target area and used their ECM to confuse, decoy and jam enemy radars. The B-26s went in low to hit the searchlights, one of their specialised attack routines. The main force of 45 B-29s came in next, made a Shoran drop, and clobbered the factory. That was the end of the last strategic target of any importance in the North.

A ten-day sustained air attack followed the strike at Namsan-ni, using Shoran for most of the drops and proving, as was found out later, that more Shoran training was necessary. New tactics evolved. The bomber stream was compressed to reduce the time gap between successive airplanes to one minute. The 91st Strategic Reconnaissance Squadron (formerly the 31st Photo Reconnaissance Squadron) flew its first 'ferret' missions to locate, monitor and analyse enemy radars. Marine night fighters operated with the B-29s in a barrier screen ahead of the main bomber stream, then added a top cover for the time on the bomb run from initial point to bombs away. Bombing altitudes were chosen carefully to avoid telltale contrail formation. Attacks were scheduled at irregular times and when the moon was dark. USAF Lockheed F-94 night fighters joined the attack, flying the barrier screen and leaving the Marine night fighters free to fly the top cover mission.

Scientific analysis of bombing began about then, and the B-29 missions were studied and restudied. From December 1952 to May 1953, the combat effectiveness of Bomber Command nearly doubled. But the war dragged on only a few more weeks. On 17 July 1953, RB-29s of the 91st SRS flew the last mission for Bomber Command, a drop of psychological warefare leaflets.

The B-29s had fought for 37 months, and had been in action on all but 26 of those days. More than 21,000 bombing sorties were logged, compared to 33,000 in World War 2, and the total bomb weight dropped exceeded 167,000 tons, compared to 147,000 tons dropped on Japan by B-29s in World War 2.

During one period from 13 July to 31 October 1950, which included the strategic bombing campaign, B-29s dropped 30,130 tons of bombs. It was a monthly average tonnage greater than the peak performance of the B-29s in World War 2. And in that earlier war, the planes were new, and maintenance was far simpler.

Bomber Command's authorised strength never exceeded 99 Superfortresses. The combat losses totalled 34: 16 lost to enemy fighters, four to enemy flak, and 14 to 'other causes'.

The B-29s in Korea were flown longer and harder and dropped more bombs, than were the B-29s in World War 2. It was an outstanding performance record for a comparative handful of planes, and it was achieved under some fairly bad conditions. Not all the bases had hot baths.

B-29s of the 92nd Bomb Wing on the high road to a target in North Korea. / *USAF via Boeing*

First Lieutenant Charles A. Stone was aircraft commander of 022, an RB-29 assigned to the 91 Strategic Reconnaissance Squadron and based as Yokota Air Base, Japan. During the Korean war, Lt Stone's crew flew reconnaissance missions above North Korea during a tour of duty that lasted from 23 October 1953 to 18 July 1954.

Stone was a good amateur photographer and he took these pictures — with the one obvious exception — of his crew during one of their missions. They were made available by Jim Cliver, then an Airman First Class and flight engineer on *Old Double Deuce*.

The crew wore baseball-style flight caps, almost covered with markings. Each man has his home state named on the visor of the cap. Over his left temple was the Circle X identifier of the 91st SRS, with the unit written out next to it. Proceeding around the cap, the next item was a red silhouette of a B-29, then his nickname at the back. Next to that was a cutout white silhouette of his home state. His name in Japanese characters was on the right temple. On the top of the hat was the base: Yokota AFB, Japan. And on Jim Cliver's cap, which is lying on the writer's desk at this moment, the top was further emblazoned with his wife's name — Coldine — and his first child, a daughter, Diane. At the front of the cap, above the visor, were the initials FE for his position of flight engineer.

Other crewmen had similar caps with different details.

*Above:* The aircraft commander, the old man, the skipper, 1st Lt Charles A. Stone, talking, listening, looking ahead and driving the airplane simultaneously.

*Far left:* 2nd Lt M. N. Hahn digs into canned rations on the long flight from Yokota. He's pilot of *Double Deuce*, flying from the right seat and — sometimes — being allowed to make the landing.

*Left:* SAC cigar tilted at a jaunty angle, 1st Lt Brackbill, the navigator, studies his charts.

166

*Above left:* 2nd Lt J. Jackson, from Louisiana, was radar operator on 022, back in the dark among the scopes, knobs and dials, making sense out of aimless squiggles on screens and weird sounds in the headphones.

*Above centre:* Airman Second Class Don Barnhart was radio operator, and he's out of uniform; his unadorned flight cap is standard unmodified issue.

*Above:* Four sets of everything confront the flight engineer, Airman First Class Jim Cliver. Cruise control is only one aspect of his job; he also must know how the pressurising system works, what that funny noise is when the wheels retract, and why isn't this damned thing working?

*Far left:* Airman Second Class Glowcheski, the left gunner.

*Left:* 1st Lt Weisburn, the bombardier, doesn't have all that much to do on a reconnaissance flight, so he often stands, hunched over, in the gap between the instrument panels and talks with Stone and Hahn. 'How the hell can you eat that stuff, Hahn?'

*Right:* Tail gunner Farley, Airman Second Class, is dressed for a long, lonely, cold ride back in the tail of the RB-29.

*Far right:* 'Hey, Sniker!' And Airman First Class Sniker, CFC gunner for *Double Deuce*, looks toward Lt Stone and the camera.

*Below:* Suited, chuted and harnessed, right gunner Airman Second Class Kleincuff backs into Korea. He's from Nebraska, and the patchwork farmland below doesn't remind him one little bit of the square-mile farms of his home state. Or of Omaha, either.

*Below left:* Lt Stone briefs the crew and inspects them before leaving on a mission over Korea. In the background is *Old Double Deuce*, the RB-29 that this crew called home for long hours at a stretch.

On 10 December 1951, Sgt William F. Dawson, then a left gunner in the 343rd Bomb Squadron, 98th Bomb Wing, left the United States aboard a DC-4 transport operated by the Flying Tiger Line. He ended his trip at Yokota Air Base, Japan, after stops at Honolulu and Wake Island. Eight days later, he was aboard *Sad Sac*, a B-29 of the 343rd BS, Capt Anthony H. Carson commanding, and they were dropping propaganda leaflets along the East coast of Korea.

Dawson completed his tour of duty in the Far East in May, 1953. During the period of his combat duty, he spent spare time photographing much of the ground activity that prepared the B-29s for their missions. All the photos shown here are from his collection, most of them taken by Dawson himself.

*Above:* Well, the first thing we gotta do is open up the accessory section panel. The mechanic on the maintenance stand is doing just that. Flow lines on the propeller blade seem to indicate trouble with the governor mechanism that would produce the leak at the hub.

*Centre left:* There's just no other way to get at the parts I need to get at! So the tail gunner goes in the turret himself, working on his twin fifties before the mission goes.

*Bottom left:* If I get a shot at any MiGs, I want to make damn sure these guns are gonna work. Before the missions, gunners load their turrets, check the gun barrels and clean or swab them with gun oil as needed.

169

*Above:* 'Sometimes we'd carry an extra pilot, or an ECM operator, or even a passenger who was observing the mission, so that's why you see twelve guys here in the crew lineup. That's Captain Carson in front, and I'm third from the right.'

*Above left:* 'Before the mission, we'd all line our gear up on a canvas mat spread out near the nose of the ship, so Capt Carson could inspect it all at the same time he inspected us.'

*Far left:* 'We're about ready to go. That's the flight engineer, figuring out how we're going to do on the fuel he's got aboard. The guns have been loaded; you can tell, because the top turret guns are pointing up in the air and the belly turret guns are pointing straight down at the ground.'

*Left:* 'That's Dupper — Cpl. H. H. Dupper — and we spent a lot of time together in the back of the B-29, sitting across the fuselage from each other. He was the right gunner and I was the left gunner.'

*Right:* 'And that's the right side of *Sad Sac*, aircraft 1676, the first one I flew in, in Korea. The 'Couldn't Care Less' on the left side was the insignia of the 343rd Bomb Squadron. I don't think it was ever the official insignia.'

# Bridge-busting in Korea

Korea's railroad system was extensive, modern and well-operated, and was probably the best in Asia at the time. It was the prime mover of people and goods in that country, both north and south of the 38th Parallel.

When the North Koreans went to war, the railroad system in that part of the country was the lifeline for their advancing forces. Only later did the famous A-frame backpacking porters become important for supply. Trucks and bicycles also later took up the transportation task as more and more bombing missions hammered the railroads into twisted rails and splintered ties.

Bridge-busting is essentially an interdiction mission, to strangle enemy troops by cutting off their main supply routes. It is not considered as a strategic mission in the classical studies of the application of airpower, yet, in the Korean conflict, strategy depended on the destruction of these railroad bridges. Bomber Command went out to hit them and to try to keep them destroyed by successive strikes on the same target bridges, rebuilt or bypassed by the energetic and tireless North Koreans.

All of the strike photos shown here were loaned by William F. Dawson, then a left gunner in the 343rd Bomb Squadron, 98th Bomb Wing.

*Right:* The modest claim of the 343rd Bomb Squadron — Bomber Command's best bridge-busters — was proclaimed on this sign at the entrance to their area at Yokota Air Base. / *William F. Dawson*

*Below:* The big raid of 25 March 1952, despatched B-29s from the 19th Bomb Group, and the 98th and 307th Bomb Wings against the railroad bridge at Pyongyang. The target was the mid-span point, and the bomber stream came in at an 18-degree angle with the bridge. Considerable damage was done, and the spans across both branches of the river were cut in several places for long distances.

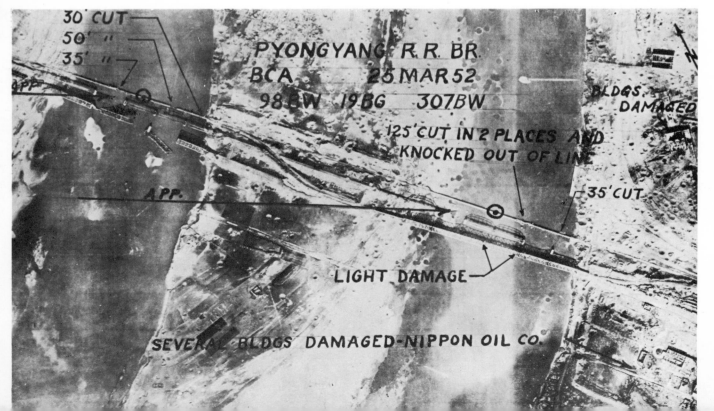

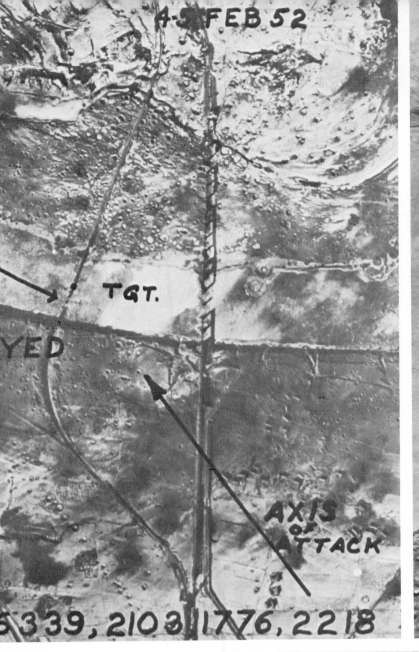

4-5 FEB 52

TGT.

...YED

AXIS of ATTACK

6339, 2103 1776, 2218

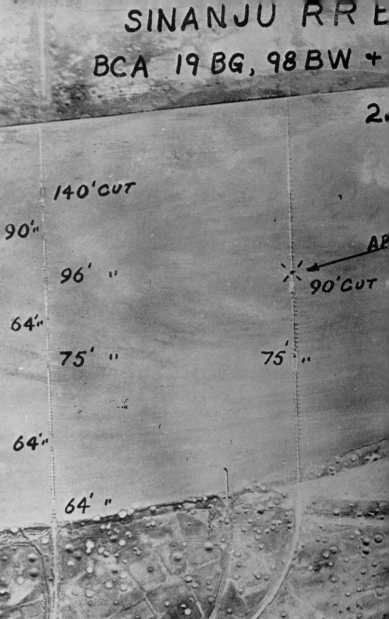

SINANJU RR E...

BCA 19 BG, 98 BW +

2.

140' CUT

90"

96' "

64' "

75' "

90' CUT

75' "

64' "

64' "

TGT #4
BCA 11 MAR 52

APP #3

CUTS IN R.R. LINE

N

ONE SPAN KNOCKED OFF THE PIERS

*Above:* This time, the three bomb wings came in at almost right angles to the bridges at Sinan-ju, and hit them hard. The span to the west was cut in seven places, varying in length from 64 feet to 140 feet, while the span to its east was cut twice.

*Above left:* With the main bridge at Sunchon knocked out by an earlier raid, the Koreans built a bypass bridge. The 98th Bomb Wing flew a mission against the bypass bridge on the night of 4 February 1952. The target was the centre of the bypass span, and the approach was made from an angle about 45 degrees to the span. The bridge was cut and portions of it were destroyed.

*Left:* The approach was from the northeast, at about 40 degrees to this railroad bridge, and the 10 B-29s from the 98th Bomb Wing cut the rail line in five places and knocked one span off its piers.

173

L'Envoi

The Superfortresses are gone now, the echoes of their roaring engines stilled, the hardstands and runways taken back by tropical vegetation.

The Japanese are allies. Korea is still a country divided. Hiroshima and Nagasaki are, to many, nightmares of conscience. Saipan is a tourist resort.

The 25-year-old Lieutenants and Captains who flew the B-29 now are nearing 60. They, and the big bomber they flew, loved and hated, belong to history.

Remember them all, and what they did, in the context of their times. Leave them there.

# Bibliography

Anderton, David A.; *Strategic Air Command;* Ian Allan Ltd, London; 1975.

Anon; *The Pictorial History of the 444th Bombardment Group;* Newsfoto Publishing Co., San Angelo, Texas.

Anon; *498th Bombardment Group;* Unknown publisher.

Berger, Carl; *B-29: The Superfortress;* Ballantine Books, New York; 1970.

Bowers, Peter M.; *Boeing Aircraft Since 1916;* Putnam and Company, London; 1966.

Brown, Anthony Cave and MacDonald, Charles B.; *The Secret History of the Atomic Bomb;* Dell Publishing Co, Inc, New York; 1977.

Carroll, John M.; *Secrets of Electronic Espionage;* E. P. Dutton & Co, Inc, New York; 1966.

Carter, Kit C. and Mueller, Robert.; *The Army Air Forces in World War II: Combat Chronology, 1941-1945;* Government Printing Office, Washington; 1975.

Collison, Thomas; *The Superfortress is Born;* Duell, Sloan & Pearce, New York; 1945.

Craig, William; *The Fall of Japan;* The Dial Press, New York; 1967.

Craven, Wesley F. and Cate, James L.; *The Army Air Forces in World War II; Volume Five: The Pacific: Matterhorn to Nagasaki;* The University of Chicago Press, Chicago; 1953.

Francillon, R. J.: *Japanese Aircraft of the Pacific War;* Funk & Wagnalls, New York; 1970.

Futrell, Robert F.; *The United States Air Force in Korea, 1950-1953;* Duell, Sloan and Pearce, New York; 1963.

Goforth, Capt. Pat E.; *The Long Haul: The Story of the 497th Bomb Group (VH);* Newsfoto Publishing Co; San Angelo, Texas.

Goldberg, Alfred; *A History of the United States Air Force, 1907-1957;* D. VanNostrand Company, Inc, Princeton, NJ; 1957.

Higham, Robin and Siddall, Abigail; *Flying Combat Aircraft of the USAAF-USAF;* The Iowa State University Press, Ames, Iowa; 1975.

Infield, Glenn B.; *Unarmed and Unafraid;* The MacMillan Company, New York; 1970.

Jackson, Robert; *Air War over Korea;* Charles Scribner's Sons, New York; 1973.

Knebel, Fletcher and Bailey, Charles W., II.; *No High Ground;* Harper & Row, New York; 1960.

Kohn, Gregory C. and Rust, Kenn C.; The 313th Bombardment Wing; *Journal, American Aviation Historical Society,* Vol 9, No 3 (Fall 1964), p 189ff.

LeMay, Gen. Curtis E. with Kantor, MacKinlay; *Mission with LeMay;* Doubleday & Company, Inc, Garden City, NY; 1965.

Maurer, Maurer; *Air Force Combat Units of World War II;* Franklin Watts, Inc, New York; 1963.

Maurer, Maurer; *Combat Squadrons of the Air Force, World War II;* Government Printing Office, Washington; 1969.

McClure, Glenn E.; *An Unofficial Pictorial History of the 500th Bombardment Group;* Rubidoux Printing Company, Riverside, Cal.

Rust, Kenn C.; Bomber Markings of the Twentieth A.F.; *Journal, American Aviation Historical Society,* Vol 7, No 3 (Fall 1962) and Vol 7, No 4 (Winter 1962).

Thomas, Gordon and Witts, Max M.; *Enola Gay;* Stein and Day, New York; 1977.